D1266305

SHAKESPEARE'S LATE PLAYS

CHARLES CROW

SHAKESPEARE'S LATE PLAYS

Essays in Honor of
CHARLES CROW

Edited by
Richard C. Tobias and Paul G. Zolbrod

OHIO UNIVERSITY PRESS : ATHENS

Copyright © 1974 by Richard C. Tobias and Paul G. Zolbrod
Library of Congress Catalog Number 74-27704
ISBN 8214-0178-5
All rights reserved
Printed in the United States of America by Oberlin Printing, Inc.
Designed by Hal Stevens

CONTENTS

PREFACE

Richard C. Tobias

JACQUES BARZUN AFFIRMED STOUTLY, IN *Teacher in America*, that a college professor publishes just as surely in his classroom as in a learned journal. He "makes public" his knowledge and understanding. Many books like this one print a careful "Bibliography of the Works of . . . ." For Charles Crow the list includes his dissertation on Emerson's versification, a lecture on Henry James' late style printed in the *English Institute Essays 1957*, and an article in *Shakespeare Survey 18*. Charles Crow did his publishing in his classes when he made his students understand and when he made newly memorable the poems and plays he discussed.

Crow has a mind ready to take pleasure and instruction from all literature. With brilliant exceptions, many professors concentrate on Poe or the astronomy in *Paradise Lost*, mining their subject with all possible industry. They may teach only Poe or Milton. A medievalist claims to read no verse after 1500 and never to look at a novel, and even if the claim is partly game, he defends a concentration that the academic community admires. Crow, on the other hand, has taught American literature, criticism, Milton, and Shakespeare. He offered seminars recently on John Dryden, Walt Whitman, Wallace Stevens, and Robert Browning. He taught for three years a sophomore Introduction to Poetry course so successfully that rising enrollments drove him away. His committee wrote a fifty-five page syllabus for a freshman writing course designed to make college writing a cultural experience rather than an exercise to be endured. Crow is the first to know the new Russian novel, the last French critic, or a fresh recording of an opera. From the early 1930's until now Crow is man thinking in a time when thought seems a commodity snatched from sick hurry. His lectures were of uncommonly high calibre because he brought so much to his classes.

Most recently he has taught criticism and Shakespeare. Students carrying ideas from these lectures to other classes testify to his effectiveness. His students talk about the plays outside class, for his teaching relates the plays to Beckett, or to a political event, or to a momentary fad, or to what is essential in the human condition. Crow's conversations and questions delight visitors. A Fulbright scholar from India—who was at Oxford during the thirties—attended Crow's Shakespeare lectures one winter and vowed they were superior to all she had known. The first two essays in this book by L. C. Knights and Kenneth Muir are glad offerings in tribute to a colleague's understanding and teaching.*

In his lectures, Crow concentrates on the text. He studies individual words and comments on their history. He relates the word to others in the speech, scene, and play, and to other plays. He uses history, psychology, and the vast commentary on the plays. He has more Greek and Latin than Shakespeare; he commands our new dictionaries and concordances. He knows where Shakespeare's Geneva Bible varies from our familiar King James version. He has a well-furnished mind, and he places what he brings out of that mind effectively in the minds of his hearers.

---

* L. C. Knights and Kenneth Muir were Visiting Andrew Mellon Professors at the University of Pittsburgh, Knights in 1961-62 and 1965-66 and Muir in 1962-63.

Richard C. Tobias

He encourages students to respond, and he finds, even in stumbling students making their first critical steps, some moments of uprightness to explain the play. In his comments on student essays, he discovers insights in their papers unsuspected by the authors. Rather than chastise for error, he makes the error an approach to new understanding. Always, whether it is the first, second, or last experience with the plays, he makes memorable and necessary revelation for the student.

As a consequence students count their classes, seminars, or conferences with Crow high points of their academic careers. They recall his habit of punctuating talk with his right hand, his habit of giving multiple-syllabled words equal intonation. They recall his remark on the travelling British company which had cast a very explicit woman as Ariel in *The Tempest*: "Well, she was quite palpable." His attention, his focus, his knowledge elevate him above others. Repeatedly in the letters answering the appeal for funds to publish this volume, his former students have said, "He was the finest teacher I had."

During his years at the University of Pittsburgh, because his department was understaffed, Crow had a heavy teaching, advising, and committee load. He taught winter and summer. His lecture on Henry James was written after he turned in his summer school grades and before the English Institute meeting in the early days of September. When resignations, illness, or deaths occurred, Crow filled in.

Teaching in the 1960's became more challenging as the university turned from its restricted elite students and opened doors to a wider range of students. With healthy skepticism, the new student demanded reasons why he should read a text. He came to the plays doubting that "Shakespearean rag." He might resent efforts to elucidate meaning: "I think it means what I feel it means." Crow added their feeling to his intelligence and continued to read as a humble man exploring with curiosity. He still sought to understand better. He listened to the protesting students, even the one who complained that Crow stifled comment because he knew too much. In such bewildering confusion, Crow still spoke quietly, with concern and dignity, to ask again what the plays said and to publish that word in the best language he could muster.   ·   ·

By the 1960's Shakespeare's last plays had caught his interest and the interest of many others. Could something in our times illuminate those plays? Older critics often thought them a descent. They preferred *Hamlet, Macbeth,* and *Julius Caesar.* They feared that the times had corrupted Shakespeare in his last plays, or that the new style of Beaumont and Fletcher and the rival tradition in the private theaters were not the mode of his genius. Was the time simply bad? Was there a drop in the creative Elizabethan protein intake? Had too many plagues exhausted London? Was it the fault of the Puritans? The Stuart Monarchy?

Whatever the explanation, the plays written after 1607 disturbed older critics, but they intrigue us in our complicated and disjunctive time. Our quite different plagues prepare us to read and experience them again. Clearly some new means seemed necessary to explore the full depth of these plays, or even to know their depth and not speculate on them as idle exercises of declining genius. *The Tempest,* of course, has always had readers and producers, but it also seems full of meaning beyond stage or language. Those who dislike critical jargon will instinctively rebel against terms like Dramatic Romance or simply Romance to describe these plays. Indeed, a contributor to this volume objects that *romance* describes a unique medieval form and has no application to Shakespeare's craft. The plays remind us of Lear's words to Cordelia:

> You do me wrong to take me out o' th' grave.
> Thou art a soul in bliss; but I am bound

Richard C. Tobias

Upon a wheel of fire, that mine own tears
Do scald like molten lead.

Even though their basic rhythm is comic (they end happily),
the plays seem to go beyond comedy and beyond tragedy to
remind us that we too are bound on a wheel of fire. Their
words are mystic and mythic and, to some modern sensibil-
ity, morbid and queer. Their actions seem silly, perverse, or
beyond imagining. Their characters seem pasteboard figures.
At the same moment the plays frighten us with lost children
and mock funerals. When we probe them, we seem to be taking them out of some grave to ask them impertinent questions. How, we must ask, are these plays examples of that ripe-
ness that Lear himself commends?

We have, therefore, asked Crow's students to honor him by
showing that his ideas have fertilized, that his insights pass
into them, and that his own special manner of teaching can
carry them through difficult times. Good teaching, good writing, civilization pass from one human being to another because a teacher, a writer, a civilized person has shown others
how to act. Such miracles must be celebrated. The best celebration is emulation; we offer humane, open, fluid essays determined to maintain the integrity of the plays. One of our
modern passions is punctilious and even pedantic concentration on minutiae or fact. It has given us more accurate texts,
more careful data about the theater. We mean no disrespect;
our aim differs. These essays offer few facts; they aim to make
newly memorable the most moving records of human experience in English. These essays are Crow's publications in the
sense that all of them—with the exception, of course, of those
written by L. C. Knights and Kenneth Muir—have grown
out of his classroom. This book is, in itself, a bibliography of
Charles Crow.

ACKNOWLEDGMENTS

WHEN WE FIRST PROPOSED THIS VOLUME, WE WENT TO Pittsburgh-based foundations, thinking that they would be interested in giving a wider audience to a native of the city. They promptly, and properly, rejected our request. They said, in effect, that funds for such a venture should come from those who had benefited from Crow's thoughts and who knew the value of them. We received one-fifth of our funding from the Faculty Grants Committee of the Faculty of Arts and Sciences, University of Pittsburgh.

All other gifts came from Crow's students and colleagues. We thank here Bernard S. Adams, Eugene R. August, Robert E. Burkhart, Mr. and Mrs. Thomas B. Carroll, Diana T. Childress, Richard C. Crowley, Montgomery Culver, Frank D. Curtin, C. J. Denne, Constance Ayers Denne, Virginia Elliott, Marian Fairman, Joseph Feltes, Judith P. Fishman, Lois Josephs Fowler, Joan B. Friedberg, Robert L. Gale, John C. Gerber, Gregory F. Goekjian, Elton D. Higgs, Ronald Huebert, Clifford Ross Johnson, Jr., Elnora Smith Jones, Dorothy Kish, Paul Loukides, Dorothy McCoy, James E. Magner, Jr., James Marino, Robert D. Marshall, William and Gertrude Mazefsky, Robert Meyers, Norman Macleod, John H. Miller, Susan Muto, Robert Reid, Ronald Ribman, Norman Rosenblood, Norman Rosenfeld, Mrs. John M. Sadler, Arthur Saxon, Helene H. Schulman, Nihalini Shetty, Ronald C. Shumaker,

Andrew Solomon, Mary T. Strauss, William Stubbs, Michael Tinker, R. C. Tobias, Elizabeth Wiley, Philip Wion, Roy Wolper, Mrs. Joseph M. Wymard, and Paul Zolbrod.

The following persons have been Special Patrons for this volume: Eben Bass, Barbara Burge, Ford Curtis, Walter Evert, George K. Hanna, Joan Huber, Robert C. Laing, Andrew Welsh, Robert Whitman, and E. J. Wasp.

Faculty members of the English Department, University of Pittsburgh, have aided us by serving as our Editorial Board. We are grateful and our contributors are grateful for their queries, judgment, and suggestions. We especially thank Virginia Elliott, Cynthia Matlack, Ed Ochester, Marilyn Papousek, Robert F. Whitman, Philip Wion.

FROM IAGO TO PROSPERO:
AN INTRODUCTORY ESSAY

Paul G. Zolbrod

A T THE BEGINNING OF ACT TWO OF *Othello,* WE OVERHEAR A discussion about a storm. "Methinks the wind hath spoke aloud at land," Montano reports to two Gentlemen watching with him for Othello's arrival on the island of Cyprus; "A fuller blast ne'er shook our battlements." The second gentleman agrees. "The chidden billow seems to pelt the clouds," he replies. "The wind-shak'd surge, with high and monstrous mane,/ Seems to cast water on the burning bear/ And quench the guards of th'ever-fixed pole." Like Montano, he too speaks of the tempest in superlative terms: "I never did like molestation view/ On the enchafed flood," he says. Perhaps the third gentleman best communicates the power of that tempest when he announces that it "hath so banged" the feared and formidable Turkish fleet "that their designment halts."

Between them, Montano and the gentlemen give us a sharply graphic conception of that storm's might. Here they identify it as a force whose impact delivers Cyprus from the menacing Turks, leaving Othello with no war to fight and consequently somewhat out of his own familiar element. In telling of it they describe a world turned topsy-turvy, where mountains tumble upon timber and where the ocean pours

1

its torrential weight upon the fixed and lofty stars. If we listen carefully to them describe it, in fact, we actually see a turbulent, capricious cosmos where unsettling agents are at work for whatever reason; and no matter how much the storm seems to have benefited Othello and his allies this time, they have no assurance whatsoever that they would not be nature's victim next time. Again and again we are reminded in this scene of storms in general and of this one in particular. And while this particular tempest seems to have a positive effect, it also transmits misgivings to the play's audience. Somehow, I would argue, it begins to anticipate the results of Iago's machinations as he creates the inversion that ruins Othello.

We can begin to see as much in the way various characters respond to the storm. To the third gentleman it is a "foul and violent tempest." When Cassio lands on Cyprus, he reports that he has "lost" Othello "on a dangerous sea." And he prays to the heavens, "Give him defence against the elements," in what is to become a futile plea. In an observation similar to the second gentleman's, he describes the storm as "a great contention of the sea and skies," adding in a statement that turns out to be ironically prophetic that it "parted our fellowship." Furthermore, in trying to explain Desdemona's quick arrival at Cyprus in the direct aftermath of such a violent storm, Cassio conjectures that tempests "do omit their mortal natures" when they encounter the likes of "The divine Desdemona," this one having let her "go safely by." Those who are too trusting, we gradually learn, become Iago's victims most easily. And in his statement here Cassio identifies himself as someone who has too much faith in so unsteady a world and consequently as someone who leaves himself open to manipulation.

The storm and some of what it implies is even duplicated in a lower, more playful key when Iago and the "divine" Desdemona themselves undertake a contention and banter with each other when Iago insists that women are inconsistent and unstable. The implication that unsteadiness exists as plentifully among people as it does in nature is repeated when Iago alleges to Rodrigo that Desdemona no longer favors Othello but now loves Cassio instead. Using language that confirms the existence of reversal and turmoil within the microcosm as directly as Montano's language testifies to its presence in the macrocosm, Iago says that once Desdemona's "blood is made dull with the act of sport," it will be inflamed "to give satiety a fresh appetite" by Cassio's attractiveness. "Her delicate tenderness will find itself abus'd," he promises, and will "begin to heave the gorge. Very nature will instruct her in it and compel her to some second choice." In the same vein he describes Cassio as "rash and very sudden in choler." Confident that the Venetian's unsteady temper can be worked to "cause these of Cyprus to mutiny," he suggests thereby that the potential for disorder always exists in individuals, just as Montano and the three gentlemen remind us of its presence in the broader sphere of external nature.

In one respect, then, the tempest becomes a keynote to the whole play and, in a less direct sense, a point of departure for this volume. The storm's destructive might has been described by several characters, and it is identified as a force with great potential for creating disorder. Likewise, an inner disorder can be created that affects the human spirit the way the wind affects the ocean's surface. Except that while battlements are shaken and clouds are pelted with a neutral, conscienceless indifference, the inner moorings of a person's mind may be destroyed with cunning and secretive design. Some humans have the ability to tamper deliberately with the fortunes of others, just as some are inclined to be tampered with, which leaves mortals as open to a subtle danger as a sea wall stands openly to be assaulted by the manifestly dangerous raging sea. And if some characters in *Othello*, trusting and benign like Cassio and Desdemona to say nothing of the Moor himself, do not recognize the more hidden danger, others like Iago do. Hence a man as clever as he can instigate anguish and turmoil ultimately as overwhelming as the stormy sea. So that in the broader sense of the play the image of the tempest establishes the precariousness of the human situation.

More narrowly, that image serves to establish the irony that frames Othello's own situation—a situation more fragile than he realizes. Consider what he says specifically to Desdemona when the two of them are reunited later in this scene:

> O my soul's joy!
> If after every tempest come such calms,
> May the winds blow till they have waken'd death!
> And let the labouring bark climb hills of seas
> Olympus-high, and duck again as low
> As hell's from heaven! If it were now to die,
> 'T were now to be most happy; for I fear,
> My soul hath her content so absolute
> That not another comfort like to this
> Succeeds in unknown fate. (II, i, 186-195)

As we are to see, Othello virtually foretells his own doom here: as the action progresses the winds *will* blow, in a manner of speaking, since they will assume the more subtle form of Iago's whispers and tauntings. Death will waken indeed, and as surely as Othello will presume to depend on Iago's word and to judge Desdemona without trial or inquiry, the "labouring bark" of his own reason will indeed "climb hills of seas" and then "duck again as low as hell's from heaven." Just as he says with such irony, his happiness at this moment is absolute. He would be better off dying now, for he will never be this happy again. Such a calm as the one he now perceives to have followed the storm so carefully described remains an illusion that conceals from him the plotting of Iago. And as we con-

4

sider this scene carefully, studying what Shakespeare does with the image of the tempest, we surely may believe Iago when he says that he can practice upon Othello's "peace and quiet even to madness." Indeed, in his own devious way Iago is a summoner of storms that can rage within the human breast.

What is so alarming about Iago's effectiveness, of course, is that Othello for all his stature cannot withstand it, perhaps all the less effectively because he does not have to fight the Turks and has time now to worry about his wife's faithfulness. Yet the Moor is as mighty as any Shakespearean hero, particularly when in his element as a fighter. Poised and full of confidence at first, he behaves with judgment and restraint. He knows fully how to act swiftly and decisively when Brabantio assaults him and accuses him, but he controls his might with the counterforce of his reason. Clearly his wits are in absolute command. Undisturbed when Iago warns him that Brabantio seeks to break up his marriage, Othello confidently observes, "My services which I have done the signiory/ Shall out-tongue his complaints." Later, when Brabantio and his officers brandish their swords against him, Othello quietly tells his father-in-law, "Good signior, you shall more command with years/ Than with your weapons." And when he stands before the Duke to account for his marriage he presents the details with a quiet, rational eloquence that displays no offence at being asked to justify his behavior. Finally, he manages to bring his ship through the storm to Cyprus and lands there poised and unshaken.

Yet just as clearly, he is sharply aware of his might. When Cassio's drunken brawling in Act Two arouses Othello from his marriage bed, he asserts his anger openly. "Now, by heaven," he says then, "My blood begins my safer guides to rule,/ And passion, having my best judgment collied,/ Assays to lead the way." Knowing full well his capacity for wrath, however, he also believes he can control it. "If I once stir/ Or do but lift this arm," he warns Montano and the others, "the best of you/ Shall sink in my rebuke." So that if he is aware that his "blood" tends to rule his "safe guides," he continues to believe that his wrath can be subdued until he wills it otherwise. Iago, whose machinations are already at work and are the ultimate cause of this disturbance, will make a shambles of that belief. At first Othello clings to the illusion of his capacity for self-control. Even as late as the third scene of Act Three, where Iago arouses the turbulence latent in him, he thinks that his reason will prevail. When Iago warns him to beware of his own jealousy, he answers, "Why, why is this?/ Think'st thou I'ld make a life of jealousy,/ To follow still the changes of the moon with fresh suspicions?" But a certain fear that he is not the master of himself after all begins more manifestly to surface. Iago suggests to him, "I see that this hath a little dash'd your spirits," and Othello replies, "Not a jot, not a jot." But the reply seems unconvincing, both to us and to himself, for a few lines later he intensifies his uncertainty by questioning his choice to marry Desdemona and by acknowledging the possibility that Iago may know more than he himself knows about his domestic situation. "Why did I marry?" he wonders aloud; "This honest creature doubtless/ Sees and knows more, much more, than he unfolds."

Thus if Othello is aware of the force latent in himself, so is Iago, who has the cunning, sinister magic necessary to arouse it; and if we see that force as a counterpart to nature's propensity for stormy destruction, Iago and *not* Othello can be seen as its absolute master. "Perdition catch my soul but I do love thee!" Othello had mused over Desdemona before any suspicion about her infidelity sullied his mind; "And when I love thee not," he then added, "Chaos is come again." However, that chaos is never his to call forth, any more than the waves on the stormy Mediterranean could have called the wind that aroused them. Instead, Iago does the summoning! "It is engend'red!" he declares in his soliloquy at the end of Act One, once he makes up his mind to ruin Othello, "Hell and night/ Must bring this monstrous birth to the world's light." So that when Othello becomes convinced of Desdemona's infidelity in the fourth scene of Act Three and cries, "Arise, black vengeance, from the hollow hell!/ Yield up, O love, thy crown and hearted throne/ To tyrannous hate! Swell, bosom, with thy fraught,/ For 'tis of aspics' tongues!" he is merely expanding Iago's earlier invocation so that it expresses his own insane rage. Iago alone arouses the propensity for that rage in mighty Othello, and once aroused it cannot be quieted until it has spent itself utterly in an orgy of total and irrational human destruction. Nor can it, once its motion begins, be reversed so that Othello's damage may be prevented or undone. The effect of Iago's cunning is absolute and eternal. We are not witnessing something cyclical like the tide; instead we pay testimony to a force rushing irretrievably in one direction only, making its way towards a frozen finality. Othello himself says as much when he declares to Iago in the climax of Act Three that his mind is now set once and for all upon Desdemona's destruction:

> Like to the Pontic sea,
> Whose icy currents and compulsive course
> Ne'er feels retiring ebb, but keeps due on
> To the Propontic and the Hellespont;
> Even so my bloody thoughts, with violent pace,
> Shall ne'er look back, ne'er ebb to humble love,
> Till that a capable and wide revenge
> Swallow them up. (III, iii, 453-60)

Here, perhaps, is where Iago's impact on Othello outdoes the effect, say, of the wind on the water's surface. After a tempest the sea grows calm again; all is as it was before. Nature replenishes herself after she works her indifferent violence. Damage is undone and restoration eventually occurs. But the effect of Othello's kind of violence endures. Once dead, Desdemona will stay dead and Othello remains indelibly wrong in killing her, even after he destroys himself in a final act of contrition. Iago's more subtly aroused man-made tempest is ultimately worse than any natural calamity, and we are left craving restitution where none is possible and wishing that nothing more than an actual storm had ravaged Othello.

The tempest-image dominates *Othello*, then, and all the more revealingly when we see it as a touchstone marking Iago's sinister progress. To be sure, its function in the other tragedies deserves special claims, also. The tempest in *King Lear*, for example, is the most directly visible among those in all the plays. The long passage which describes it in Act III generates some of Shakespeare's most remarkable poetry. Storms permeate *Macbeth* to the point that the tempest there becomes synonymous with murder, with "Lamentings heard i' th' air," and with "strange screams of death." G. Wilson Knight, in fact, demonstrates how central that image is throughout Shakespeare and how specifically it serves the tragedies in *The Shakespearean Tempest* (London, 1953). But I would argue that in *Othello* the tempest becomes an unparalleled image of natural and man-made forces at work to test a man. And given the way the image functions in that particular play, I would argue that Othello remains less responsible for his own undoing than Shakespeare's other tragic heroes; as we watch Iago do to him what the wind does to the sea, and as we acknowledge the finality of the results, we discover how tenuously fixed even the mightiest, most self-controlled man can be. The stars themselves can be subdued by the ocean in this play where, we might argue, the tragic vision extends to a point of distortion, transforming itself into a view of a universe where stability is ultimately unavailable to men and where lost harmony can never be restored.

Paul G. Zolbrod

Suppose that *Othello* were Shakespeare's final play. Written during the period of his mature tragedies, it is the most straightforward drama among them, with no subplot such as we find in *Lear*, and with nothing to divert our attention from its unrelenting progress towards the conclusion. Singular in its theme, swift in its development, offering few metaphysical ambiguities, it makes its way directly from beginning to end on the basis of Iago's progress. Here is the clearest expression we find in Shakespeare—and one of the clearest we find anywhere in literature—of an entirely evil man working out his absolute will on people nearly innocent of everything beyond human trust and characteristically human self-delusion. We are left with very little by way of hope for reassurance or redemption. In a manner of speaking we see the wreckage of a hurricane with nothing left to salvage: Shakespeare at his most abjectly and realistically pessimistic. If, during the years of his writing the late tragedies, Shakespeare was, as Peter Quinnell has said, "exploring the dark universe," he manages to penetrate the most remote and the most despairing recesses of that darkness in *Othello*, where one man incites a psychic storm in another, who in turn becomes tempest-driven in the uncharted sea of his own chaotic anguish.

Othello was not Shakespeare's last play, however, any more than the tragedies stand as his final set of works. During the period of the tragedies he may have attained an artistic maturity that commands attention and awe, but only by our assuming that artistic maturity and the tragic view necessarily go hand in hand. It depends, of course, upon taste and attitude. As for Shakespeare's own taste and attitude, they apparently did not harden and cease to change with the last of the tragedies. The late plays seem to mark a process—and perhaps even what we might ultimately decide to call a progress of withdrawal from so dark a view expressed in *Othello*. And that withdrawal culminates in the *Tempest*, which *is* the final play and which marks the absolute distance of Shakespeare's movement away from darkness and despair.

As G. Wilson Knight demonstrates, and as we can easily see for ourselves, Shakespeare continues to find plenty of work for the tempest-image in the late plays. In *The Winter's Tale*, for example, a tempest "flapdragons" the ship that brings Antigonus to Bohemia with the infant Perdita. Likewise, the tempest-images in *Cymbeline* remind us constantly that powerful men have a capacity for creating instability and for suffering it. Imogen says that Cymbeline, "like the tyranneous breathing of the North, shakes all our buds from growing." Shakespeare does not forget that some men have power over others and that mortals can be more destructive of one another than nature is of itself. Throughout the last plays the vicissitudes of the elements remain as an index of man's unsteadiness. However, the late comedies still differ in their use of the tempest-image from the way it is used in the tragedies. While storms create disaster in both sets of plays, and while they serve in both to remind us that man himself can create disaster, in the tragedies that disaster is real and permanent. If things go wrong in the late comedies, however, they are ultimately set right again. Othello's mood is, as we have seen, like the sea whose currents rush "to the Propontic and the Hellespont." But in the last plays, where we find a more cyclical kind of movement promising new life wherever destruction occurs, moods and attitudes are more like tides wherein flow follows ebb. Readers and viewers would do well to consider that difference. In the third scene of Act Three of *The Winter's Tale*, for instance, the Clown speaks to the Shepherd of the death of Antigonus on land while a storm sinks his ship in the sea. To the Clown's report the Shepherd replies:

> Heavy matters! heavy matters! But look
> thee here, boy. Now bless thyself; thou

met'st with things dying, I with things
newborn. Here 's a sight for thee; look
thee, a bearing-cloth for a squire's child!
Look thee here; take up, take up, boy;
open 't. So, let 's see: it was told me
I should be rich by the fairies. This is
some changeling; open 't. What 's within,
boy? (III, iii, 115-123)

If the tempest here marks Antigonus' destruction, it also
brings Perdita to Bohemia, where she will grow into the young
woman who restores her father's battered senses. Terror and
destruction can be reversed, we find; new life follows old; the
dead can be brought back to life; awful undoings can be re-
done again. More significantly, attitudes do change, and an
artist's perceptions never cease to evolve.

Miranda, in the opening lines of the second scene of Act
One in *The Tempest*, best presents the distance between the
atmosphere of *Othello* and that of Shakespeare's last plays.
"If by your art, my dearest father, you have/ put the wild
waters in this roar, allay them," she begs, naively secure in
the belief that he has such absolute control. And her father's
immediate response reinforces that belief. "Lie there, my art,"
he says, and then he tells her:

> Wipe thou thine eyes; have comfort.
> The direful spectacle of the wrack, which touch'd
> The very virtue of compassion in thee,
> I have with such provision in mine art
> So safely ordered that there is no soul—
> No, not so much perdition as an hair
> Betid to any creature in the vessel
> Which thou heard'st cry, which thou saw'st sink . . .
> (I, ii, 25-32)

Thereupon he tells Miranda their story, a story of others con-
spiring against him which begins with his own careless pur-

suit of impractical things. But all that error is to be revised by the very storm he has created, which is only temporary, which is illusive in its appearance of doing damage, and which in fact will enable him to remedy the mistakes of his own past, to say nothing of altering the lives of men who have heretofore worked mischief upon others. Like Iago, we find, Prospero tampers with the lives of men. But unlike Iago he works *through* nature instead of trying to short-circuit her. Beyond saying that much, I leave exploration of this very important difference to the accompanying essays. But I do assert that somewhere in the world that Shakespeare creates for us the unrelenting flow of human misery is reversed; the black magic of Iago has its counterpart in the more positive and appealing magic of Prospero, whose storms are an antidote to the more malevolently conceived sort of tempest that can destroy an Othello. If one kind of violent disturbance turns the world upside down, another disturbance rights it again with a power that heals, cleanses and restores: which places a special emphasis indeed upon Prospero and upon his kind of art, and which invites us to take very seriously Shakespeare's growth beyond the tragedies.

That growth is—directly or indirectly but always concertedly—the first thing that the essays herein collected have in common. The writers whose work is represented here are all concerned with what Shakespeare ultimately becomes as he seeks to transcend the dark vision of his tragedies. Cumulatively, these essays celebrate growth and restoration as our greatest poet presents them in some of his most challenging and engaging plays. The essays here have a second thing in common as well, written as they are by former students and colleagues of Charles Crow. They testify to the effectiveness of a man whose career as a teacher has displayed a certain artful provision of his own to perform magic. A subtle thing, that magic encourages us never to think in terms of finality: never

12

Paul G. Zolbrod

to accept a last word on any play or set of plays, on any matter of judgment or on any point of interpretation. Consequently Professor Crow has secured continuing growth and development among generations of students who have learned from him, among other things, that a Shakespeare play renews itself each time it is read or seen. Hence it seems to us that a set of essays dealing with Shakespeare's last plays—with the particular quality of their message of renewal—might serve as an appropriate token of his lifelong professional contribution. For above all his is a contribution that will never cease to replenish itself in the minds of those who have had the pleasure of studying with him.

Allegheny College
Meadville, Pa.

1

THE TEMPEST

L. C. Knights
(i)

O F ALL THE GREATEST WORKS OF ART IT SEEMS TRUE TO SAY that they contain an element of paradox, that what imposes itself on our imaginations as a unified and self-consistent whole contains contradictory elements tugging our sympathies—and therefore our judgments—in different ways: part of the continuing life of the great masterpieces is due to the fact that they will not allow the mind of the reader to settle down comfortably with the sense that he has finally reached *the* meaning which can now be put in a pocket of the mind with other acquired certainties producible at need. More than is the case with any other of Shakespeare's plays, with the exception of *King Lear*, paradox is of the essence of *The Tempest*, a fact that is reflected in the history of Shakespeare criticism. I am not referring to the truism that every work of art, without exception, 'means' something different for every age and every reader, but to the completely contradictory accounts that have been given of this play. It is not so long since critics, identifying Prospero with Shakespeare, saw the play

15

either as embodying the serene wisdom of age or as a deliberate turning aside from the harsh realities of life to the more easily manageable world of romantic fantasy. More recently the views to which I have alluded have been sharply challenged, most notably by Jan Kott,—in *Shakespeare our Contemporary*—for whom *The Tempest* is "a great Renaissance tragedy of lost illusions," its ending "more disturbing than that of any other Shakespearean drama." Others have written to much the same effect. And even for those who are not unduly swayed by critical opinion there is difficulty in saying simply and clearly where one feels the play's greatness to reside. Because of its obvious impressiveness and mystery, and because it is probably Shakespeare's last play without a collaborator, there is a temptation to read in large significances too easily, as I think we may tend to do with *Cymbeline*. On the other hand, to say that *The Tempest*, like *Cymbeline*, points to more than it contrives to grasp and hold in a unified dramatic structure—that also feels wrong. Perhaps we should start by pondering what everyone would agree to be there, in the play: I mean prominent aspects of the play's dramatic mode, its technique. Not everyone will agree as to the significance to be attached to these, but to consider them may clear the ground for criticism. I. A. Richards has remarked of the interpretation of poetry that "whatever accounts are offered to the reader must leave him—in a very deep sense—free to choose, though they may supply wherewithal for exercise of choice." This, he added, "is not . . . any general license to readers to differ as they please. . . . For this deep freedom in reading is made possible only by the widest surface conformities"; for "it is through surfaces . . . that we have to attempt to go deeper."[1]

There are four aspects of "surface" technique that deserve attention. The play observes the unities of time and place; it is related to the contemporary masque; it makes great use of

16

music and song; it employs a very great variety of modes of speech.

Alone among Shakespeare's plays the action of *The Tempest* keeps well within the limits of a natural day: indeed Prospero is rather insistent on getting the whole business completed in three or four hours. Clearly this means compression, and it is compression of a particular kind. There are plays that keep the unities that obviously have great depth and spaciousness, for example *Oedipus*, or *Phèdre*. Here the effect is different—as though important experiences were rendered by a rather spare, and at times almost conventional, notation, that only gets its effect when the reader or spectator is prepared to collaborate fully, to give apparently slight clues full weight. We notice in particular two things. (i)There is a form of symbolism developed out of the earlier plays (notably *King Lear*), as when Stephano and Trinculo fall for the "trumpery" hung up on the lime (or linden) tree; and the potentially healing and cleansing power of the tempest is indicated by the information about the shipwrecked party—"On their sustaining garments not a blemish, But fresher than before"; and "Though the seas threaten, they are merciful" (which it may not be fanciful to associate with Jung's dictum, "Danger itself fosters the rescuing power"). Or again, love's labours are simply represented by Ferdinand carrying logs. (ii) Psychological states are briefly, even if pungently, represented. We know that Antonio was ambitious ("So dry he was for sway") and that Sebastian is a would-be murderer; but neither state of mind is developed as it might have been in the tragedies. Alonso undergoes a storm in which he learns to listen to his own guilt; but this is reduced to,

O, it is monstrous, monstrous!
Methought the billows spoke, and told me of it;
The winds did sing it to me; and the thunder,

17

That deep and dreadful organ-type, pronounc'd
The name of Prosper: it did bass my trespass.
(III, iii, 95-99)

So too with the young lovers: compared with Florizel and
Perdita they have very little to say to or about each other,
but what they do say is often telling and beautiful; and the
harmony in diversity of the sexes is given in a simple tableau
—"Here Prospero discovers Ferdinand and Miranda playing
chess." It remains to be seen whether we are justified in giving
to these brief "notations" the kind of weight that I have implied we should give.

The Tempest is also distinguished from Shakespeare's other
late plays in its relation to the contemporary masque. Apart
from the formally presented masque of Ceres at the betrothal in Act IV, there are various masque-like tableaux, as when
"several strange shapes" bring in a banquet for the shipwrecked party, and then, as they approach it: "Thunder and
lightning. Enter Ariel like a Harpy; claps his wings upon the
table; and, with a quaint device, the banquet vanishes." This
has been often noticed;[2] and indeed Shakespeare had often
used what is seen on the stage to emphasize what is said, as in
the formal and ceremonious grouping of his characters, their
pairing off or drawing apart; but *The Tempest* puts a special
emphasis on modes of formal, masque-like, presentation, and
we need to be fully aware of the language of visual suggestion that is developed in the play.

"Suggestion": the critic does well to be careful when he
uses the word, but he can hardly avoid it when speaking of a
play in which music and song have so important a part. Ariel
sings to Ferdinand, to the sleeping Gonzalo, to Prospero as
he robes him and anticipates his own freedom; Stephano sings
"a scurvy song"; Caliban sings. At key points in the action
Ariel plays music to the actors. The banquet is presented to
the King's party with "solemn and strange music" and van-

18

ishes to the sound of thunder. The masque of Ceres is accompanied by "soft music" and vanishes "to a strange, hollow and confused noise." In short "the isle is full of noises. . . ." Now not only is music—harmony—the polar opposite of tempest, as Professor Wilson Knight has rightly and so often reminded us,[3] it is the art furthest removed from the discursive mode. In all Shakespeare's plays music and song had been functional to the action, and so they are here; but they make their contribution to the changing moods of the play by unexpected and almost undefinable means, as W. H. Auden has pointed out in his essay, "Music in Shakespeare."[4] Perhaps we may have to allow to the play as a whole a power of controlled suggestion greater than any formulable meaning we can attach to it.

Finally, in this brief glance at "technique"—the surface characteristics which everyone would agree to be there, whatever the interpretation attached to them—we should notice the great range of style and manner: from the delicate allusiveness of Ariel's songs to the decidedly *not* delicate speech of the "low" characters; from the slightly stylized verse of the masque to the passionate intensity of some of Prospero's speeches. Nor is it only the low characters who command a pithy idiom directly related to everyday speech. It is Antonio who gives us,

> For all the rest,
> They'll take suggestion as a cat laps milk;
> They'll tell the clock to any business that
> We say befits the hour; (II, ii, 287-90)

and it is Ariel himself who describes the effect of his music on the drunken butler and his followers—"they prick'd their ears. . . . lifted up their noses As they smelt music." In the poetry of the play there is at least as much of the earthy as there is of the ethereal.

With this, of course, we find our attention focusing on far

19

more than "technique." To the range of style there corresponds an equal range of interest and awareness. It is well known that the play makes direct reference to contemporary matters. It is, among many other things, a contribution to the debate on "nature" and "nurture"; and F. R. Leavis, making the point that *The Tempest* is "much closer [than *The Winter's Tale*] to the 'reality' we commonly expect of the novelist," is clearly right in saying that "Caliban . . . leads the modern commentator, quite appropriately, to discuss Shakespeare's interest in the world of new discovery and in the impact of civilization on the native."[5] Important as this is, it is even more important to see how much of "the real world" comes into the play by way of reference, imagery and allusion. The opening storm proves to be merciful, but, as Gonzalo says,

> Our hint of woe
> Is common; every day, some sailor's wife,
> The masters of some merchant, and the merchant,
> Have just our theme of woe. (II, i, 3-6)

Ariel's songs are balanced by the coarse life of Stephano's song. Gonzalo's Utopia, remembered from Montaigne, inevitably calls to mind its opposite—the more familiar world of "sweat, endeavour, treason, felony, Sword, pike, knife, gun. . . ." The masque of Ceres conjures up images of the English countryside at its most peaceful:

> You sunburn's sicklemen, of August weary,
> Come hither from the furrow, and be merry:
> Make holiday; your rye-straw hats put on, . . .
> (IV, i, 134-6)

but we are also reminded of the wilder, undomesticated, aspects of nature—not only the storm-tossed waves, the "roarers" that "care nothing for the name of King," but "long

heath, broom, furze . . .", "the green sour ringlets . . . whereof
the ewe not bites," the lightning-cloven oak. The island, for
all its magical qualities, is very much a part of the everyday
world: even one of the most delicate of Ariel's songs has for
burden, "Bow wow" and "Cock a diddle dow . . . the strain of
strutting chanticleer," as though it were dawn in an English
village. And at the centre of these specific references is a vision of "the great globe itself," which, with all its towers, palaces and temples, as Prospero reminds us, is as transient as
"this insubstantial pageant faded." In other words, the island
mirrors, or contains, the world; what we have to do with is
not exclusion and simplification but compression and density,
vibrant with its own unique imaginative life. The point has
been well put by Dr. Anne Barton:

> Spare, intense, concentrated to the point of being riddling, *The
> Tempest* provokes imaginative activity on the part of its au-
> dience or readers. Its very compression, the fact that it seems to
> hide as much as it reveals, compels a peculiarly creative re-
> sponse. A need to invent links between words, to expand events
> and characters in order to understand them, to formulate
> phrases that can somehow fix the significance of purely visual
> or musical elements is part of the ordinary experience of read-
> ing or watching this play.[6]

(ii)

With so much, perhaps, all readers would agree. Any attempt to say more, to define the centre of interest to which
these different aspects of Shakespeare's technique direct our
attention, is unavoidably personal and partial. As so often
when a play has made a strong impact on the mind and we
know we are still far from understanding, it is useful to face
directly the more obvious difficulties. Consider, for example,
the abrupt ending of the masque that Prospero had arranged
for Ferdinand and Miranda.

Enter certain Reapers, properly habited: they join with the Nymphs in a graceful dance; towards the end whereof Prospero starts suddenly, and speaks; after which, to a strange, hollow, and confused noise, they heavily vanish.

Pros. [*Aside*] I had forgot that foul conspiracy
Of the beast Caliban and his confederates
Against my life: the minute of their plot
Is almost come [*To the Spirits*] Well done! Avoid; no more!
Fer. This is strange: your father's in some passion
That works him strongly.
Mir.   Never till this day
Saw I him touch'd with anger, so distemper'd. (IV, i, 138-45)

It is indeed strange, and Professor Kermode finds the motivation inadequate, wondering "that Prospero should so excite himself over an easily controlled insurrection."[7] But it is only strange if we forget that Caliban, like Ariel, stands in some kind of special relationship with Prospero. ("We cannot miss [i.e. do without] him," and, near the end of the play, "This thing of darkness I Acknowledge mine.") Caliban, although his mother was a witch, is also a "native" of new-found lands who raises the whole question of man before civilization and of the relation of "natives" to European settlers. It is also Caliban, who knows the island better than anyone else, who speaks some of the most beautiful poetry in the play:

Be not afeard; the isle is full of noises,
Sounds and sweet airs, that give delight, and hurt not.
Sometimes a thousand twangling instruments
Will hum about mine ears; and sometimes voices,
That, if I then had wak'd after long sleep,
Will make me sleep again: and then, in dreaming,
The clouds methought would open, and show riches
Ready to drop upon me; that, when I wak'd,
I cried to dream again. (III, ii, 144-52)

But he is also a brute "on whose nature nurture can never stick"; and the play gives us no warrant for supposing that

22

each man has not a Caliban inside himself—even Prospero. In the passage I have referred to we have had an elaborate, slightly artificial masque of Ceres—a vision of nature fertile and controlled. But life isn't as simple as that: Caliban, pure instinct, is still plotting; and it is the sudden memory of this that puts Prospero into a "passion That works him strongly." No one is put into that kind of temper by external danger (especially when the danger, such as it is, is largely represented by a couple of drunks), only by self-insurrection. Perhaps we have here an explanation of Prospero's tensed-up attitude towards Caliban at the beginning of the play and his spiteful and childish punishings of him—"I'll rack thee with old cramps, Fill all thy bones with aches. . . ." What I am suggesting is that the play is mainly the drama of Prospero, a man who, even by Elizabethan standards, is not old, but one who is looking towards the end of his days, trying to sort out and to come to terms with his experiences. Prospero is not simply above the action, controlling it, he is intimately involved. The play is about what Prospero sees, and, above all, what he is and has it in him to become. "Prospero," says Harold Goddard, "when expelled from his dukedom, is a narrow and partial man. Thanks to his child, the island, and Ariel, he gives promise of coming back to it something like a whole one. But an integrated man is only another name for an imaginative man."[8]

I have said that no single, clearly defined interpretation can be extracted from—much less put upon—this play. But when it is seen in some such way as this the action at least falls into an intelligible shape, which still allows the working of other promptings. Consider briefly a few major phases in the action. The play opens with a storm, conjured up by magic, but real enough not to make its nautical technicalities out of place. In some sixty lines Shakespeare—as in all his masterful openings —is doing several things simultaneously. The human characteristics of various people who will play a part in the subsequent action are revealed—from the detachment of Gonzalo to the panicky blustering of Antonio and Sebastian. The storm is also a reminder of fundamental equalities—"What care these roarers for the name of King?" But like all Shakespearean storms it carries overtones: indeed it is explicitly related (I, ii, 207 ff.) to inner storms. The second scene is sometimes regarded as a contrast to the first, and so—in some ways—it is; but it is also a continuation. The storm has prepared us for something in the mind of Prospero, a mental turmoil that is sharply contrasted with the music of Miranda's compassion —"O, I have suffered with those that I saw suffer." The tortured syntax of many of his speeches, with their abrupt dislocations, his interjections to Miranda (more, surely, than a clumsy attempt by the dramatist to hold the attention of the audience throughout a long exposition)—these mark the tumultuous strength of his anger against his brother: "I pray thee, mark me, that a brother should Be so perfidious," "Thy false uncle—Dost thou attend me?" And underneath the anger (which to be sure is natural enough) is an admission of at least partial responsibility.

> I pray thee, mark me.
> I, thus neglecting worldly ends, all dedicated
> To closeness and the bettering of my mind
> With that which, but by being so retir'd,
> O'er-prized all popular rate, in my false brother
> Awak'd an evil nature. . . . (I, ii, 88-93)

The New Arden note on this passage, rightly admitting that "no paraphrase can reproduce its involved urgency," offers as the main sense: "The fact of my retirement, in which I neglected worldly affairs and dedicated myself to secret studies of a kind beyond the understanding and esteem of the people, brought out a bad side of my brother's nature. . . ." Apart from the fact that a ruler's business is to rule—not at all events to be "all dedicated" to study—the paraphrase misses the point. In the phrase, "in my false brother Awak'd an evil nature," the verb has a subject, and it is not "the fact of my retirement" but the pronoun "I." W. H. Auden is surely right when, in *The Sea and the Mirror*, he makes Prospero say, "All by myself I tempted Antonio into treason." From at least as early as *Richard II* Shakespeare had used incoherence *dramatically*; and Prospero's involutions contain at least some admission of hidden guilt.

The main movement of the play, it has been suggested, is Prospero's movement towards restoration, renewal of the self. He is certainly human enough—not simply the wise controller of other people's fate—to make us interested in his fluctuations of mood. True, as white magician he is in some ways analogous to the artist, and within the conventions of the play his magic can control much of the action. But even within the play magic cannot do what is most essential. It is not magic that determines Gonzalo's decency or the falling in love of Ferdinand and Miranda. Magic can help to demonstrate how evil mistakes the goal or desires what proves to be trash, just as art can set out telling *exempla*. But magic cannot help Prospero in his most extreme need. When, in the passage already referred to, he breaks off the masque because he has recalled the "foul conspiracy of the beast Caliban and his confederates," his "old brain" is genuinely "troubled," and he needs to walk "a turn or two. . . . To still my beating mind." The conspiracy, as it turns out, is easily dealt with: the conspirators are very stupid, and Prospero certainly puts too much effort and too much venom into punishing them. To "a noise of hunters heard," Caliban and his associates are hunted by dogs, one of whom is called "Fury" and another "Tyrant." Prospero clearly relishes the hunting:

> Go charge my goblins that they grind their joints
> With dry convulsions; shorten up their sinews

With aged cramps; and more pinch-spotted make them
Than pard or cat o' mountain. (IV, i, 259-62)

It is not the first time that he has appeared like a bad-tempered
martinet, so that you want to ask, What is he afraid of? It is
immediately after his grim enjoyment at handing out punishment that he announces,

> At this hour
> Lies at my mercy all mine enemies. (IV, i, 263-4)

Any actor playing the part of Prospero would have to ask himself, What is the *tone* of this? It certainly isn't a calm an-
nouncement of a further stage in the magician's demonstra-
tion: to my mind it is very close to the lines immediately
preceding. The question of what Prospero intends to do with
his enemies (which means also, What is he going to do with
himself?) is a genuine one, and at this stage we have no right
to assume that the answer will be comfortably acceptable.

If we agree that in this play comparatively slight clues do
in fact bear a great weight of implication, then the opening
of Act V, which immediately follows the hounding of Prospero's minor enemies, is a genuine crisis, and we miss what
Shakespeare is doing if we see it as leading smoothly into a
pre-ordained "happy ending." Everything now depends on
how Prospero handles the situation. When the Act opens he
is tugged two ways. Miranda—"a third of mine own life"—
loves his enemy's son, and he furthers and approves, though
putting mock obstacles in the way. But he has been in a thun-
dering bad temper (which he has tried to overcome); he wants
to get his own back—to hunt his enemies with the dog, Fury.
The question is whether he can stop dwelling on his own
wrongs, real as these are, stop nagging about Caliban, and
trust his best self. That, surely, is the significance of the opening exchange with Ariel—his intuitive self. Ariel describes the
plight of the King of Naples and his party.

26

L. C. Knights

> Your charm so strongly works 'em,
> That if you now beheld them, your affections
> Would become tender.
> *Pros.*   Dost thou think so, spirit?
> *Ari.*   Mine would, sir, were I human.
> *Pros.*   And mine shall.
> Hast thou, which art but air, a touch, a feeling
> Of their afflictions, and shall not myself,
> One of their kind, that relish all as sharply
> Passion as they, be kindlier mov'd than thou art?
> Though with their high wrongs I am struck to th' quick,
> Yet with my nobler reason 'gainst my fury
> Do I take part: the rarer action is
> In virtue than in vengeance: they being penitent,
> The sole drift of my purpose doth extend
> Not a frown further. Go release them, Ariel:
> My charms I'll break, their senses I'll restore,
> And they shall be themselves.[9] (V, i, 17-32)

It is *after* this—and in the acting there should be a marked pause before "And mine shall"—that Prospero can "abjure" "this rough magic," and we hear the "heavenly music" that he has called for. As Goddard points out, not only does Prospero obey Ariel, instead of commanding him—"Music replaces magic."[10]

What follows is of great importance. Once more, music and formal movement add an undefinable suggestion to the spoken word. But the words are clear enough. The royal party shepherded by Ariel, enter to "a solemn music," Alonso "with a frantic gesture," and "all enter the circle which Prospero has made." As they come to themselves the feeling is of a more-than-individual return to consciousness.

> The charm dissolves apace;
> And as the morning steals upon the night,
> Melting the darkness, so their rising senses
> Begin to chase the ignorant fumes that mantle
> Their clearer reason. (V, i, 64-68)

(It is the same image as in George Herbert: "As the sun scatters with his light All the rebellions of the night.")

> Their understanding
> Begins to swell; and the approaching tide
> Will shortly fill the reasonable shore,
> That now lies foul and muddy. (V, i, 79-82)

Prospero is not simply *arranging* this: as "one of their kind, that relish all as sharply Passion as they," he is himself involved. As the King's party come to themselves, so he resumes his full human nature, not as magician but as man:

> I will discase me, and myself present
> As I was sometime Milan. (V, i, 85-6)

The often quoted "the rarer action is In virtue than in vengeance" is of course the key. Prospero has come to terms with his experience, and—so far as their individual natures permit —with his enemies. There is a special emphasis on the rejoicings of the good Gonzalo.

> O, rejoice
> Beyond a common joy! and set it down
> With gold on lasting pillars: in one voyage
> Did Claribel her husband find at Tunis,
> And Ferdinand, her brother, found a wife
> Where he himself was lost, Prospero his dukedom
> In a poor isle, and all of us ourselves
> When no man was his own. (V, i, 206-13)

Prospero "found his dukedom" in a more than literal sense "in a poor isle," and you certainly have to include him among those who "found" themselves "when no man was his own." But Gonzalo is not Shakespeare's chorus to the play. Antonio makes no reply to the "hearty welcome" that Prospero offers all (V,i,110-111), and it is his silence that comes between Prospero's first address to him—"Flesh and blood, You, brother mine. . . . I do forgive thee"—and the second, where "forgive" is used in the barest legal sense:

> For you, most wicked sir, whom to call brother
> Would even infect my mouth, I do forgive
> Thy rankest fault,—all of them; and require
> My dukedom of thee, which perforce, I know,
> Thou must restore. (V, i, 130-34)

It is with some reason that Auden, quoting these lines, finds that the play ends "more sourly" than *Pericles, Cymbeline,* or *The Winter's Tale.* I myself don't feel that "sourly" is the word. The harmony that is achieved is valuable—but there is no final all-embracing reconciliation. Prospero may draw his circle of relationship, but some people will choose to stay outside, and Prospero will somewhat tartly respond. The music remains something that Caliban dreams of, and that humans hear from time to time—and can sometimes actualize in their own lives. The play claims no more than that. The end is an acceptance of the common conditions and common duties of life: "Every third thought shall be my grave." Those characters who have proved themselves capable of it have undergone a transforming experience. Now they go back to the workaday world, to confront once more the imperfect, paradoxical and contradictory nature of life.

Paradox runs through the play. Again and again the double and contradictory nature of things is insisted on. To Miranda's question, "What foul play had we, that we came from thence? Or blessed was't that we did?," Prospero answers, "Both, both, my girl." Miranda's "O brave new world, That has such people in't" is counterpointed by Prospero's "Tis new to thee," which is not merely cynical and disillusioned. And the great speech in which Prospero dwells on the transience of all things human, which it would be both perverse and simple-minded to see as "pessimistic,"[11] begins,

> You do look, my son, in a mov'd sort,
> As if you were dismay'd: be cheerful, sir . . .
> (IV, i, 146 ff.)

It is in these tensions that man has to live. Gonzalo, we remember, had tried to cheer up his king by painting a picture of the ideal commonwealth:

> All things in common Nature should produce
> Without sweat or endeavour: treason, felony,
> Sword, pike, knife, gun, or need of any engine,
> Would I not have; but Nature should bring forth,
> Of its own kind, all foison, all abundance,
> To feed my innocent people. (II, i, 159-64)

Life, however, is more stubborn and intractable than that, and part of the greatness of *The Tempest* is that it forces us to recognize it. It helps us to face with something that is neither wishfulness nor despair—with something that is both resigned and positively affirming—the intractabilities and the limitations of our lives.

1. I. A. Richards, *Internal Colloquies: Poems and Plays*, (Proem to 'Goodbye Earth and Other Poems', 1958), pp. 76-77.
2. For example, by Enid Welsford in *The Court Masque*, chapter 12, "The Masque Transmuted," and by Frank Kermode in the Introduction to his New Arden edition of the play.
3. Especially in *The Shakespearean Tempest*.
4. The essay was first published in *Encounter*, December, 1957; it is reprinted in Auden's collection of critical essays, *The Dyer's Hand* and in the World's Classics volume, *Shakespeare Criticism, 1935-60*, ed. Anne Ridler.
5. F. R. Leavis, 'Shakespeare's Late Plays,' *The Common Pursuit*, p. 179. See also Kermode's Introduction to the New Arden edition; D. G. James, *The Dream of Prospero*; Philip Brockbank, 'The Tempest: Conventions of Art and Empire', *Shakespeare Survey* 8; and the commentary of Henri Fluchère, *Poèmes de Shakespeare, Suivis d'Essais Critiques sur l'Oeuvre Dramatique*, (Bibliothèque de la Pléiade), pp. 581 ff.
6. Anne Righter (Barton), Introduction to the Penguin edition of *The Tempest*, p. 19.

L. C. Knights

7. Frank Kermode (ed.), *The Tempest*, p. 103.

8. Harold Goddard. *The Meaning of Shakespeare* (Chicago University Paperbacks), Vol. II, p. 290.

9. It is interesting—though not, I think, essential for our understanding of the play—to note that some of Prospero's lines are a direct translation from the opening paragraph of Montaigne's essay "Of Cruelty." I owe this reference to Miss Eleanor Prosser; see her *Hamlet and Revenge* (Stanford U.P.), pp. 83-4, and "Shakespeare, Montaigne and the 'Rarer Action,' " *Shakespeare Studies*, I (1961), 261-6. The reference appears not to have been noticed previously by English scholars.

10. *Op. cit.* p. 284.

11. "Prospero's great speech is an utterance neither of pessimism nor of ennui but of awe":—Enid Welsford, *The Court Masque*, p. 346.

2

THEOPHANIES IN THE LAST PLAYS

Kenneth Muir

EVERYONE NOTICES THAT, WHEREAS NO GODS OR GODDESSES appear in any of Shakespeare's plays written before 1607, there is hardly a play written after that date in which the gods do not intervene. This can partly be accounted for by the fact that nearly all the early plays are set in the Christian era. Hymen appears in *As You Like It*, but he is presumably played by one of the cast. In *King Lear*, when Albany prays for the safety of the King and Cordelia, he gets a notoriously dusty answer. Macduff wonders, after the murder of his family, at the non-intervention of the Heavens, but comes to the conclusion that his family were punished for his sins. In *King Lear*, as William Elton has urged, *deus* remains *absconditus*.[1] In *Coriolanus* the hero rhetorically pretends that the gods laugh at his surrender to Volumnia's pleading, though the general tone of the play is entirely secular. In *Antony and Cleopatra*, however, there are intimations of immortality, and it could almost be said that the protagonists are manifestations of pagan gods. It is not accidental that Cleopatra should be identified with Isis; that the meeting of the lovers on the river Cyd-

nus should lend in Plutarch to a rumour that Venus and
Bacchus had met "for the general good of all Asia" and that
Enobarbus should describe the meeting in hyperbolic terms
with Cleopatra "o'erpicturing" Venus; that Antony should refer to his ancestor, Hercules; that there should be supernatural music when the god deserts him; and that after his death
Cleopatra should depict him as a demigod. But we are left
at the end with the feeling that the lovers, who have been
playing such exalted roles, may after all have been self-de-
luded and self-deceiving.

When we turn to *Pericles* there is a very great difference.
We no longer see human beings aspiring to be demigods: we
see the gods sporting with powerless human beings. Behind
the actions of the characters, and despite the textual uncertainties, we can see the controlling power of Diana. Thaisa,
before her hasty marriage to Pericles, has vowed, according
to her father, to wear Diana's livery for a year:

> This by the eye of Cynthia hath she vow'd
> And on her virgin honour will not break it.
> (II. v. 11-12)

Diana, it would seem, punishes her for taking her name in
vain by making her die in childbirth, despite Pericles' prayer
to his "divinest patroness," Lucina, one of Diana's names.
Thaisa's first words when she is brought back to life are

> O dear Diana, where am I? (III. ii. 110).

She decides to adopt the vestal livery she had formerly promised to wear; and she wears it for some sixteen years as a
priestess in Diana's temple at Ephesus. Marina in the brothel
appropriately prays to the same goddess to protect her virginity (IV.ii. 149). After Pericles has recovered his daughter
and heard (as he thinks) the music of the spheres, Diana ap-

pears to him and commands him to visit her temple, so that in the end he is reunited to Thaisa too. He might exclaim in the words of the Bible, "Great is Diana of the Ephesians!" It should be added that neither Gower nor Twine refers to Diana, except in connection with the temple where Thaisa serves the goddess. In the good physician, Cerimon, we see "a heavenly effect in an earthly actor"; or, as Thaisa puts it: "this man Through whom the gods have shown their power" (V.iii. 61).

Apart from Diana, the god who most affects the fortunes of Pericles, though he does not make a personal appearance, is Neptune. Pericles is wrecked on the shore at Pentapolis, where he meets Thaisa. On the voyage from Pentapolis there is a storm, during which Marina is born and Thaisa is cast overboard, apparently dead. Thereafter, we are told, Pericles gives himself up "to the mask'd Neptune"; and, after the report of Marina's death, he arrives at Mytilene, his ship adorned with sable banners, while the city is celebrating the feast of Neptune. It cannot be accidental that this is the beginning of the end of his trials and tribulations.

The misfortunes of Pericles, at least in the play as we have it, seem too arbitrary, and it is possible, as I have suggested elsewhere,[2] that Shakespeare made more than either the reporter or the compositor did of the broken vow to Diana, her punishment and ultimate forgiveness of Thaisa. But the new dimension apparent in *Pericles* can be seen by comparing it with one of Shakespeare's earliest plays, *The Comedy of Errors*. In its source, the father of the twins had died long before: Shakespeare begins his play with Ægeon, condemned to death in the opening scene, and reprieved in the last. Memories of the story of Apollonius of Tyre lie at the back of the denouement. The scene is set, like the final scene of *Pericles*, at Ephesus. The lost wife has become, not a priestess in the temple of Diana, but an abbess in an anachronistic priory; and

34

she is reunited to her husband, like Thaisa, after a lapse of many years. Yet Shakespeare is vague about her religion and there is no suggestion that the reunion of husband and wife is due to the workings of providence. God—and the gods—are excluded from the play, except for a reference by Ægeon in the first scene to their mercilessness.

In *Cymbeline*, which probably followed soon after *Pericles*, Shakespeare avoided the mistake of having a nearly guiltless hero as the plaything of the immortals—a tennis-ball was the favourite Renaissance analogy—by making Posthumus Leonatus doubly guilty: of betting on his wife's chastity and of ordering her murder. The play, as has too often been demonstrated, is close in certain respects to *Philaster*; but neither in *Philaster*, nor in the Boccaccio story which provided Shakespeare with his main source, nor in *Frederyke of Jennen*, nor in the historical material taken from Holinshed, could he have found the vision of Jupiter in the last act. Mr. J. M. Nosworthy has convincingly shown that Shakespeare remembered an old play, *The Rare Triumphs of Love and Fortune*, which opens with a quarrel between the gods and their attempted pacification by Jupiter:

Ye Gods and Goddesses, whence springes this strife of late?
Who are the authors of this mutenye?
Or whence hath sprung this civill discorde here:
Which on the sodaine strooke vs in this feare.
If Gods that raigne in Skyes doo fall at warre,
No meruaile then though mortall men doo iarre . . .
Ye powers deuine be reconcilde againe,
Depart from discorde and extreme debate:
Within your breasts let loue and peace remaine,
A perfect patterne of your heauenly state.

In the last act of the play, Jupiter intervenes; the lovers, Hermione and Fidelia, are reconciled with the King, who had previously banished Hermione as Posthumus had been banished in *Cymbeline*, and the King is reconciled with Hermione's father, the exiled Bomelio.

The vision vouchsafed to the sleeping Posthumus has not found many admirers.[4] The ghosts squeak and gibber in the metre that Chapman used when he spoke out loud and bold in his translation of the *Iliad*; and, though Jupiter is given the dignity of rhymed pentameters, both they and the ghosts' fourteeners seem wooden, coming as they do after the colloquial ease of Shakespeare's later blank verse. Still, when all is said, there is no reason to drag in a hypothetical collaborator to bear the responsibility of passages we happen to dislike. When one considers the other plays of Shakespeare's final period, one is not surprised to find Jupiter making a personal appearance in *Cymbeline*. Shakespeare knew that in such a scene the spectacle and the music were more important than the words, and he realized that the descent of Jove on the eagle would keep the audience interested. What he was writing was hardly more than a libretto, and we may suppose that both the ghosts and Jupiter would adopt a special manner of delivery, perhaps to a musical accompaniment.

The message conveyed by Jupiter is essentially the same as that given in *The Rare Triumphs of Love and Fortune*:

> But when the Sunne after a shower of raine,
> Breakes through the Clowdes, and shows his might againe,
> More comfortable [is] his glory then
> Because it was a while withheld of men.
> Peace after warre is pleasanter we finde,
> A ioy differd is sweeter to the minde.

So Jupiter tells the ghosts:

> Whom best I love I cross; to make my gift,
> The more delay'd, delighted. Be content . . .
> He shall be lord of Lady Imogen,
> And happier much by his affliction made.

"The Lord Loveth whom he chasteneth," we are assured. Whether Posthumus will really be happier in his marriage when he and Imogen both know he had tried to have her murdered is a question which should not be asked in the world of the play. But at least Posthumus forgives Imogen and admits she is his superior even when he still believes her guilty of adultery; he forgives freely the man who has tricked him into this belief; and Imogen forgives both the men who have wronged her.

This process of forgiveness, which is the main theme of the play, had been set in train before Jupiter's appearance which, it would seem, has no real influence on what happens: it merely informs the audience that all will come right in the end. Nevertheless one gets the impression that the Gods have been watching over their mortal favourite and that what ultimately happens is in accordance with the divine will.

There is no actual theophany in *The Winter's Tale*, but we have a greater sense than in *Cymbeline* that human lives are watched over by the gods. This is due partly to what appears to be a direct intervention when Leontes denies the oracle and is immediately informed of the death of Mamillius. But it is also due to the way in which the riddling oracle holds out a promise that Perdita will be restored and to the providential shipwreck on the coast of Bohemia so that Perdita, when she grows up, can reconcile Polixenes and Leontes by marrying Florizel.

There are other factors which have to be borne in mind. The Christian undertones of a pagan play have often been pointed out—the references to Judas, to original sin, to the need for repentance, to purgatory and redemption. Then there is Antigonus' vision of Hermione which is comparable in some ways to the vision of Diana in *Pericles*. There is also, as critics have pointed out, a curious suggestion that underneath the conscious level of the play is a vegetation myth. Leonard Digges, Shakespeare's neighbour, published his translation of *The Rape of Proserpine* in 1617, not long after the first performances of *The Winter's Tale*, and his account of the significance of the poem contained nothing that was unfamiliar to the educated Jacobean reader. Apart from the allegorical significance, Digges points out that Ceres stands for tillage, Proserpine for the seeds, and Pluto for the earth. It is difficult to believe that some of Shakespeare's original audience would not have noticed his references to the story of Proserpine. Perdita plays as she has seen others do in Whitsun pastorals; she is called Flora by Florizel and the sheep-shearing

> Is as a meeting of the petty gods,
> And you the Queen on't.

She confesses that as the mistress of the feast she is "most goddess-like prank'd up." When she is distributing the summer flowers, she wishes she had spring flowers to distribute to her fellow-maidens and she refers directly to the Proserpine story:

> O Prosperpina,
> For the flowers now that, frighted, thou let'st fall
> From Dis's waggon!—daffodils
> That come before the swallow dares, and take
> The winds of March with beauty . . . .

When she arrives in Sicilia, Leontes immediately greets her as "goddess" and that he is thinking of the spring goddess can be seen from his next speech:

> Welcome hither,
> As is the spring to th' earth.

It is hardly too fanciful to suggest that the theophany in *The Winter's Tale* is the appearance of Perdita; and that the "death" and "resurrection" of Hermione provide a parallel to

38

the period spent by Proserpine in the underworld and her return to earth.

There is no actual theophany in *The Tempest*, but Juno and Ceres are among the characters in the masque performed by the spirits. Prospero is the controller of the spirits and the deviser of the masque, as he is also the controller of the inhabitants and visitors of his island. It may be said, indeed, that the visitors are compelled to come and that they enact their own roles but in a plot devised by Prospero so that, in relation to them, Prospero is omnipotent and omniscient, and to the audience he seems to shadow forth divine qualities because he wills himself to be controlled by "god-like reason." To perceptive members of the audience, therefore, there need not be any other manifestation of the divine. In *Cymbeline* Jupiter promises that all shall be well; and Imogen and Posthumus make it well by their acts of forgiveness. In *The Tempest* the rarer action of Prospero does not require a heavenly validation.

The vision of paradise granted to Queen Katherine in *Henry VIII* is another example of the masque elements in the plays of the period; but much more interesting from our point of view is *The Two Noble Kinsmen*. There is a kind of antemasque in Act III (for which Fletcher or Beaumont was doubtless responsible), and the scene in Act V, in which the kinsmen and Emilia offer prayers to Mars, Venus and Diana and all receive apparently favourable answers, is an impressive example of theophany. There is virtual unanimity that the scene was Shakespeare's own, and that even the stage directions bear marks of his hand. Arcite's prayer to Mars contains some of Shakespeare's characteristic imagery and vocabulary:

> Thou mighty one, that with thy power hast turn'd
> Green Neptune into purple . . . .
>   who dost pluck

39

With hand armipotent from forth blue clouds
The mason'd turrets, that both mak'st and break'st
The stony girths of cities . . . .
       that heal'st with blood
The earth when it is sick, and cur'st the world
O' th' pleurisy of people.

The other speeches are equally Shakespearian, although Palamon's to Venus reveals an extravagant satirical power unlike anything he had written before, even the satirical scenes of *Troilus and Cressida.* The gods do not make an appearance on the stage—their statues are an adequate substitute for that —but they manifest themselves by the signs they give their worshippers:

> there is heard clanging of armour,
> with a short thunder, as the
> burst of a battle . . . .
>
> Here music is heard and doves are
> seen to flutter . . . .
>
> Here the hind vanishes under the
> altar and in the place ascends
> a rose-tree, having one rose upon it . . .
> Here is heard a sudden twang of
> instruments and the rose falls from
> the tree.

Arcite takes Mars's signs auspiciously; Palamon gives Venus thanks for "this fair token"; and Emilia declares that Diana's "signs were gracious." As it turns out the prayers are all answered literally: Arcite wins the fight but loses the lady; Palamon wins the lady despite his defeat in battle; and Emilia secures as husband the man who loves her best and incidentally the man who loves her first. It is no wonder that Theseus at the end of the play speaks of men as the playthings of the

40

gods and decides to give up the attempt to understand their mysterious ways:

> with you leave dispute
> That are above our question.

We are left with the question why Shakespeare in his last four or five plays introduced such scenes. The first and most obvious reason, as many critics have suggested, is that the use of Black-friars made possible more spectacular scenes than the Globe had done, even though these plays were also staged at the Globe. Two of them were seen by Simon Forman there; *Henry VIII* was certainly staged there; and *The Tempest* may well have been. But it is difficult to imagine the masque in *The Tempest* being done adequately except in a covered theatre.

The second reason which has been advanced is the popularity of court masques in the reign of James I and the wish of the King's Players to cater for the fashionable taste. (There may even have been the possibility of using costumes which had already seen service at court). Against this it must be admitted that there were plenty of masques, or entertainments of a masque-like character, at the court of Queen Elizabeth and, moreover, that some Elizabethan dramatists introduced such entertainments into their plays. It is true that Jacobean masques were often concerned with divine or supernatural characters, and this may have encouraged Shakespeare to follow suit.

He may also have been influenced by the kind of material he was dramatizing. It would have been clearly wrong to have introduced theophanies in plays set in the Christian era. One cannot imagine the appearance of God to Richard III, to Richard II, or even to the saintly Henry VI. Viola and Beatrice were too self-reliant for divine revelations; and in the comedies written in the sixteenth century things work out happily without the need of divine intervention. Ghosts and apparitions influence the action of *Hamlet* and *Macbeth*. Despite Albany's prayer for direct intervention and his confidence that Cornwall's death was a sign that the gods had indeed punished the sinners, they do not prevent the death of Cordelia. Tragedy is possible only if the gods do not save human beings from the consequences of their actions. But when Shakespeare, influenced by the success of revivals of old romantic plays, went in search of similar material, happy endings were imperative and they could be brought about only by giving the protagonists a second chance. Pericles has lost his wife and daughter: he regains them both by the help of Diana. Posthumus thinks he has murdered Imogen but she is restored to him by the help of Jupiter. Leontes thinks he has killed Hermione and Perdita: he regains them both by the working out of Apollo's oracle. Prospero loses his dukedom and recovers it after fifteen years of exile. It is sometimes said, and often assumed, that the tragic view is truer to real life than the happy endings based on second chances; and that Shakespeare was escaping from reality in his last plays: the tragic loading of Desdemona's bed is the inevitable result of Iago's villainy and Othello's credulity, whereas Hermione's recovery and Imogen's escape are improbable to say the least. But, as Calderón puts it, the worst is not always certain.

The pagan gods who watch over the actions of men in the last plays are a means of showing—as Professor William Elton thinks *King Lear* does not—that the universe is under the government of providence. This does not necessarily mean that Shakespeare's views on the matter underwent a change between 1605 and 1608; it means rather that in writing tragicomedy he was able to present a different emphasis, the more freely because of the pagan settings. But it may be noted that although one gets the impression of a theocentric universe in which things are working together for good—and although this was clearly intentional—nevertheless the happy endings depend equally on the actions of the characters themselves. One could almost say that although the same endings could happen without divine intervention, they could not happen without positive virtuous action or repentance by the main characters. *Pericles*, as we have seen, is a special case; and *Henry VIII* and *The Two Noble Kinsmen* are not wholly Shakespeare's. But in the other three plays the happy endings depend on repentance and forgiveness.

Although there is no reason to doubt that Shakespeare was at least a nominal Christian, it is apparent from what has been said that the happy outcome is determined more by human character and conduct than by divine omniscience and omnipotence, especially in the plays which followed *Pericles*. Nevertheless the theophanies are important, and they may be taken to signify that the virtuous actions of human beings are the best validation of the providential government of the world. The reunion of Pericles and Marina which makes him hear the music of the spheres, the resurrections of Thaisa and Hermione, the joy of reconciliation and forgiveness cemented by the marriage of children, are symbols of what might be, and should not be dismissed as sentimental day-dreaming by a dramatist declining into dotage.

1. William Elton, *King Lear and the Gods* (San Marino, Calif.: Huntington Libr., 1966), p. 63.
2. Kenneth Muir, *Shakespeare as Collaborator* (London: Methuen, 1960), p. 81.
3. In the Arden edition of *Cymbeline*, ed. J. M. Nosworthy (London: Methuen, 1955), pp. xxiv-xxviii.
4. G. Wilson Knight defends it convincingly and brilliantly in *The Crown of Life* (London: Oxford U.P., 1947), pp. 129-202.

3

ARE SHAKESPEARE'S LATE
PLAYS REALLY ROMANCES?

D. T. Childress

IT HAS BECOME COMMONPLACE IN SHAKESPEAREAN CRITICISM
to refer to the late plays as romances. Yet Shakespeare
never used the word in any of his plays, nor did any of his
contemporaries refer to these works as romances, for the term
"romance" was used more strictly in the critical vocabulary of
the English Renaissance than it is today. It was not used in
or to describe the *Faerie Queene*, nor was it applied to pastoral poetry (except by Fulke Greville, who refers to Sidney's
"Arcadian Romanties"),[1] for the Elizabethans regarded the
Arcadia and the *Faerie Queene* as epics. The epic was to them
a nobler, more aristocratic, more sophisticated, and more edifying form; romances were old-fashioned tales in verse, hold-
overs from the Middle Ages, which circulated among the
lower classes and country dwellers in cheap, slightly modern-
ized quarto editions and usually received critical attention
only in the form of disparagement, whether on moral grounds
—for being bawdy and Papist—or literary—for being full of
improbabilities and rhyme tags.[2] Even the late medieval

works we today call prose romances were dissociated from the metrical versions by their publishers; Caxton advertised his sumptuous folio translations from French romance as "books" or "histories," never romances, and his successors followed suit.[3]

We have, then, no contemporary evidence that Shakespeare wrote romances. It is not, of course, necessary to limit ourselves to contemporary generic labels when discussing literary works; however, if we are going to make certain assumptions about a literary work because we believe it belongs to a certain genre, then we must stop to consider whether these assumptions are valid. It is my feeling that to apply the term "romance" to Shakespeare's later plays—to *Pericles, Cymbeline, The Winter's Tale,* and *The Tempest* in particular—as has so often been done, is not only anachronistic but also very misleading.

One of the difficulties with discussing Shakespeare's late plays is that no contemporary label exists. The editors of the First Folio put *Cymbeline* with the tragedies—a classification no modern critic seems willing to accept—and *The Winter's Tale* and *The Tempest* with the comedies—a grouping more easily agreed with, especially by anyone who has seen these plays performed. Their similarities to Beaumont and Fletcher's tragicomedies are apparently not strong enough for most critics to accept that name. "Romance" thus fills a gap.

"Romance" is also popular as a label for these plays because of the breadth of interpretation that the term permits. It is not a generic term at all. Even in the Middle Ages it was used for a rather wide variety of fictional works, although as Hoops has shown, it was limited to verse narratives, of which many if not all do bear some resemblance to each other.[4] But it is the later meanings added to "romance" that have made the term so plastic. Any poet who draws his inspiration from medieval romance is assumed to be writing romances, even though he may be using romance materials to quite different ends—for an allegory, an epic, or a play; any literary form containing motifs from folklore tends to be classified as a romance.

Nor is much distinction made between "romance" and "romantic," an adjective coined in the middle of the seventeenth century to describe the qualities in all earlier literature which the "age of reason" found unreasonable, unnatural, ridiculous, and childish, only to be given much more positive connotations by the antiquarians of the eighteenth. As W. P. Ker points out, the discrepancy between "romance"—the medieval genre—and the modern meanings of "romantic" are enormous;[5] yet Northrop Frye, E. C. Pettet, R. G. Hunter, and others use it apparently as an adjective for romance, that is Shakespearean "romance," and let the connotations fly. There is a difference. Can we afford to ignore the historical meaning of the word romantic, especially the significance given to the word by the Romantic poets and critics? Romanticism is itself a difficult movement to define, but it is only blurring valuable distinctions to assume that all romancers are romantics. It may be, as J. P. Brockbank has suggested, that Shakespeare *is* a "romantic," that he is not writing romances but looking back to medieval stories from a sympathetic but sophisticated distance.[6] Brockbank is using these terms more clearly and precisely than most, and his suggestion concerning *Pericles* is one I will return to later.

The broad view of romance as a major literary category that transcends generic boundaries has been with us at least since Clara Reeve observed that romance is "of universal growth";[7] but it is especially through the work of Northrop Frye that its validity as a term describing one of four basic "modes" of literature has been widely accepted. One of the advantages of the larger idea of romance is that it enables us to see likenesses among a wide variety of works. When we call

Shakespeare's last plays "romances," we evoke vibrations reaching back to the *Odyssey* and the Book of Job and forward to (as Norman Rabkin suggests)[8] *The Confessions of Felix Krull*. It relates these plays to a certain kind of fiction that delights in the marvelous or the improbable and ends happily, but that is singularly hard to define. In one recent effort, Gillian Beer admits that most of the traits she lists as typical of romance apply to fiction generally, and she sidesteps the issue of definition by asserting that "romance is an inclusive not a defining term."[9]

If we do not try to define romance too narrowly, then it is easy enough to apply the term to the later plays. Marvelous incidents do occur—there are the dream messages, the theophanies, Prospero's magic—all four plays end happily, and the events are certainly improbable. Furthermore, each play provides an interlude of pageantry—the tournament and dancing in *Pericles*, the vision of Jupiter in *Cymbeline*, the festival in *The Winter's Tale*, and the masque in *The Tempest* —which suggests the dramatic equivalent of the descriptions of ceremony and feast in medieval romances; and the main characters are aristocratic and apparently "flat" (although not all critics would agree on this). But if we look at some of the characteristics of romance as discussed by Frye in *The Anatomy of Criticism*,[10] important discrepancies become obvious. Frye's description of the romance hero as a human being who performs marvelous actions (p. 33) can apply only to Prospero; Leontes, Posthumus, Cymbeline, and Pericles, like Frye's heroes of epic and tragedy, are all subject to the order of nature. None of the plays seems to "lean heavily on miraculous violations of natural law" (p. 34), except perhaps, again, *The Tempest*. The themes of romance—the myth of the birth of the hero, the hero's innocent youth in a pastoral world, the quest, the struggle to maintain "the integrity of the innocent world against the assault of experience" (p. 201)—are touched on, but none seems to be the basis of any of Shakespeare's plots. These assumptions about romance are not particularly helpful. There is no doubt that Shakespeare is using "romance" (or folklore) materials, but what is he doing with them? The most crucial question and the most difficult to answer concerns Shakespeare's attitude to these plays, or more accurately, the response he seems to seek from us. Almost all definitions of romance stress its subjectivity. Frye writes, "Everything is focussed on a conflict between the hero and his enemy, and all the reader's values are bound up with the hero" (p. 187). If romances are analogous to rituals and dreams, if the romance world is idealized and the characters are "stylized figures which expand into psychological archetypes" (p. 304), then romance must be naive, primitive, unself-conscious, and we must participate imaginatively and sympathetically in it. Many critics will agree that these qualities are definitely characteristic of these late plays. Such a view is basic to the "allegorical" interpretations of G. Wilson Knight and Derek Traversi. Frye, too, in his lectures on the late plays emphasizes their "primitive, mythical dimension"; the only way of looking at the statue scene in *The Winter's Tale*, he asserts, is as a "dramatic exhibition of death and revival."[11]

But such a view overlooks a great deal of evidence that Shakespeare's attitude in these plays is more ironic, that the response he elicits from us is less participatory and naive. For even though these plays have marvelous incidents and happy endings, pageantry and folklore plots, there are many devices which tend to alienate us, as spectators, from the action taking place on stage and prevent us from being absorbed into the dramatic illusion. Several studies have called attention to some of these devices. The most obvious is the use of the narrator in *Pericles*. As Francis Berry has pointed out, Gower's role serves to "frame" the play; he stands downstage between the audience and the action and directs our attention back in time and in distance to the events taking place upstage.[12] That Gower is himself resuscitated "from ashes" and speaks in an archaic manner distances the play still further from us. The self-conscious theatricality of *Cymbeline* noted by many critics serves the same purpose. Soliloquies are used not to reveal character but to present information essential to the plot, ironic asides tell us what to think about some of the characters, entrances and exits are unnecessarily emphatic; even the exaggerated rhetoric of the poetry calls attention to the play as a work of art. In *The Winter's Tale* the references to old tales, coming as they do at points where our willing suspension of disbelief is already strained, stress the improbability of the action. The role of Time, although briefer than that of Gower in *Pericles*, is similarly that of a narrator; he reminds us the events are fictitious. Prospero's long narrative in the second scene of *The Tempest* is sometimes compared to the narrations of Gower and Time; but here the "narrator" is part of the main action and his speech is expository. Nevertheless, the exaggerated effort to observe the unities may itself have a distancing effect on a sophisticated audience.

Another means by which the audience is held back from participating in the fantasy "myths" of these late plays is the abundant humor. As Charles Crow has observed, critics who emphasize the solemnity of *The Winter's Tale* have difficulty finding a place for Autolycus in their interpretations.[13] Yet Simon Forman in the earliest description we have of the play was apparently more vividly impressed by this rogue than by the "dramatic exhibition of death and revival" in the statue scene (assuming the play he saw had the same final scene we have now), since he devotes a paragraph to Autolycus and makes no mention whatsoever of Hermione's resuscitation. J. R. Brown has shown the importance of laughter in the late plays, especially that occasioned by Autolycus but also that

49

evoked by the rustics, by Paulina and the timid courtiers, by Boult and the brothel scenes in *Pericles*, by Cloten (at first) and the jailer in *Cymbeline*, and by the drunken villains in *The Tempest*.[14]

Brown offers the interesting suggestion that laughter helps us to accept the dream fantasies of the plots of these plays, since "laughter and dreams alike release our fantasies from the restrictive control of our censoring minds."[15] If this theory is true, it means that our censoring minds must be caught off guard, that we—and the Elizabethans and Jacobeans— must be primed by laughter before we will watch a manifestly unrealistic scene. We can accept the "miraculous" revival of Hermione because we are at a bemused distance from it. This use of humor (if it is so intended) is sophisticated. We are no longer in the subjective world of romance where the laws of nature are "slightly suspended,"[16] where dragons are real dragons, and our hopes, fears, and dreams are bound up with those of the bold hero who sets out to face the unknown. Clowns who comment ironically on the values of the principal characters, who parody or make fun of the main action, or who trip up the naive are rare in romance. Sir Dinadan is the exception, not the rule. There are fools in romance, there are even sympathetic comic characters, like the giant Ascopard in *Bevis of Hampton*, and there is much laughter in the form of a happy acceptance of life expressed usually at court feasts and banquets celebrating the return of the hero, his victories, or his marriage. The laughter that greets Gawain's return in *Sir Gawain and the Green Knight* is of this kind. But few efforts are made to evoke laughter from the audience unless it is derisive laughter directed at some fool, such as Sir Kay in the later Arthurian romances, who acts as foil to the hero. (Cloten plays something of this role.) Romance does not use laughter to release us from our censoring minds; perhaps this is one reason many modern minds reject romance and relegate romances to the realm of children's literature.

One of the most remarkable uses of laughter in the final plays, a use that is most alien to romance and that is especially effective in distancing the spectator from the action, is Shakespeare's use of what I think can best be called the grotesque. In his study on the grotesque in literature and art, Wolfgang Kayser describes the grotesque in terms of its effect on the reader or spectator: it applies to a scene or incident or character which seems funny at first so that we start to laugh but which is actually so horrifying and is presented so impersonally that the laughter dies in our throats. It is a mingling of comedy and horror that leaves us basically unable to respond. It is not comic, satiric, or tragic; it is "the estranged world"—"incomprehensible, inexplicable, and impersonal."[17]

Three scenes in particular in the late plays seem so estranged to me. Judging from the critical censure and apologia that they have received, I suspect that others have been similarly disturbed. These are the brothel scenes in *Pericles,* Imogen's soliloquy over Cloten's headless body in *Cymbeline,* and the death of Antigonus in *The Winter's Tale.* In each case our sympathies are engaged and yet disengaged; comedy undercuts a grim reality, yet the grimness remains to undercut the comedy. Almost every critic has something to say about these scenes, usually (more recently) to explain or justify their existence, but these apologies tend to simplify what is by nature complex. If we regard Imogen's soliloquy as farcical (as Nosworthy does)[18] or Antigonus as an evil character justly punished (as Cutts does),[19] we are denying some very real feelings that these characters have previously evoked. On the other hand, if we see Marina, Imogen, and Antigonus only as "good" romance characters, then these scenes are unforgivable. Scenes like these have no place in the world of romance.

In *The Tempest* it is not a scene but a character who creates a similar kind of distance for us. Caliban may or may not be derived from romance monsters, but he is much more difficult to deal with. He is monstrous but not altogether unreasonable; he is comic and offensive; it is not clear at the end whether he will be regenerated or not. He, too, is the focus of critical arguments. Yet these grotesque elements could all be derived from romance; the difference lies in Shakespeare's handling of them. Marina's fate greatly resembles that of the heroines of the exemplary romances in Middle English literature, such as *Emare* and *Bone Florence of Rome*; but no comic scenes intrude on the sufferings of those heroines. The mistaken corpse in *Cymbeline* is anticipated in the Middle English romance *The Squyr of Lowe Degre*, in which the heroine cares for a body she supposes is that of her lover, but again the humorous possibilities are not developed; the bizarre incident simply reveals the extreme loyalty of the heroine. These incidents are treated seriously in romance; there is no attempt to disengage our feelings for the heroine. The task assigned to Antigonus is commonplace in romance; however, in romance, the loyal courtier does not carry it out but saves the child and protects him from danger. Grim takes Havelok with him into exile; Saber hides Bevis of Hampton from his evil stepfather. Those who do expose royal children are disobeying orders to kill them, as Markus does in the *Chevalers Assigne* when his villainous heart is softened by pity. Thus in romance the situations are simpler. Antigonus, by romance standards, is cowardly and unfeeling, and his loyalties are misplaced. But the punishment that follows his misdeed is too swift, too cruel, and too comic. He is no villain. Even if he were, the comedy surrounding the scene would still cut across our sense of justice. If we laugh, it is with some embarrassment, for we are left disoriented. His death is not tragic, nor comic, nor satiric: it is grotesque.

The distance between romance and these last plays is greatest in these scenes. The plays as a whole are less disorienting, for they end happily; the main characters are re-united, sins are forgiven, and new hope for the future arises with the marriages of Marina and Lysimachus, Perdita and Florizel, and Miranda and Ferdinand, and the reunion of Imogen and Posthumus. Yet even here our rejoicing may be subdued by our misgivings about earlier events, the deaths of Mamillius, Antigonus, even Cloten; the calumniation of Hermione; the long separations of Pericles and Thaisa and Leontes and Hermione; the degradation of Marina and the questionable morality of Lysimachus; the harsh exchanges between Prospero and Caliban; the violent jealousies of Leontes and Posthumus; the threats of Polixenes. The elab-orate contrivances in the last acts of *Pericles, Cymbeline,* and *The Winter's Tale* to bring about the happy reunion might even strike some viewers as mockery, like the rescue of Macheath at the end of *The Beggar's Opera,* but if parody were intended, one would hope that it would be more ob-vious. The plays can be produced as parodies on the stage, but that is only simplifying and flattening these plays to make them easier to digest. The optimistic endings—if they are optimistic—are not altogether satisfying, nor do I think they are intended to be satisfying.

The differences between *The Tempest* and the other three plays are especially obvious here. The wrong done to Pros-pero took place twelve years before, and the plots to murder him and Alonso which we do see take place are kept safely comic; we witness no terrible passions and no one is killed —not a hair is harmed in the shipwreck, as we are twice told (I. ii. 30 and 217). Although Caliban remains a grotesque character, we suffer none of the embarrassment of children dying, women being calumniated and sold into white slavery, headless corpses being made love to on stage, violent jeal-ousy, incest, and bears dining on gentlemen.

The late plays, then, cannot fairly be called romances. We

are oversimplifying and overlooking a great deal when we do so. It is difficult, of course, to find another category so convenient. One is tempted to see the distance with which Shakespeare treats his romance materials as a kind of romantic irony, with Shakespeare, like Schlegel's romantic poet, hovering above the world on the wings of poetic reflection. Brockbank's suggestion that these plays show a "romantic response to romance" is similar, but his idea that Shakespeare is looking back "to the Middle Ages in search of rich simplicities" makes the plays sound sentimental.[20] If Shakespeare were simply recreating romance and distancing it to remind us that we are only watching a play, there would be no need for the grotesque scenes just discussed. He is not treating romance sympathetically, nor is he being satiric. Clearly a new terminology is needed. Perhaps we need to recognize, as Schlegel did, that tragicomedy is not a mixture of genres but a consistent and independent form, which, as Kayser observes, is conceptually related to the grotesque.[21] But whatever we call the plays, and however we account for, or try to account for, the detachment Shakespeare seeks to establish between play and audience, we must recognize that it is there and that these final plays are something other than "romances."

1. See Reinald Hoops, "Der Begriff 'Romance' in der mittelenglischen und frühneuenglischen Literatur," *Anglistische Forschungen* 68 (Heidelberg, 1929), 65-76.
2. Ronald S. Crane, *The Vogue of Medieval Chivalric Romances during the English Renaissance* (Menasha, Wisc., 1919).
3. According to Hoops, p. 79, the first prose work referred to as a romance is Henry Reynolds' *Mythomystes* in 1633. A glance through Arundell Esdaile's *List of English Tales and Prose Romances before 1740* (London: The Bibliographical Society, 1912) readily reveals that before 1642 most such works were called novels, novelles, histories, or tales. On the other hand, Part II, which covers the years 1643 to 1739, has many titles containing the word romance.
4. "Der Begriff 'Romance,' " pp. 46-54.

5. W. P. Ker, *Epic and Romance* (1908; rpt. New York: Dover, 1957), pp. 321-327.

6. J. P. Brockbank, *"Pericles* and the Dream of Immortality," *Shakespeare Survey* 24 (1971), 105-116.

7. Clara Reeve, *The Progress of Romance* (Colchester, 1785; rpt. New York: The Facsimile Text Society, 1930), p. xv.

8. Norman Rabkin, "The Holy Sinner and the Confidence Man: Illusion in Shakespeare's Romances," *Four Essays on Romance*, ed. Herschel Baker (Cambridge, Mass.: Harvard University Press, 1971), pp. 35-53.

9. Gillian Beer, *The Romance* (London: Methuen, 1970), p. 24.

10. Northrop Frye, *The Anatomy of Criticism* (Princeton: Princeton University Press, 1957). Subsequent references to this study will appear in the text.

11. Northrop Frye, *A Natural Perspective: The Development of Shakespearean Comedy and Romance* (New York and London: Columbia University Press, 1965), pp. 70, 113.

12. Francis Berry, "Word and Picture in the Final Plays," *Later Shakespeare*, ed. J. R. Brown and Bernard Harris, Stratford-upon-Avon Studies, 8 (London and New York, 1966), 81-101.

13. Charles Crow, "Chiding the Plays: Then Till Now," *Shakespeare Survey* 18 (1965), 1-10.

14. J. R. Brown, "Laughter in the Last Plays," *Later Shakespeare*, pp. 103-125.

15. Brown, p. 119.

16. Frye, *The Anatomy of Criticism*, p. 33.

17. Wolfgang Kayser, *The Grotesque in Art and Literature*, trans. Ulrich Weisstein (Bloomington: Indiana University Press, 1963), p. 184.

18. J. M. Nosworthy, Introduction in *Cymbeline*, The Arden Shakespeare (London: Methuen, 1955), p. lxv.

19. John P. Cutts, *Rich and Strange: A Study of Shakespeare's Last Plays* (Washington State University Press, 1968), p. 78.

20. Brockbank, *"Pericles* and the Dream of Immortality," p. 108.

21. Kayser, p. 54.

4

EARLY MODERN ENGLISH
IDIOM IN A PROSE
PASSAGE FROM *KING LEAR*

Alex Newell

THE SPEAKER OF MODERN ENGLISH IS FREQUENTLY TROUBLED by the meanings of words in Shakespeare's plays, but the semantic difference is, of course, merely one among many changes that set off Shakespeare's language from English as we use it today. Unless he is making a special study, the contemporary reader usually deals with the plays in texts that have been rendered into modern spelling, and practically the only time he suspects that English pronunciation might have sounded different 370 years ago is when he encounters two words that apparently should rhyme but do not in modern pronunciation. Occasionally an editor will call attention to a phonetic matter like the pun on *raisin* and *reason* when Jaques in *As You Like It* says to Orlando: "An you will not be answered with reason, I must die." If the two words were not outright homonyms in Elizabethan English, the pun must have been sustained by a pronunciation of *reason* that was at least obliquely similar to *raisin*. Since significances based on phonological changes are often not included by editors in their notes, most readers of Shakespeare are unaware of meanings and poetic currents determined by Elizabethan pronunciation in all its variety. For a richer example than Jaques' pun, consider the opening of Sonnet CXXIX: "The expense of spirit in a waste of shame / Is lust in action." In Shakespeare's time, there are reasons to think, *expense* and *expanse* might have been pronounced alike, and *shame* was possibly (even if unintentionally) a homonym with *sham*, a slang word of obscure origin that designated a city woman of pleasure who pretended to country innocence.[1] The opening statement of Sonnet CXXIX becomes much more alive poetically as soon as the double meanings can be included: an apparent expansion is really a wasteful expenditure, a sham that is a shame.

While on the one hand the modern reader or viewer of Shakespeare's plays usually remains unschooled in—and therefore oblivious to—orthographic and phonological changes that have taken place, he cannot avoid noticing and sensing the host of idiomatic differences springing from Shakespeare's language. Some of these differences seem accountable at first on the ground that their medium is poetry, and indeed this could be a valid explanation for many deviations from familiar usage, as we know from the work of Gerard Manley Hopkins, Dylan Thomas, and other poets who have come centuries after Shakespeare.[2] But when the speaker of modern English reads or hears a passage of prose in Shakespeare's plays, the poetic factor largely disappears, the separations from modern idiom become unquestionable, and it is quite clear that English as it was used at the end of the reign of Elizabeth I is different in quite a number of small but significant ways from English as it is spoken in the time of Elizabeth II. It should be a useful exercise, therefore, to examine a passage of Shakespearian prose dialogue to recognize and describe some of the lexical, semantic, and syntactic differences that are unavoidably present in Shakespeare's plays, unlike the more remote matters of differences in orthography and phonology.[3] The second scene of *King Lear* provides a passage that seems especially suitable because it is free of conspicuous idiosyncracies of individual speech.[4] Except for short speeches at the beginning and end of this scene, it is all in prose; and the language of the characters—Edmund, Gloucester, and Edgar—probably represents the usage of educated men, or at least Shakespeare's version of it in a style suitable for his dramatic purposes.

> *Glou.* Why so earnestly seek you to put up that letter?
> *Edm.* I know no news, my Lord.
> *Glou.* What paper were you reading?
> *Edm.* Nothing, my Lord.
> *Glou.* No? What needed then that terrible dispatch of it into your pocket? The quality of nothing hath not such need to hide itself. Let's see: come; if it be nothing, I shall not need spectacles.
> *Edm.* I beseech you, Sir, pardon me; it is a letter from my brother that I have not all o'erread, and for so much as I have perus'd, I find it not fit for your o'erlooking.
> *Glou.* Give me the letter, sir.
> *Edm.* I shall offend, either to detain or give it. The contents, as in part I understand them, are to blame.
> *Glou.* Let's see, let's see.
> *Edm.* I hope, for my brother's justification, he wrote this but as an essay or taste of my virtue.
> *Glou.* [*Reads.*] *This policy and reverence of age makes the world bitter to the best of our times; keeps our fortunes from us till our oldness cannot relish them. I begin to find an idle and fond bondage in the oppression of aged tyranny, who sways, not as it hath power, but as it is suffer'd. Come to me, that of this I may speak more. If our father would sleep till I wak'd him, you should enjoy half his revenue for ever, and live the beloved of your brother, Edgar.*—Hum!—Conspiracy! "Sleep till I wak'd him,—you should enjoy half his revenue." My son

Edgar! Had he a hand to write this? a heart and brain to breed it in? When came you to this? Who brought it?

Edm. It was not brought me, my Lord; there's the cunning of it; I found it thrown in at the casement of my closet.

Glou. You know the character to be your brother's?

Edm. If the matter were good, my Lord, I durst swear it were his; but, in respect of that, I would fain think it were not.

Glou. It is his?

Edm. It is his hand, my Lord; but I hope his heart is not in the contents.

Glou. Has he never before sounded you in this business?

Edm. Never, my Lord. But I have heard him oft maintain it to be fit that, sons at perfect age, and fathers declin'd, the father should be as ward to the son, and the son manage his revenue.

Glou. O villain, villain! His very opinion in the letter! Abhorred villain! Unnatural, detested, brutish villain! worse than brutish! Go, sirrah, seek him; I'll apprehend him. Abominable villain! Where is he?

Edm. I do not well know, my Lord. If it shall please you to suspend your indignation against my brother till you can derive from him better testimony of his intent, you should run a certain course; where, if you violently proceed against him, mistaking his purpose, it would make a great gap in your own honour, and shake in pieces the heart of his obedience. I dare pawn down my life for him, that he hath writ this to feel my affection to your honour, and to no other pretence of danger.

Glou. Think you so?

Edm. If your honour judge it meet, I will place you where you shall hear us confer of this, and by an auricular assurance have your satisfaction; and that without any further delay than this very evening.

Glou. He cannot be such a monster—

Edm. Nor is not, sure.

Glou.—to his father, that so tenderly and entirely loves him. Heaven and earth! Edmund, seek him out; wind me into him, I pray you: frame the business after your own wisdom. I would unstate myself to be in a due resolution.

Edm. I will seek him, Sir, presently; convey the business as I shall find means, and acquaint you withal.

Glou. These late eclipses in the sun and moon portend no

good to us: though the wisdom of Nature can reason it thus and thus, yet Nature finds itself scourg'd by the sequent effects. Love cools, friendship falls off, brothers divide: in cities, mutinies; in countries, discord; in palaces, treason; and the bond crack'd 'twixt son and father. This villain of mine comes under the prediction; there's son against father: the King falls from bias of nature; there's father against child. We have seen the best of our time: machinations, hollowness, treachery, and all ruinous disorders follow us disquietly to our graves. Find out this villain, Edmund; it shall lose thee nothing: do it carefully. And the noble and true-hearted Kent banish'd! his offence, honesty! 'Tis strange.

Exit.

Edm. This is the excellent foppery of the world, that, when we are sick in fortune, often the surfeits of our own behaviour, we make guilty of our disasters the sun, the moon, and stars; as if we were villains on necessity, fools by heavenly compulsion, knaves, thieves, and treachers by spherical predominance, drunkards, liars, and adulterers by an enforc'd obedience of planetary influence; and all that we are evil in, by a divine thrusting on. An admirable evasion of whoremaster man, to lay his goatish disposition to the charge of a star! My father compounded with my mother under the dragon's tail, and my nativity was under *Ursa major*; so that it follows I am rough and lecherous. Fut! I should have been that I am had the maidenliest star in the firmament twinkled on my bastardizing. Edgar—

Enter Edgar.

and pat he comes, like the catastrophe of the old comedy: my cue is villanous melancholy, with a sigh like Tom o' Bedlam. O! these eclipses do portend these divisions. Fa, sol, la, mi.

Edg. How now, brother Edmund! what serious contemplation are you in?

Edm. I am thinking, brother, of a prediction I read this other day, what should follow these eclipses.

Edg. Do you busy yourself with that?

Edm. I promise you the effects he writes of succeed unhappily; as of unnaturalness between the child and the parent; death, dearth, dissolutions of ancient amities; divisions in state; menaces and maledictions against King and nobles; needless diffidences, banishment of friends, dissipation of cohorts, nuptial breaches, and I know not what.

60

Edg. How long have you been a sectary astronomical?
Edm. When saw you my father last?
Edg. The night gone by.
Edm. Spake you with him?
Edg. Ay, two hours together.
Edm. Parted you in good terms? Found you no displeasure in him by word nor countenance?
Edg. None at all.
Edm. Bethink yourself wherein you may have offended him; and at my entreaty forbear his presence until some little time hath qualified the heat of his displeasure, which at this instant so rageth in him that with the mischief of your person it would scarcely allay.
Edg. Some villain hath done me wrong.
Edm. That's my fear. I pray you have a continent forbearance till the speed of his rage goes slower, and, as I say, retire with me to my lodging, from whence I will fitly bring you to hear my Lord speak. Pray ye, go; there's my key. If you do stir abroad, go arm'd.
Edg. Arm'd, brother!
Edm. Brother, I advise you to the best. I am no honest man if there be any good meaning toward you; I have told you what I have seen and heard; but faintly, nothing like the image and horror of it; pray you, away.
Edg. Shall I hear from you anon?
Edm. I do serve you in this business.
Exit Edgar.

The most obvious differences that set Shakespeare's language off from modern idiom are the lexical and semantic changes that have occurred in the English vocabulary since Shakespeare wrote *King Lear* sometime between 1603 (the year Queen Elizabeth died) and 1606. Throughout his vocabulary we find all degrees and types of shifts in the meanings of familiar words. At times the change has the extremity of opposite poles, as we see in Edmund's statement, "This is the excellent foppery of the world," where excellent means "exceeding" (in a bad sense).[5] Some other examples of word changes in the scene being considered are *fond* meaning foolish; *suf-*

fer meaning to allow; *closet*, room; *perfect*, full, mature; *resolution*, certainty, conviction; *lose*, to cause (a person) the loss of; *diffidence*, distrust, suspicion; *mischief*, misfortune, calamity; *fitly*, at a fitting time. Sometimes the former meanings still communicate figuratively, as in *taste* meaning trial or test and *hollowness* meaning insincerity. Not infrequently we meet words no longer current, words like *sirrah, fain, anon,* and *withal.* And sometimes a lost meaning is further obscured by a strange construction, as when Gloucester says to Edmund, "Wind me into him," in which wind is a reflexive verb meaning to insinuate oneself, and *me* is a dative of interest meaning "for me." The sense of the statement in modern English is: "Worm your way into his confidence for me."[6] In Shakespeare's time the debate over the use of inkhorn terms was still very much alive, but in his use of language Shakespeare was always guided by his conception of character and is not likely to be guilty of inkhorn flamboyance. In the present passage, only *auricular* strikes a conspicuous Latin note, and perhaps a Greek note is detectable in Edmund's technical use of *catastrophe* when he says: "He comes like the catastrophe of the old comedy." But both words have a dramatic context that makes them suitable: "auricular assurance" relates to the legal concept of auricular confession and Edmund wants his father to have formal proof of Edgar's treachery; Edgar's timely appearance gives Edmund his chance to complete the outline of his plot.[7] Edmund's allusion to drama in his remark, which could be an effective aside addressed to the audience, perhaps gives him a suggestive touch of the vice figure from "the old comedy."

In a highly analytic language like English it is useful to recognize the difference between words that may be said to "contain" meaning and structure words that do not contain meaning in themselves but help to express the relationship between the words with meaning. The former type are sometimes called categorematic words and the latter are called syncategorematic. In addition to the changes that have occurred in Shakespeare's categorematic vocabulary (in words like *closet* and *wind*), a number of differences are apparent in his use of prepositions, compared to modern usage. The phrase "confer of this" illustrates a common early modern English way of expressing "about." The expression "*in* respect *of* that" has become "*with* respect *to* that" in modern English, and today people part *on* good terms, not "in good terms," as Edmund says. "Has he never before sounded you in this business?" is an expression that is still current but in a modified form. Shakespeare's version is faithful to the nautical metaphor involved, *in* expressing the notion of depth or penetration. Transposed into modern colloquial English, the question would be: "Has he (n)ever before sounded you *out about* this business?" The modern version has shifted away from the idea of plumbing the interior to the idea of extracting sounds out of a person.

As the last example shows, idiomatic changes in the use of prepositions affect the ways in which words may be related to each other and the sense determined by the relationships. The replacement of *in* by *out* illustrates a radical alteration. Other noteworthy differences in Shakespeare's use of prepositions in the passage are the use of *at* in the modern sense of "through"—"I found it thrown in at the casement of my closet"—and *on* in the sense of "by"—". . . as if we were villains on necessity." In the first example there may possibly be a bit of ambiguity in *at*, which may be seen to convey not only the notion of "through" but also the notion of location near the window. However, since "thrown in" stresses the idea of entry and the action behind it, *at* would seem to continue and fulfill the notion of "through" initiated by *in*. The idea of a passage through is much stronger here than in a modern locution like, "Come in at the back door," in which *at* primarily specifies the place where the entry is to be made. The crux of the problem may be seen in the difference in modern idiom between "He came in *at* the back door" and "He came in *through* the back door." The former expresses the notion of location; the latter points up the means of entry. Edmund is explaining how the letter came to him and has probably used *at* because it had a stronger meaning of "through" than it does today.[8]

In the other example, the use of *on* to express "by" seems curious in the text because it starts a prepositional series in which *by* immediately takes over: ". . . as if we were villains on necessity, fools by . . . heavenly compulsion, knaves . . . by spherical predominance . . . ." Because it seems to inject the broad notion of "on the basis of," the use of *on* to start the series can be seen to enrich the function of *by* in the succeeding phrases. In connection with Shakespeare's use of *on* and *upon* in ways very similar to the example just cited, Wilhelm Franz explains the change in usage that has taken place: "*Upon* ist in dieser Funktion im 17. Jahrhundert noch ganz geläufig. Die neure Sprache bezeichnet in diesem Falle das Motiv vornehmlich durch *out of, from (by): out of kindness* (*malice*), *by* (*from*), *instinct, from fear*, indem der Bewusstseinszustand als die Quelle einer Handlung und nicht als der Boden vorgestellt wird, dem sie als Untergrund entsprossen ist."[9]

In the use of second person pronouns in the passage, Shakespeare conforms to modern practice except for two instances, one involving the use of *ye*, the other involving the use of *thee*. By Shakespeare's time *ye* and *you* were used interchangeably for the most part, though *ye* was supposedly the nominative form and *you* the accusative. The fact that pronouns were used interchangeably may be all that is needed to explain why Edmund, in urging Edgar to find safety, shifts from "I pray you" at the beginning of one speech to "Pray ye, go" at the end of it. E. A. Abbott, however, points out that *ye* is the form frequently used in entreaties.[10] If the shift from *you* to *ye* could have intensified Edmund's appeal, it is possible that he injected the shift as a special verbal gesture to help express urgency and concern. (In his next speech, he shifts back to "Pray you, go.") However the case may be, *ye* was destined to fade out of the language because it was not really essential as a word and because it was often pronounced like an unstressed *you*: [jə].

The occurrence of *thee* in the passage is more interesting because in Shakespeare's time the forms of the second person singular (*thou, thy, thee*) were used among familiars and in addressing children and persons of inferior rank.[11] *Thee* occurs when Gloucester says to Edmund, "It shall lose thee nothing."[12] What may give special significance to Shakespeare's use of *thee* is that Edmund, through his "Thou, Nature, art my goddess" soliloquy, has charged the action with the idea of social status. Rebelling against his "base" position, he has apostrophized the gods to "stand up for bastards!" When his father enters and the two men talk, they address each other with the polite pronoun *you*. There are only three speeches out of Edmund's fourteen when, in talking to his father, he does not acknowledge Gloucester's superior rank, beginning with his deferential, "So please your Lordship." As we know from Gloucester's conversation with Kent at the very beginning of the play, the father is also quite conscious of his illegitimate's son's inferior social status, for he claims emphatically to be as fond of him as of Edgar, his son "by order of law." These ideas concerning social status are part of the play's larger concern with order based not only on law but especially on observed and respected familial relations. Midway in his conversation with Edmund, believing that Edgar is treacherous, Gloucester says to his illegitimate son, "Go, sirrah, seek him," using a term that designates inferiority in the person addressed. One may ask whether Gloucester's use of *sirrah* at this point is related subsequently to his use of *thee* in his final remark to Edmund: "Find out this villain, Edmund, it shall lose thee nothing." Or is his later use of the familiar pronoun solely an expression of the new or heightened affection he intends for Edmund as a loyal son? If the familiar pronoun *thee* has special significance in the context, it would seem to exist subtly on two levels. Coming after *sirrah* in a repetition of the same instruction, *thee* appears on one level to carry the import of a superior addressing an inferior. At the very same time, the use of *thee* signals a promise of reward from a father who, in a sudden expression of affection, wants to be sure of at least one loyal son. Since Shakespeare's audience would be attuned to nuances of social distinction and affection in the use of second person pronouns, it is possible that they found significant expressive values in Gloucester's use of *thee*.[13]

While Shakespeare's use of second person pronouns in the passage seems for the most part to foreshadow modern practice, his use of the relative pronouns *who* and *that* is appreciably different from modern idiom. In Chaucer, the relative pronoun *who* is never used in the nominative case, and the "almost universal" relative is *that*.[14] In early modern English *who* has assumed a nominative function, but the Shakespeare passage indicates that it has a broader reference than it does today. In present day English *who* is used only to refer to people. It would not be used as we find it in the letter Edmund gives to Gloucester: ". . . aged tyranny, who sways, not as it hath power, but as it is suffer'd." In this instance we may have encountered a stylistic trait of Shakespeare, as we gather from Abbott's comment about *who*: "It is especially used after antecedents that are lifeless or irrational, when personification is employed, but not necessarily after personal pronouns."[15] Even if we accept *who* as a personification of "tyranny," the subsequent incongruity with *it* suggests a freer reference in the use of *who*. *That* in the passage is also playing a broader role than it has now, though its current function is still quite versatile. When Edmund says, "I should have been that I am had the maidenliest star in the firmament twinkled . . .," the pronoun *that* seems to have a double reference. In one sense it is a relative expressing "what" or "who" (or both); and in another sense it is a demonstrative expressing *that*. The combined aspects give a special forcefulness to the word. Today we would use *what* as the pronoun combining the demonstrative sense of *that* and the relative sense of *who*.

In her excellent essay titled, "Shakespeare and Elizabethan English," Gladys Willcock stresses a point worth recalling: "Custom was the only guide the Elizabethan possessed . . . We should be chary of imputing to the Elizabethan any habit of grammatical analysis such as we make in answering syntactical questions, however little grammar of the parsing variety we have learnt at school."[16] The incongruity between *who* and *it* clarified in the analysis above perhaps illustrates Miss Willcock's point about Elizabethan freedom from our type of grammatical analysis—and our notions of correctness. The Elizabethans also did not apply our algebraic rule about double negatives to language, as we may gather from the two examples of double negatives in the passage. When he intends to affirm his father's exclamation that Edgar cannot be an evil monster, Edmund says, "Nor is not, sure." And after asking Edgar if he left his father on good terms, Edmund asks again: "Found you no displeasure in him by word nor countenance?" Both of these instances demonstrate the clear emphasis that can be achieved through the double negative. Edmund's question, ending with a return to the negative aspect of his interrogation, shows the refined rhetorical use that can be made of the double negative.

Edmund's question, with its subject-verb inversion, also

brings us to the important matters of word order and the use of verbs in Shakespeare's English. Because the verb is such a frequently used part of speech and has so many functions, even short conversations like those Edmund has with his father and brother are enough to reveal a variety of idiomatic features. These features concern the patterns of word order, the use of *do* as an auxiliary, the occurrence of progressive constructions, and the status of certain verb forms. The subject-verb inversion in Edmund's question illustrates a device commonly used in some languages (German, for example) to construct an interrogative sentence. Several questions in the passage show such inversion: "Spake you with him?" "Parted you in good terms?" "Why so earnestly seek you to put up that letter?" A characteristic of all these examples is that they avoid *do* as an auxiliary. Such avoidance also occurs in Gloucester's negative construction when he says: "The quality of nothing hath not [does not have] such need to hide itself." This apparent avoidance of *do* seems to reserve the use of that word as a means of expressing emphasis, as in Edmund's statement, "I do serve you in this," and in Edgar's question, "Do you busy yourself with that?"

Subject-verb inversion reveals something more fundamental about English idiom in Shakespeare's time than a way of framing questions without using *do*, which thereby seems to acquire additional strength as an intensifier. The orientation of people then to patterns of word order different from present-day English is a definite implication of such inversion, whether or not it represents actual colloquial usage. If Edgar's question did have extra intensity because it begins with *do* (it is really not necessary to insist that it did), this was so partly because there existed a familiar verb-subject pattern to construct interrogatives, a pattern that was idiomatic then —or at least was conventional as stage language—but which has faded out of modern English. Modern English idiom strives to preserve a subject-verb sequence and restricts inversion to certain verbs used as auxiliaries when questions are asked: When *did* you go? *Is* he coming? *Shall* we go? *Can* he come? It is not only the omission of *did* in forming the interrogative that makes us sensitive to the construction of "When saw you . . . .?"; it is also the unfamiliar verb-subject sequence of the word pattern. This pattern is one of several in the passage that differ from patterns of modern idiom. Other examples are: "We make guilty of our disasters, the sun, the moon, and stars . . . ." (in modern word order: "We make the sun, the moon, and stars guilty of our disasters") and "How long have you been a sectary astronomical?" in which the position of the adjective after "sectary" may be a trace of French influence (although Edgar may here be using an established technical term, possibly with derision of its inflated quality produced by the word order). The presence of such unfamiliar patterns in the passage, *in addition to* the patterns of modern idiom, suggests that English in Shakespeare's day was oriented either to a less rigid sense of word order (a possible implication of Miss Willcock's remarks above) or to a greater variety of patterns—or more probably both.

Several other features of verbs in the passage need to be noticed before concluding this brief study of the characteristics of idiom in a specimen of Shakespeare's prose. "Hath writ" illustrates a confusion in the use of preterite and past perfect forms, and together with *spake* it suggests the fluid state of many strong verbs in the sixteenth and seventeenth centuries. What seems to be confusion, however, was probably freer acceptable usage in Shakespeare's time, for Shakespeare has no strict consistency in the use of verb forms. The use of the *-th* form, as seen several times in *hath* and once in *rageth*, was a residue from Middle English in early modern, and Professor Baugh says, "It is altogether probable that during Shakespeare's lifetime *-s* became the usual ending for this part of the verb in the spoken language."[17] In distinct contrast with the greater frequency of progressive verb constructions in modern idiom, there are only two progressive verb constructions in the passage, one in the present tense ("I am thinking, brother . . . .") and one in the past ("What paper were you reading?").

Together with the infrequent use of *do* as an auxiliary and the complete absence in the passage of compound participles, the dearth of progressive forms suggests that there has been a general increase in periphrastic verb constructions since Shakespeare's time. Gloucester's use of the subjunctive *be* in his remark, "If it be nothing . . . ," was common in Elizabethan idiom but is now archaic. When Edmund says, "If the matter were good, my Lord, I durst swear it were his," we see a conditional form of *dare* that is no longer idiomatic—*durst* expressing "would dare." Finally, genitive-gerundive constructions like "not fit for your o'er-looking" and "on my bastardizing" seldom occur in modern idiom, which would probably use an infinitive construction in such expressions—*not fit for you to see.*

"There is no question relating to Shakespeare as a writer which does not involve his style," says M. C. Bradbrook.[18] It is an axiom with which I am fully in accord. In the passage there are stylistic matters as well as lexical, semantic, and syntactic ones which determine the difference between Shakespeare's language and ours. We therefore should also recognize a difference in stylistic idiom as distinct from linguistic or grammatical idiom, although the two are not always separable, especially when we are concerned with the poetics of Shakespeare's art. Matters like the infrequency of progressive verb constructions and the use of subject-verb inversion or the genitive-gerundive construction, for example, may very well be grammatical attributes of relatively formal discourse, so that in the scene Shakespeare may be modulating a seemingly colloquial tone with formal-sounding notes. Similarly, to choose random examples from the passage, we become conscious of non-colloquial qualities in the rhetorical flourishes and harmonies of Edmund's ridicule of astrology, and in the alliteration and parallelism and balances of phrasing in an utterance like Gloucester's question: "Had he a hand to write this? a heart and brain to breed it in?" Distinctly rhetorical characteristics such as repetitions, balances, symmetrical and antithetical constructions, elaborately extended series, pointed-up logicality, and others, are reminders of what Professor Kenneth Muir has stated in a discussion of "Shakespeare and Rhetoric": "Shakespeare was in no danger of becoming too colloquial in his dialogue. Even his apparently colloquial prose is a good deal further from actual Elizabethan speech than the dialogue of Middleton or Jonson."[19] As will be explained shortly, the determination of colloquial idiom is complicated by the fact that the art of rhetoric played an important role not only in stage-language but also in educated usage, especially when the language of men from the court was involved, as in the case of the Gloucester family.

The passage has not been exhausted in this examination, but by now it has become clear that Shakespeare's language is set off from modern English idiom, not by big differences but by the cumulative effect of a large number of small ones. Since the passage is not a transcription of spoken speech but rather artistically created dialogue for personages in a drama, matters of style and artistic purpose inevitably prevent us from regarding the dialogue as a representation of actual speech. Many readers and viewers and actors, however, regularly make the mistake of equating the dialogue Shakespeare wrote for his characters with colloquial Elizabethan speech. Such an error, which has no bearing on the analysis of idiomatic differences between Shakespeare's English and ours, is probably determined by the very popular and perhaps prevalent convention of naturalism in modern drama, supported by an ignorance of Elizabethan dialects and Elizabethan traditions in education, literary language, dramatic writing, and the art of acting. Unavoidably, therefore, an interesting question to ask about the passage is: how much of a departure, if any, is the speech of Gloucester, Edmund, and Edgar from what was likely to have been the colloquial speech of educated men of their station in Shakespeare's time? Even if it is difficult to arrive at a conclusive answer, the question is of special interest because in the present passage we are concerned with prose dialogue that appears to be the colloquial speech of persons who circulate at court, written at a time when the language of educated people at court and in London had established itself as standard English.[20]

From what we know of Elizabethan practices in education, the language used by educated people like the Gloucesters was strongly influenced by the instruction they received in formal logic and rhetoric, or what may be comprehensively called the arts of language. These arts of language, resting on Greek and Latin bases, formed the subject of many books with titles like *The Arte of Rhetorique* by Thomas Wilson, *The Artes of Logike and Rhetorike* by Dudley Fenner, and *The Arte of English Poesie* by George Puttenham. The arts of language became part of an educated person's idiom of thought and expression; they entered naturally into the written language and became inextricably part of Elizabethan prose style, complementing the tradition in literary language. Shakespeare's grammar school education in the arts of language has been documented at length by T. W. Baldwin in *William Shakespeare's Small Latine and Lesse Greeke*; his use of what he learned in school has been studied by Sister Miriam Joseph in her valuable book, *Shakespeare's Use of the Arts of Language*. Given the great importance of the arts of language in Shakespeare's time, we cannot always draw a line easily between good colloquial language with its rhetori-

Alex Newell

cal qualities and stage language with its own long-standing tradition of rhetoric as a stylistic convention, not only in dramatic dialogue but also in the art of acting. It is therefore important to be aware that an intimate relationship existed between educated speech and stage speech through their common strong interest in the arts of language. Furthermore, the highly stratified class structure of Elizabethan society, regulated in every sphere by a sense of "degree," exerted a considerable force on the way language was used. It forced speech into formalized patterns and conventions with which Shakespeare's audience felt quite at home. "The artificial and rhetorical aroused no instinctive distrust," Miss Willcock reminds us.[21] Whatever the distance might have been between stage speech and the colloquial speech of educated people, there was no essential incongruity of style such as sets off Elizabethan standard English from the standard forms of the language used today in the English-speaking world. The linguistic and rhetorical characteristics of stage speech that represented the upper classes of society were the richer, more formalized extensions in art of the language educated people valued and cultivated in writing and speaking.

1. E. J. Dobson makes an observation that is pertinent to this possibility: "There is no reason to suppose that an Elizabethan in punning would not take full advantage of all the variant modes of speech then current." "Early Modern Standard English," *Transactions of the Philological Society* (Oxford: Basil Blackwell, 1955), p. 46. It is also worth noting that the double meanings of *expense* are further enriched if we know that *spend* in Shakespeare's time could mean "to expend sexually; to discharge seminally," as Eric Partridge points out in *Shakespeare's Bawdy* (New York: E. P. Dutton, 1960), p. 161.

2. Because word order in poetry is freer than in prose, Wilhelm Franz makes the following prefatory comments in the chapter on word order in his study of Shakespeare's language: "Nachstehende Beobachtungen über die Wortstellung bei Sh. gründen sich vornehmlich auf die Prosa, weil an ihr am besten der Entwicklungsgang der Stellung des Wortes im Satz klargelegt werden kann. Die gebundene Rede kommt für vorliegenden Zweck erst in

zweiter Linie in Betracht, da hier der Subjectivismus des Dichters in der Handhabung der metrischen Form eine zu hervorragende Rolle spielt und die Wortstellung in der Poesie notwendigerweise eine freire sein muss als in der Prosa." *Die Sprache Shakespeares in Vers und Prosa* (Halle, Salle, Germany: Max Niemeyer, 1939), p. 575.

3. Matters of orthography and phonology have been studied by E. J. Dobson, *English Pronunciation, 1500-1700* (London: Oxford University Press, 1957) and Helge Kökeritz, *Shakespeare's Pronunciation* (New Haven: Yale University Press, 1953).

While the English language today has many dialectal differences in different parts of the English-speaking world, and while there is no one normative dialect which can be said to be more representative of Modern English than any other, it seems safe to say that English as it was used in Shakespeare's time is set off in quite a number of small but significant ways from any present-day English dialect. Unavoidably, the explanations of idiomatic differences in this essay are based on English as I know it and use it. For this reason certain explanations may not be in accord with dialectal usage other than my own. Nonetheless, these explanations may serve as illustrations of differences that have occurred one way or another during the course of almost four centuries. They should also help persons speaking other dialects of English to identify and clarify specific differences between Early Modern English idiom and English as they know it and use it.

4. The text used is the Arden paperback edition: William Shakespeare, *King Lear*, ed. Kenneth Muir (New York: Random House, 1964). "The present text of the play," Professor Muir explains in his Introduction, "is based on F; but since the F texts of other plays contain numerous errors and 'sophistications' (i.e. unauthorized 'improvements'), we shall accept Q readings not only where the F readings are manifestly corrupt, but also where Q seems palpably superior." In his Preface Professor Muir cites materials he used in preparing his edition: "This revision of W. J. Craig's edition has been rendered simpler than it would otherwise have been by the publication of the Shakespeare Association Facsimile of the First Quarto, Dr. J. Dover Wilson's facsimile of the Folio text, Sir Walter Greg's *The Variants of the First Quarto of "King Lear"* (1939-40), and Professor G. I. Duthie's splendid edition (1949). I have used all these; and I have consulted the works listed in Tannenbaum's useful *Bibliography*, besides many more books and articles since published." After checking Professor Muir's text of the passage (and the textual notes he provides) against the Shakespeare Association Facsimile of the First Quarto and the Norton Facsimile of the First Folio, prepared by Charlton Hinman, I decided to use Professor Muir's text as it stands. Needless to say, for the purposes of this study, both Q and F represent the English of Shakespeare's time perfectly, even if they are not transcriptions of spoken English and even if in isolated instances they may not represent perfectly what Shakespeare wrote or intended.

5. C. T. Onions, *A Shakespeare Glossary* (Oxford: Clarendon Press, 1949). This glossary and the *New English Dictionary* are the sources for all historic definitions given.

6. Editorial note, *King Lear*, p. 30.

Alex Newell

7. John Crow Ransom has an interesting article discussing Shakespeare's artistic juxtaposition of Latin words with native ones: "On Shakespeare's Language," *Sewanee Review*, 55 (1947), 181-198.

8. Wilhelm Franz does not say anything about *at* in this sense. What he says about *out at* and *forth at* suggests indirectly—though insufficiently—the explanation I have attempted. E. A. Abbott in *A Shakespearian Grammar* (London: Macmillan, 1881) also does not comment on *at* in this sense.

9. Franz, p. 382.

10. Abbot, p. 236.

11. Professor Albert Baugh thinks English practice in the use of pronouns seems to have been suggested by French usage. *A History of the English Language* (New York: Appleton-Century Crofts, 1957), p. 281.

12. According to Abbott, *thee* in such instances is a reflexive.

13. That Shakespeare was probably managing the use of pronouns for expressive purposes in *King Lear* is supported by the following information Gladys Willcock provides: "Elizabethan letters and many recorded scraps of conversation show continual 'my lordings' and 'your gracings' between equals, with the appropriate adaptations of diction and sentence-structure, and children were expected to express themselves with almost grovelling servility." "Shakespeare and Elizabethan English," *Shakespeare Survey* 7 (Cambridge: Cambridge University Press, 1954), p. 13. In an earlier essay, also entitled "Shakespeare and Elizabethan English," Miss Willcock makes a critical comment related to this matter: "In Lear there is something peculiarly horrible in the manner in which Goneril and Regan preserve hollow forms of filial respect: 'O Sir, you are old . . . .'" *A Companion to Shakespeare Studies*, ed. Harley Granville-Barker and G. B. Harrison (Cambridge: Cambridge University Press, 1934), p. 133.

14. Baugh, p. 296.

15. Abbott, p. 176.

16. *Shakespeare Survey* 7, p. 22.

17. Baugh, p. 298.

18. M. L. Bradrook, "Fifty Years of the Criticism of Shakespeare's Style: A Retrospect," *Shakespeare Survey* 7 (Cambridge: Cambridge University Press, 1954), p. 1.

19. *Shakespeare Jahrbuch*, 90 (1954), 60.

20. See E. J. Dobson, "Early Modern Standard English," for evidence that "from early in the sixteenth century there was in being an idea that there was a correct way of speaking English" and that it was based on the speech of London as a geographic region but with "the more precise observation that it was the language of the Court, i.e. of the highest social classes and of the administration."

21. *Shakespeare Survey* 7, p. 13.

5

THEME IN *TIMON OF ATHENS*

Michael Tinker

Timon of Athens HAS PROVOKED AN EXTRAORDINARY DIVER-
gence of critical opinion.[1] Contrary to those critics who
find *Timon* incomplete and disorganized, I believe the play
is highly structured. The theme, simply stated, is "Man shall
not live by bread alone." That theme is brought out by the
imagery, the plot structure, and the inversion of the theme in
the protagonist, that is, by the representation of a man who
does live by bread alone.

With regard to the structure of the play, Una Ellis-Fermor
calls *Timon* "a design not fully comprehended."[2] David Cook
considers the play to be "powerfully conceived, but not realized in fully developed dramatic terms."[3] Even J. C. Maxwell,
the best critic on this play, states that Shakespeare "did not
bring his own work on the play to a satisfying state of completion."[4] I submit that for an incomplete play it shows a remarkable amount of structural unity. It is divided into two distinct
halves of almost exactly the same length (I.i to III.v, III.vi to
V.iv).[5] Each of these halves has near its beginning a banquet
given by Timon, and each ends with Alcibiades talking to the

Senators of Athens. In the first part of the play we have the entrances of the Poet and Painter, Apemantus, and Alcibiades, in that order. In the second half these characters reappear in precisely the opposite order. Moreover, there is a point about Timon's behaviour critics have apparently overlooked: namely, that his munificence is not confined to the first half of the play. In the second half he continues to give away gold: to Alcibiades, to the prostitutes, to the Banditti, and to Flavius. In short, the whole play seems to be a carefully balanced whole of parallels and contrasts. If we accept the thesis, that the play is unfinished, it seems to me that we must admit that a play with so many obvious and carefully developed structural elements must have been very near to completion.

Earlier critics tended to think of Timon as a noble man who, betrayed by his friends, rejected mankind entirely and became a misanthrope.[6] More recently critics perceive that there is really nothing essentially noble about Timon in the first half of the play. As Cook comments, "Timon is not discriminatingly or positively generous."[7] Maxwell astutely observes that Timon "has no true sense of reciprocity in friendship: 'there's none Can truly say he gives if he receives,' and if he seems to recant that later in the scene—'what need we have any friends, if we should ne'er have need of them?'— the contradiction merely emphasizes his irresponsible attitude."[8] The first passage Maxwell quotes is ironic: among Timon's friends "none can truly say he gives" since each receives back more than he gives.

One of the problems is that Timon's generosity is effortless. O. J. Campbell has remarked about the early scenes of the play that the various people who come to Timon "are arranged as a procession of individuals, each one serving as the illustration of the same vice. . . . The similarity of his response to each of these adulators in turn makes his generosity seem automatic and therefore ridiculous."[9] Timon's bounty does not require him to strain himself at all; at a later time his misanthropy will be equally effortless.

In the play Timon's bounty is consistently associated with eating, a natural but necessary function that we tend to think of largely as a pastime, until we are hungry. Timon tells the Painter: "We must needs dine together" (I.i.167). Only a short time later he tells the messenger from Alcibiades: "You must needs dine with me" (I.i.243). Timon's generosity is represented by his feasts. Nobles come to "taste Lord Timon's bounty" (I.i.273). The eating images emphasize what I see as the basic theme of the play. Food becomes a metaphor for material values. Timon and his friends do live by bread alone: indeed, they see the world as a dining hall.

Timon, for all his talk of friendship, does not really understand what friendship is. He thinks friendship lies solely in giving, that because he gives he is good, and that all other men are equally good. It is important to stress Timon's opinion of himself in the first part of the play, because it contrasts sharply with his opinion later. The failure to understand what Timon thinks about Timon has led many critics astray. Almost his first words in the play are "I am not of that feather to shake off / My friend when he must need me" (I.i.103-104). Timon clearly has a high opinion of himself at this point. But why this high opinion? Because he is bountiful, and as he says, "We are born to do benefits" (I.ii.99-100). His high opinion of himself is unjustified, and Timon will learn its falseness all too soon.

Timon's concept of friendship is contrasted with that of Flavius. The steward, who has no bounty, is nevertheless more capable of friendship than is Timon. Any sensible person would have deserted Timon as soon as the course of Timon's fortunes became clear. Most of the sensible people do just that. But sensible people live by bread alone, and Flavius does not. That Flavius is meant to contrast with the flat-

terers of Timon is obvious; that he is meant to contrast with
Timon himself may be overlooked. When Flavius distributes
his own savings among the other servants, R. P. Draper thinks
that Flavius' action "is a notable instance of the servants' dis-
cipleship of the master's idealism and practice."[10] The critic
has missed the point. Flavius' action is not motivated by any
desire to give *per se*. He says, "The latest of my wealth I'll
share amongst you" (IV.ii.23). "Share" is a word significantly
absent from Timon's vocabulary. As Maxwell points out, in
Flavius "we see genuine personal affection, contrasting
strongly with Timon's automatism."[11] It is Flavius' acceptance
of non-material values that makes him considerably more
than a disciple of Timon.

The other major contrast in the play is between Timon and
Alcibiades. The first encounter between Alcibiades and the
Senate, which Miss Ellis-Fermor finds so hard to account for,
is one of the more significant scenes in the play.[12] It illustrates,
among other things, the quite specific differences between Alcibiades and Timon. Alcibiades, like Timon, is prepared to
give his possessions for his friends: "I'll pawn my victories,
all / My honours to you, upon his good returns" (III.v.82-83).
However, although Alcibiades and Timon are both willing to
give up their possessions, Alcibiades' giving is towards a specific end. Timon gives indiscriminately, Alcibiades for a purpose. There is another crucial difference between Alcibiades
and Timon; Alcibiades has no illusions about mankind. He
realizes that men are sometimes less than noble: "To be in
anger is impiety; / But who is man that is not angry?" (III.v.
57-58). Timon, on the other hand, thinks men are faultless
and never doubts that his friends will help him until they have
in fact not helped him. Alcibiades displays what Maxwell
calls "balanced humanity" in contrast to Timon's "inhuman
excess."[13] I find in this scene a confrontation between the
two opposing sets of values: Alcibiades representing non-

material values, and the Senate representing purely material
ones. Alcibiades is willing to give up his material possessions
for the freedom of his friend. This contrast between values
will be further developed in the confrontations between Timon and Alcibiades and Timon and Flavius.

In the second half of the play we find Timon outside
Athens. A significant element of Timon's change is his self-
condemnation. In his first impassioned soliloquy outside the
wall, he says:

> Timon will to the woods; where he shall find
> The unkindest beast more kinder than mankind.
> The gods confound—hear me, you good gods all—
> The Athenians both within and out that wall!
> (IV.i.35-38)

Such a curse must, of necessity, include Timon himself, who
is an Athenian. Having previously seen all men as good, Timon now sees all men as evil. And since all men are evil, and
Timon is a man, he must accept himself as evil, too. David
Cook thinks that "when Timon finds his new supply of gold,
his condemnation of the malpractices it could foster is elo-
quent, but he conveniently overlooks the fact that his own
abuse of wealth is to be included in the indictment."[14] I do not
think that Timon "conveniently overlooks" anything. Only a
few lines earlier he has said, "There's nothing level in our
cursed natures / But direct villainy" (IV.iii.19-20). Among the
"cursed natures" Timon includes his own. He believes that
his only recourse after the loss of his fortunes is to despise
himself: "Not nature, / To whom all sores lay siege, can bear
great fortune, / But by contempt of nature" (IV.iii.6-8). He
has no values other than material ones to uphold him in his
time of need. Timon among men assessed himself and others
materially; Timon in exile continues to do so.

The entrance of Alcibiades shortly after Timon's discovery

of the gold is crucial. "What art thou there?" asks Alcibiades. "A beast, as thou art" (IV.iii.49-50), replies Timon. Timon again includes himself in his general damnation of mankind. When Alcibiades asks how Timon has changed, Timon tells him:

> As the moon does, by wanting light to give.
> But then renew I could not, like the moon;
> There were no suns to borrow of. (IV.iii.68-70)

Clearly Timon is not talking about money here. He has money. He has found the gold. "Suns" must refer, not to men with money, but to good men. Timon is saying that there are no good men from whom he may draw kindness. It is highly ironic that one of the few kind people in the play is standing before him, yet Timon cannot recognize the kindness of Alcibiades:

> *Alcib.* Noble Timon, what friendship may I do thee?
> *Tim.* None, but to maintain my opinion.
> *Alcib.* What is it, Timon?
> *Tim.* Promise me friendship, but perform none.
> If thou wilt not promise, the gods plague thee,
> for thou art a man! If thou dost perform,
> confound thee, for thou art a man! (IV.iii.71-77)

Timon's reply to the first question is, of course, exactly, what he demanded of friendship before his change of fortune: maintenance of opinion. Just as he previously demanded kindness of men and could see no evil, now he demands evil and can see no kindness. In his reply to the soldier's second question, he damns Alcibiades for his very humanity.

I would argue that part of the difficulty is that Timon has not really changed. The word "bounty" was associated with Timon in the first half of the play, and now the two prostitutes call him "bounteous Timon" (IV.iii.169). It is as easy for

81

him to be misanthropic as it was for him to be generous. It requires no more effort on his part to give stones than it formerly required to give gold. Only material things motivate Timon. In the first half of the play those things took the form of feasts; in the second half they take the form of roots. Timon laments "That nature, being sick of man's unkindness, / Should yet be hungry" (IV.iii.178-179). Only hunger moves Timon. He truly lives on bread alone. Timon is unwilling to accept anything other than material wants in man's nature. He has rejected everything else.

The next person to come in is Apemantus. The contrast set up here is a minor but important one. Apemantus chides Timon for his misanthropy. Furthermore, Apemantus claims that "Thou'dst courtier be again, / Wert thou not beggar" (IV.iii.243-244). The statement is of course false: Timon is at this point neither beggar nor courtier. Apemantus does not have the insight to see through Timon. Timon, however, sees through Apematus very well.

> *Apem.* I love thee better now than e'er I did.
> *Tim.* I hate thee worse.
> *Apem.* Why?
> *Tim.* Thou flatter'st misery.
> (IV.iii.235-236)

Timon realizes that Apemantus is, in his own way, just as much a flatterer as all the others: "If thou hadst not been born the worst of men, / Thou hadst been a knave and a flatterer" (IV.iii.277-278). Apemantus is what he is because he cannot be what he wants to be. Timon, however, with his new found gold, can be whatever he wants to be. He is what he is by choice.

The conversation continues:

> *Apem.* Art thou proud yet?
> *Tim.* Ay, that I am not thee.

Michael Tinker

Apem.   I, that I was
      No prodigal.
Tim.   I, that I am one now.
Where all the wealth I have shut up in thee,
I'ld give thee leave to hang it. Get thee gone.
That the whole life of Athens were in this!
Thus would I eat it. [*Eating a root*] (IV.iii.278-284)

There are several insights to be found in these lines. Timon realizes that Apemantus is in some sense worse than Timon is, because Apemantus holds the same views but does not follow them through to the same conclusion—self-exile. Timon also recognizes that his own apparent change is only superficial: he is still prodigal. The irony is that given these realizations Timon cannot advance beyond them. Cook observes, "Timon has found a much more secure retreat than in his previous dream of perfect living. . . . Timon will not accept the human condition with its confusions and compromises. He must be more, or less, than man."[15] The last line Timon speaks above again shows his determination to see the world as food. Just before Apemantus leaves, he confirms that determination: "I am sick of this false world, and will love nought / But even the mere necessities upon't" (IV.iii.378-379). Timon again denies non-material values and demonstrates his conviction to live by bread (or roots). He lacks the strength to go beyond "mere necessities." It is precisely this lack of strength that differentiates him from Alcibiades and Flavius, both of whom recognize values beyond the material.

Apemantus leaves and the Banditti enter. Timon immediately condemns them for the same fault that he condemns all others for: "You must eat men" (IV.iii.428). He soon launches into a long description of nature as a thief:

> The Sun's a thief and with his great attraction
> Robs the vast sea; the moon's an arrant thief,
> And her pale fire she snatches from the sun;

83

> The sea's a thief, whose liquid surge resolves
> The moon into salt tears; the earth's a thief
> That feeds and breeds by a composture stol'n
> From general excrement; each thing's a thief.
>   (IV.iii.439-445)

It is quite in character that Timon must extend this monomaniacal point of view to everything. In the words of Maxwell: "Since for Timon giving must be only giving, receiving only receiving, even if he has in his adversity expected a reversal of the roles, the normal processes of give-and-take in nature, appear as thievery, on the analogy of the corrupted society of Athens, which has also lost the notion of reciprocity."[16] Timon has again refused to see the world as anything but evil.

The appearance of Flavius after the Banditti leave seems to me to be the crux of the play. Flavius does not understand what has happened to Timon. He makes the same mistake that Apemantus made: "What an alteration of honor has desp'rate want made!" (IV.iii.465). There is no "desp'rate want," although Flavius cannot know that. When Timon first sees Flavius he treats him as he treats all other men:

> *Tim.*   Away! What art thou?
> *Flav.*   Have you forgot me, sir?
> *Tim.*   Why dost ask that? I have forgot all men;
> Then, if thou grant'st th'art a man, I have forgot thee.
>   (IV.iii.475-478)

Flavius, like Alcibiades, is condemned for being a man. There is a notable difference, however, between this confrontation and the others. Flavius weeps, and Timon is moved: "Had I a steward / So true, so just, and now so comfortable? / It almost turns my dangerous nature mild" (IV.iii.494-496). Almost—but not quite. Timon very nearly accepts values beyond material ones. But he does not. And his refusal to do so is tragic.

84

Michael Tinker

The existence of Flavius gives the lie to Timon's neat little syllogism: all men are evil; I am a man; therefore, I am evil. But all men are not evil. Flavius is good. Timon totters for a moment on the brink of humanity:

> Forgive my general and exceptless rashness,
> You perpetual-sober gods! I do proclaim
> One honest man. Mistake me not, but one;
> No more, I pray—and he's a steward.
> How fain I would have hated all mankind!
> (IV. iii. 499-503)

The tragedy lies in Timon's inability to reject the syllogism even after its major premise has been proven false. If he accepts the possibility that man can be good, then he must also accept the responsibility to be good himself. He must give up the easy life of Misanthropos. He must accept values beyond bread—beyond the material world. And he cannot. Timon drives Flavius away, but not before Flavius has pointedly remarked: "You should have fear'd false times when you did feast" (IV.iii.517). I have pointed out that Timon has not really changed. Flavius does not realize that Timon is still feasting; but Timon does realize it, and in so doing pronounces his own damnation. He has seen someone whose values are not wholly material, recognized those values, (as he did not in the case of Alcibiades), and refused to accept them. Timon has not missed, but rejected, his chance to rise above himself. His self-condemnation is complete.

The next scene serves to emphasize the tragedy. The Painter says:

> Promising is the very air o' the' time it opens
> th' eyes of expectation. Performance is ever the
> duller for his act; and, but in the plainer and
> simpler kind of people, the deed of saying is
> quite out of use. (V.i.23-26)

Flavius is one of "the plainer and simpler kind of people" and it is precisely the lack of "performance" which has led to Timon's tragedy. "Have I once liv'd to see two honest men?" (V.i.55) cries Timon. The answer is no. But he has lived to see one, and he knows it. Throughout his conversation with the Painter and the Poet he plays on the word "honest," and in so doing he curses himself. It is the very word he used to describe Flavius, but, in his refusal to admit the failure of his own logic, he has ceased to be honest himself. When he comments to the two, "Each man apart, all single and alone, / Yet an arch-villain keeps him company" (V.i.106-107), the remark applies equally well to himself.

The entrance of the Senators heaps irony upon irony:

> *First Sen.*   Worthy Timon—
> *Tim.*   Of none but such as you, and you of Timon.
>   (V.i.133-134)

Timon explicitly lumps himself in with those whom he formerly cursed for betraying him. Later he says,

>   You witch me in it;
> Surprise me to the very brink of tears.
> Lend me a fool's heart and a woman's eyes,
> And I'll beweep these comforts, worthy senators.
>   (V.i.154-157)

This speech is a grotesque parody of Flavius' earlier weeping before Timon. Timon, himself incomplete, can only ape the complete man. In his next speech he announces repeatedly that he "cares not" (V.i.167-183), and we know that it is because he has rejected the responsibility of caring. Caring for others implies values beyond those of the material world. Timon's choice is a conscious one. Having seen Flavius, he knows that it is possible to care, and he chooses rather to live by bread.

In the last act Timon admits the failure of his own value system: "My long sickness / Of health and living now begins to mend, / And nothing brings me all things" (V.i.185-187). And indeed it has been a sickness. Timon recognises his own lack of completeness, but we have seen that he has refused to cure himself. The only solution left to him is death. "Man shall not live by bread alone," and having tried bread alone, Timon may not live. Timon's next to the last words are: "Graves only be men's works and death their gain" (V. i. 221-222). So they must be for Timon, but having proclaimed one honest man, Timon knows that there are possibilities of values beyond graves and death.

Timon is dead. Alcibiades returns to Athens, not to destroy it, but to restore it. Cook suggests that "the burden of the play, positively expressed in Alcibiades, is the need to accept and love man as he is, and to acknowledge our human condition."[17] I would suggest also that Alcibiades in sparing Athens affirms the basic theme. He acts with mercy, a decidedly non-material value. Alcibiades is not perfect. We have seen him with his prostitutes. He is, however, capable of recognizing and accepting humanity in others, as Timon is not. He is even capable of recognizing the humanity in Timon:

> Though thou abhorr'ds in us our human griefs,
> Scorn'dst our brains' flow and those our droplets which
> From niggard nature fall, yet rich conceit
> Taught thee to make vast Neptune weep for aye
> On thy low grave, on faults forgiven. (V. iv. 75-79)

It is the ultimate irony that Timon, who could not forgive himself, is forgiven by something even more impersonal than himself—the sea. But he is also forgiven by Alcibiades, who at the end calls him "noble."

At the beginning of this essay I asserted that *Timon of Athens* was a complete, or nearly complete play, and that it could be treated as a unified whole. The unity is principally thematic, and the theme is brought out through the eating imagery associated with material values, through such plot elements as the confrontations between characters holding opposing views, and through the character of Timon—the completely material man. The ending of the play emphasizes the theme by suggesting that insofar as man rises above the level of the beasts—above the level of Timon—he does so by acts such as Alcibiades', by the deliberate choice not to live by bread alone. Alcibiades, by affirming those values that Timon sought to deny, brings humanity back to the world.

1.   It is appropriate that this essay should appear here, since I first studied *Timon* in an undergraduate seminar with Dr. Crow, and it was he who first pointed out to me the significance of the word "bounty" in the play. My ideas were further developed in a graduate course at the University of Wisconsin under Professor Robert Kimbrough. I would also like to acknowledge the helpfulness of the referees for this volume, whose comments contributed greatly to the clarity of the essay.

2.   Una Ellis-Fermor, "*Timon of Athens*: An Unfinished Play," *Review of English Studies*, 18 (1942), 283.

3.   David Cook, "*Timon of Athens*," *Shakespeare Survey*, 16 (1963), 94.

4.   J. C. Maxwell, "*Timon of Athens*," *Scrutiny*, 15 (1948), 208.

5.   All references to the play are to the New Arden edition of *Timon of Athens*, ed. H. J. Oliver (London: Methuen, 1959; rpt. with minor corrections 1963).

6.   A good example of this viewpoint is found in G. Wilson Knight's "The Pilgrimage of Hate: An Essay on *Timon of Athens*," *The Wheel of Fire* (London: Methuen, 1954).

7.   Cook, p. 85.

8.   Maxwell, p. 200.

9.   Oscar James Campbell, *Shakespeare's Satire* (London: Oxford University Press, 1943), p. 187.

10.   R. P. Draper, "*Timon of Athens*," *Shakespeare Quarterly*, 8 (1957), 196.

11.   Maxwell, p. 207.

12.   Ellis-Fermor, pp. 277-288.

13.   Maxwell, p. 206.

14.   Cook, p. 91.

15.   Cook, p. 92.

16.   Maxwell, p. 201.

17.   Cook, p. 84.

6

HERITAGE IN *PERICLES*

Andrew Welsh

IT'S AN OLD TALE, TOLD AGE AFTER AGE IN LANGUAGE AFTER
language. It was probably first told to eastern Greeks by a
romance written no later than the third century A.D. The
Greek romance has been lost, but a Latin prose version made
sometime between the third and the sixth centuries A.D. carried the tale throughout Europe, and many manuscripts of
this popular version still survive. The Latin version entered
Godfrey of Viterbo's twelfth-century *Pantheon* and the four-
teenth-century collection of tales *Gesta Romanorum*. The tale
was told in most of the vernacular languages of Europe as
well, and versions of it have been found in Old English, Pro-
vençal, French, Italian, Spanish, Portuguese, German, Dan-
ish, Swedish, Dutch, Polish, Russian, and Hungarian.[1] In the
twentieth century it has been found in oral tradition in Modern Greek, told as a folktale in the islands and on Asia Minor,
sung as a ballad by wedding processions in Crete.[2] Chaucer
knew the tale, and Gower, and Sidney. And Shakespeare.
Like any traditional story, it changed often through many
retellings: names were changed, incidents dropped out and

other incidents were attracted from other stories, thematic meanings or moral lessons were developed and then forgotten or misunderstood by the next story-teller. Manuscripts of the many variant versions proliferated and then were damaged, surviving only in fragments. Time, with its anonymous accidents, was always to be counted among the many authors of this tale, and these conditions remain when we try to focus on a particular version of it in England at the beginning of the seventeenth century. The play *Pericles, Prince of Tyre* was from its first appearance attributed to Shakespeare, but it was not included in the First Folio. All texts of the play are based on a quarto published in 1609, badly printed and full of mistakes. The quarto, in turn, was based on seriously corrupt reported copy, perhaps pirated from a performance of the play. No other play of Shakespeare's has such an unreliable textual base.[3] To what extent it is in fact a play of Shakespeare's has been clouded as well, and at different times the play has been regarded as one of his early works, as a work that was composed at two periods of his life, as a play by someone else that Shakespeare partially revised, and as a collaboration in which Shakespeare wrote the last half. Yet the tale survives.

And that is the point: of all the plays, the hand of Shakespeare has suffered the most obliteration in this one, and of all the plays this one is based on a story that has in its own right shown an amazing vitality through its long history. It was no obscure incident from English or Roman history to which Shakespeare turned in this first of his four romances, but an old, fantastic tale that had pleased many and pleased long. Its enduring vitality, critics have speculated, may have been the main reason for Shakespeare's attraction to it just at the time he was leaving the great tragedies behind and searching out new forms for his late plays. This tale, so close to the traditional motifs of folktales, brought to him basic, archaic patterns of the story-telling imagination. From them he could expand into the themes that resonate more and more in his late plays, themes which involve the spreading out of time through long journeys and many incidents during which people age and learning becomes much more of a ripening than a catastrophic tragic recognition. The ways in which the tale's thematic concerns of loss and recovery, fathers and daughters, tempests and music, death and rebirth become the central themes of the late plays have been followed by such critics as G. Wilson Knight, Derek Traversi, and Northrop Frye, among others.[4] In addition to these major themes, however, there are other elements, smaller ones associated with different periods in the tale's long tradition, that Shakespeare also inherited and put to use. They are like the armor that Pericles recovers from the sea after his shipwreck—"part of mine heritage," he calls it[5]—something passed on to him by his father, known by a certain mark, a little rusty now, perhaps, but helpful and even necessary for him to accomplish the prize. Some small heritages that this centuries-old tale passed on to Shakespeare, and what he did with them, are my subject. There are four of them that I shall look at, and each one was put to new use by Shakespeare. Throughout most of the play they remain submerged, but in the central recognition scene between Pericles and Marina these external heritages of the tale's long tradition are gathered up by Shakespeare and used within the play in such a way that the theme of heritage—something passed on from one generation to another —itself becomes one more of the play's central themes.

The first heritage is the tale itself, the old story that carries the sense of being told by one generation to another. For fourteen hundred years the tale had been told as a narrative rich in incidents extending over many places and a long period of time. The incidents themselves show the tale's closeness

91

to the motifs of folktales and popular literature—the riddle-tests, shipwrecks, banquet scenes, disguised or unknown princes, abductions of virgins by pirates, lost children, recognition tokens and remarkable reunions that story-tellers have always used, from prehistory up through the novels of Sir Walter Scott and James Fenimore Cooper. Shakespeare's first problem must have been in deciding how to change the manner or mode of the tale, in Aristotle's terms, from narrative to drama. He solved the problem by respecting the tale and keeping the older narrative mode importantly present in the play in the figure of Gower. There is no character quite like Gower in any other Shakespeare play. The Prologues in *Henry V* and *The Winter's Tale* perform the same necessary function of turning over the hour glass, but Gower's part in *Pericles* goes far beyond—and behind—this. He has usually been seen as a classical chorus in the play, or as an illusion-breaking stage manager, but when he steps forward to begin the tale he tells us very simply who he is:

> To sing a song that old was sung,
> From ashes ancient Gower is come,
> Assuming man's infirmities,
> To glad your ear, and please your eyes. (I.Cho.1-4)

He is the ancient story-teller whose job it is to pick up this echoing tale from the even more distant past and to pass it on. As the narrator who spins out a tale of voyages and marvelous incidents, he represents a tradition that goes back to Homer standing forward and beginning a story about a man who wandered far and saw much in his sea travels. When Gower begins, he is making a claim for attention not on behalf of himself but on behalf of the old tale. He goes on to say that

> It hath been sung at festivals,
> On ember-eves and holy-ales. (I.Cho.5-6)

The tale belongs to festival times, story-telling times, and we should remember this if we find it a bit naive in places. It is meant to entertain us, not with its realism but with its truth: "The purchase is to make men glorious" (I.Cho.9). In an Elizabethan version of his rough old language, Gower then begins the tale, pointing to the long line of story-tellers behind him: "I tell you what mine authors say" (I.Cho.20). Shakespeare, or whoever is the author of this passage, is also pointing back here to the long tradition behind him, a tradition that includes the poet John Gower himself, whose *Confessio Amantis* (1393) is one of the play's two known sources. In the *Confessio*, John Gower had in turn pointed back to the long tradition behind his version, the twelfth-century *Pantheon* and other "olde bokes."[6] As a character in the play, Gower embodies an important meaning that this old tradition represents: the very survival of the tale, in spite of centuries of accidents and changes in its transmission, is a conquest of devouring time by the human imagination. Just as the story-teller within the play controls time and space—

> Thus time we waste, and long leagues make short;
> Sail seas in cockles, have and wish but for't;
> Making, to take our imagination,
> From bourn to bourn, region to region. (IV.iv.1-4)

—so as one in a long line of story-tellers the poet Gower has conquered time with the story itself.

Within the play, the conquest over time by the human spirit is a meaning that Pericles must find; without this, the final reunions hardly pay him back for the fourteen years of wandering, loss, and sorrow that he has suffered. The meaning is found by bringing the external sense of the continuing tradition of the old tale into the play itself. Twice, the telling of the story is used as an element of the plot, in both cases as a recognition device that brings about a restoration and a triumph over the long years of separation and loss. The retelling of the story within the story was a conventional feature of Greek romance, but this tale is nearly unique in using it as a recognition device. It is used in the earliest surviving versions of the tale, and Shakespeare kept this heritage as an important working element of his play, a recognition device more powerful than Pericles' ring or any other token. When Marina tells her story to Pericles in the harbor of Mytilene, the tale is both a means by which the father recognizes the daughter and a means by which the daughter restores the father to new life. Later, when Pericles retells his story in the temple of Diana at Ephesus, the telling is once more a means of recognition and restoration, this time for the lost husband and the lost wife and for the lost mother and the lost daughter. What is recognized through the tellings, we must believe, is that time has brought not merely suffering and loss but also ripening and regeneration. With this recognition, one generation is able to look to the next: Pericles' last words in the play look forward to the marriage of Marina and to the continuation of the story. If we listen to other versions of the story, such as Book VIII of Gower's *Confessio Amantis* or Laurence Twine's novel *The Patterne of painefull Adventures* (1576)— Shakespeare's other main source for the story—we can see the tale's sense of its own tradition raised to a further power, looking back at itself as it set out on its long journey. Gower tells us that the citizens of Ephesus had gathered at the temple of Diana to see the great king, and when they heard his story from his own lips they began to tell it over and pass it on,

> And al the toun thus sone it wiste.
> Tho was ther joie manyfold,
> For every man this tale hath told
> As for miracle, and were glad,

and Twine tells us that "when report heereof was spread abroad, there was great joy throughout all the Citie of Ephesus, and the report has blowen about in everie place."[7] They are the first of the many story-tellers who, like Gower, have assumed the responsibility of making the tale's hopeful recognition of the possibilities of restoration part of the human heritage.

In addition to the tale's hope for the triumph of the human spirit over annihilating time, another characteristic of the original romance was passed on to Shakespeare. The story had always been a sea tale, a story of voyages and tempests and shipwreck. G. Wilson Knight has pointed out that Shakespeare's imagination, from *The Comedy of Errors* onwards, had been attracted to tempests and sea-voyages, and that in choosing the story of *Pericles* he found a new structure for his last plays that was based on "his most instinctive symbol" (*The Crown of Life*, p. 36). A sea tale poses another particular problem for a dramatist, yet Shakespeare kept this characteristic of the tale as a powerful and important element throughout the play. The sea is always there for Pericles, and he finally becomes lost in it. At first, following the almost casual advice of Helicanus to "go travel for a while" (I.ii.106), Pericles turns to the sea as an escape from the wrath of Antiochus—

> So puts himself unto the shipman's toil,
> With whom each minute threatens life or death.
> (I.iii.23-24)

It saves him by taking him to his false hosts in the city of Tharsus. The next time he uses the sea as an escape he is shipwrecked and loses everything. Later, in a second tempest, Pericles loses his wife Thaisa in childbirth, and it is the law of the sea that she must go overboard. Pericles' lines at her sea burial are the occasion for one of Shakespeare's finest elegies:

A terrible childbed hast thou had, my dear;
No light, no fire: th'unfriendly elements
Forgot thee utterly; nor have I time
To give thee hallow'd to thy grave, but straight
Must cast thee, scarcely coffin'd, in the ooze;
Where, for a monument upon thy bones,
And e'er-remaining lamps, the belching whale
And humming water must o'erwhelm thy corpse,
Lying with simple shells. (III.i.56-64)

Years later the child born during the tempest, Marina, is captured on the sea shore by pirates who take her back to the sea on their ship. Finally Pericles, who believes that she is dead, inexplicably rushes back onto the sea that has brought him such painful losses. There he is a victim of a third tempest which, in Shakespearean fashion, is both external and internal:

> He bears
> A tempest, which his mortal vessel tears,
> And yet he rides it out. (IV.iv.29-31)

Pericles, Thaisa, and Marina are all lost to the sea—Pericles twice, the second time by a kind of suicide. Yet the sea gives back too: Pericles is saved after his shipwreck by three fishermen, three men of the sea, and the sea returns the lost armor. It pays for Thaisa's death with the birth of a daughter, a "fresh-new seafarer" whom Pericles—in one of the most striking changes in the tale made by Shakespeare—names "Marina." Thaisa's coffin, like Ishmael's in another sea tale, is cast up by the sea onto the shores of Ephesus, where Cerimon revives her. Marina's abduction by pirates who come off the sea saves her from the murderer Leonine, and the third tempest that wracks Pericles and his ship drives him to the harbor of Mytilene on the feast day of Neptune and to Marina who restores him. As critics have noticed, the sea in this play is "the mask'd Neptune" that has the essential ambiguity of Fortune: it brings both loss and restoration, dealing indifferently with human beings without regard for their virtues or vices. The world of *Pericles*, however, is not a Lear universe, and Shakespeare was careful to keep another original element of the old tale in the figure of the goddess Diana, who by the end of the play has become the story's controlling deity. As the chaste goddess she is Marina's patron saint; as the cult-goddess of Ephesus she provides a haven for sea-buried Thaisa; as the bright "goddess argentine" associated with the moon there may be the suggestion that she brings Pericles help in the form of some control over the sea's indifferent blows—not control over the deep-sea tempests that have battered him, but at least a knowledge that applies to the shores and harbors where most of the human life in this tale is lived, transition zones whose tidal rhythms follow the moon's own rhythms of death and rebirth.

A second heritage that the tale brought to Shakespeare came not from the original Greek romance but from the early Latin version made sometime between the third and sixth centuries A.D., the *Historia Apollonii Regis Tyri*. During this early Latin period echoes of Virgil, Ovid, and Roman comedy appeared in the tale, and at some point ten literary riddles composed by Symphosius in the fourth or fifth century were also brought into the story. They are asked by Marina (or Tharsia, as she is known in the *Historia*) when she comes on board the ship in the harbor of Mytilene, and they are part of her attempt to heal Pericles (Apollonius). Before we look at this scene, however, we should recall the important riddle that begins the play.

Pericles at the court of Antiochus finds himself in an old folklore situation: like Oedipus, he faces a riddle for which he must find the answer or lose his life. It is, moreover, a double-edged riddle, for if he does give the answer he will still lose his life. In the *Historia,* Antiochus himself is the speaker of the riddle, which is convincingly difficult: *Scelere vehor, materna carne vescor, quaero fratrem meum, meae matris virum, uxoris meae filium; non invenio* ("I am carried along by crime, I feed on my mother's flesh, I seek my brother, my mother's husband, my wife's son, and I do not find him").[8] The answer turns on the various in-law relationships that Antiochus and his daughter have created by their incest, and this riddle tests Pericles' skill much more than the relatively transparent one given in the play:

> I am no viper, yet I feed
> On mother's flesh which did me breed.
> I sought a husband, in which labour
> I found that kindness in a father.
> He's father, son, and husband mild;
> I mother, wife, and yet his child:
> How they may be, and yet in two,
> As you will live, resolve it you. (I.i.65-72)

In addition to simplifying the riddle, the play makes one other small change: the answer depends on realizing that the speaker of the riddle is not Antiochus but his daughter, a change that emphasizes Marina's very different use of riddles and her very different relationship to her father.

Pericles' skill with riddles was itself a heritage passed on to his daughter. Like her musical skill and her other graces, Marina's cleverness with riddles is a birthmark by which she is recognized. The skill is much more obvious in the older versions of the tale, but it still survives in Shakespeare's play through submerged allusions, as when Marina diverts an attack on her virginity (something Antiochus' daughter could not do) by asking Boult an enigmatic question, "What canst thou wish thine enemy to be?" (IV.vi.157), or when Gower tells us that in addition to educating the young ladies of Mytilene in music, dance, and needlework, she was also outwitting the city's scholars with riddles they could not answer: "Deep clerks she dumbs" (V.Cho.5). In the Latin *Historia*, when Marina comes to heal Pericles, she first sings to him: he thanks her, gives her gold, and sends her away. She comes a second time and asks him her ten riddles. Pericles easily finds the answers: 1) the wave and fish, 2) the river-reed, 3) a ship, 4) a bath, 5) an anchor, 6) a sponge, 7) a ball, 8) a mirror, 9) wheels, and 10) the steps of a ladder (Haight, pp. 168-70). He then asks her again to leave, and it is only after he strikes her and she cries out her story that he recognizes her. Although it is tempting to notice that half of the riddles are connected with sea imagery, in the *Historia* they remain obvious inter-polations that contribute very little to the progress of the scene. This is also true in Shakespeare's two sources: Gower tells us that Marina asked the riddles, but he does not give them, while Twine keeps three of the original ten—the sea, a ship, and a bath. Shakespeare, then, finished a job begun a thousand years before when he made Marina's riddles an in-tegral part of the recognition scene (V.i). Groping his way out of his isolation, Pericles sees a woman standing before him; to find out who she is he questions her, asking first about her parentage and birthplace:

> What countrywoman?
> Here of these shores?

She answers with a riddle based on the condition of her birth at sea:

> No, nor of any shores;
> Yet was I mortally brought forth, and am
> No other than I appear.

He next asks her where she now lives, and she answers, "Where I am but a stranger." To this apparent contradiction she adds a further ambiguity:

99

> from the deck
> You may discern the place.

She is pointing toward the land, where she obviously lives but which, she says, is not her home; something else in the scene, however, is pointing in another direction. As the recognition and Pericles' restoration proceed, he asks her to sit by him, to tell him her story and her name. She answers this time not with puzzles but with a simplicity that resolves all ambiguities:

> My name is Marina.

She could be pointing toward the sea now. When the riddles of her birth and her presence in Mytilene are finally resolved, Pericles embraces the final recognition with a return of his old skill:

> O, come hither,
> Thou that beget'st him that did thee beget;
> Thou that wast born at sea, buried at Tharsus,
> And found at sea again.

"Thou that beget'st him that did thee beget" cannot but recall the riddle of Antiochus' daughter, but this is a "restored" version of that riddle. At the beginning of the play the riddle's deception overshadowed all, and the ugly incest it concealed presented Pericles with the first of many false appearances that were to plague him. The daughter of Antiochus, Pericles learned, was a "glorious casket stor'd with ill" (I.i.78), the music she entered with was false music, and her "graces" (I.i.14) were equally false. Marina's riddle skill, however, is used not to conceal but to reveal. She is as she says, "No other than I appear," and, like her other heritage, the gift of music, her riddles are not deceptions but healing graces. The situation concealed by the riddle of Antiochus'

Andrew Welsh

daughter has led to the destruction of Antiochus and his daughter, but the "birth" riddles of Marina and Pericles express a resurrection of both the daughter, "buried at Tharsus, And found at sea again," and of the father. Where the first riddle marked a corrupt father-daughter relationship, Pericles, begotten by his daughter, uses a riddle to mark the restoration of a healthy father-daughter relationship in which he can do what Antiochus could not do: give away his daughter to a husband. Pericles, the riddle shows, has engendered a future, whereas Antiochus, like the cannibalistic parents in famine-stricken Tharsus, has devoured his future.

The tale's long passage through the Middle Ages brought with it another heritage known by its mark in Shakespeare's play, the tradition of the seven capital sins. Originating with the early desert fathers, the scheme of the capital sins was developed by Gregory the Great and Thomas Aquinas into an important element of medieval Christian theology and—more importantly for our purposes—medieval Christian iconology.[9] It was known and used by Dante, Langland, Chaucer, and Spenser, and John Gower organized the tales in his *Confessio Amantis* according to the sin each tale exemplified. In Gower's order, the seven sins are Pride, Envy, Wrath, Sloth, Avarice, Gluttony, and Lust. The last sin was understood as excessive or illicit sexual desire, and it was under "Lust" that Shakespeare found in the *Confessio* the long story that became *Pericles*, placed there by Gower because of the unlawful love of Antiochus and his daughter—the "foul incest" (I.i. 127) and "heinous capital offence" (II.iv.5) that opens the play. The sins were called "capital" sins not in the sense that they were the most serious sins (as in "capital punishment"), but because they were considered to be the fountainheads (*capita*) from which all other sins spring. Antiochus' incest, Pericles knows, will easily lead to wrath and then to homo-

101

cide (a sin of wrath, in the medieval classification), once Antiochus is aware that the first sin has been uncovered:

> One sin, I know, another doth provoke;
> Murder's as near to lust as flame to smoke. (I.i.138-39)

This is not to say that *Pericles* is a medieval Christian play. Gower's external framework of the seven capital sins and his reading of the Pericles story as an example of incest were not explicitly adopted by Shakespeare, but the entire artistic tradition of the sins could not help but influence this play which, on one level, reads like a psychomachia of the virtues and vices. The tradition remains beneath the surface in Shakespeare's play, integrated like the other heritages of the tale into the plot, diction, and imagery, but it is nevertheless present. T. S. Eliot sensed this, and his poem "Marina," based on the play, brings the capital sins to the surface again, each sin associated with an animal in good medieval fashion.

References to the sins occur throughout the play, but there are three scenes in particular in which the author brings the medieval tradition to the surface. The corresponding passages in the play's two principal sources, we note, make no such use of the capital sins. The first scene is at Tharsus before the arrival of Pericles; the governor, Cleon, and his wife, Dionyza, are recounting to each other the pitiful state of their city, contrasting it with its former prosperity:

> A city on whom plenty held full hand,
> For riches strew'd herself even in her streets;
> Whose towers bore heads so high they kiss'd the clouds,
> And strangers ne'er beheld but wond'red at;
> Whose men and dames so jetted and adorn'd,
> Like one another's glass to trim them by—
> Their tables were stor'd full to glad the sight,
> And not so much to feed on as delight:
> All poverty was scorn'd, and pride so great,
> The name of help grew odious to repeat. (I.iv.22-31)

This is not a picture of a prosperous city, but a city wallowing in pride, vainglory, wasteful gluttony, sloth, lack of charity (the contrary virtue of envy, in Gower) and, in general, a sense of *luxuria* and "superfluous riots" (I.iv.54). This pride has had its fall, but it is in the same city that another capital sin later arises, "That monster envy" (IV.Cho.12) that leads to the attempted murder of Marina. The capital sin is once again the source of other sins: envy breeds wrath in Dionyza, who sends Leonine, "The pregnant instrument of wrath" (IV.Cho.44), to commit homocide.

If Tharsus is a city of pride, gluttony, and envy, a society of avarice is the subject of the little allegory overheard by Pericles on the shores of Pentapolis. Patch-breech, a fisherman, tells his head fisherman that he marvels at "how the fishes live in the sea." The master answers,

Why, as men do a-land: the great ones eat up the little ones. I can compare our rich misers to nothing so fitly as to a whale: a' plays and tumbles, driving the poor fry before him, and at last devours them all at a mouthful. Such whales have I heard on a'th' land, who never leave gaping till they swallow'd the whole parish, church, steeple, bells, and all. (II.i.28-34)

"A pretty moral," observes Pericles in a play full of pretty morals.

The moral of a later scene, however, is less pretty. From primitive religion onwards the concept of sin has been associated with disease, and through the Middle Ages specific correspondences were made between particular capital sins and particular diseases. In English literature, the sin of lust had been associated with a wounded foot in the *Ancren Riwle*, with dropsy in the Northern Homily Cycle MS., with leprosy by Gower in the *Mirour de l'omme*, and with venereal disease by Spenser in Book I of the *Faerie Queene*. Shakespeare darkened the comedy of the brothel scenes in *Pericles* with images of disease, emphasizing the inevitable associations of lust with the rotting, wasting effects of syphilis. By the conventions of this kind of romantic tale, the abducted virgin must pass through the trials of not simply any brothel, but the lowest of the low, and there is a feeling in the play that the brothels of Mytilene, like the brothels of Veracruz, were proverbial. The three girls of the brothel, the Bawd complains, are "rotten" with disease and "sodden" from attempts to control the disease with sweat tubs. The language of this scene brings out a sense of decay and disintegration behind the comedy:

> *Bawd.* What else, man? The stuff we have, a strong wind will blow it to pieces, they are so pitifully sodden.
> *Pandar.* Thou sayest true; there's two unwholesome, a' conscience. The poor Transylvanian is dead, that lay with the little baggage.
> *Boult.* Ay, she quickly poop'd him; she made him roastmeat for worms. (IV.ii.17-23)

In her attempts to encourage Marina, the Bawd tells her that she will live in pleasure, "taste gentlemen of all fashions" and "have the difference of all complexions" (IV.ii.74-76), but all that the scene shows of these gentlemen is a Transylvanian dead from the disease, a Frenchman weak in the legs from it, and a Spaniard whose slavering mouth and premature heat also show suspicious signs of disease as well as of lust. Even Lysimachus, as a customer, is aware of the dangers in the pleasures of the brothel ("How now, wholesome iniquity, have you that a man may deal withal, and defy the surgeon?" —IV.vi.23-25); it is a "sty," Marina tells him, where "Diseases have been sold dearer than physic" (IV.vi.97). The scenes show that the brothel deals not in pleasure but in disease, and into this situation Marina comes anticipating her later role as a healer. She wreaks havoc by treating not the symptoms of the disease but the cause, converting the men who visit her from vice to virtue. Chastity triumphs over Lust, and we see two of the customers abandoning the girls of the brothel for healthier pursuits—they are going to hear the vestal virgins sing. The clear definitions of morality in the play often lend themselves to simple conflicts of Virtue and Vice, such as a figure representing Chastity conquering the contrary Vice of Lust. If this is a common pattern in medieval literature, it should still be remembered that conflicts between figures representing the seven capital sins and figures representing contrary virtues were meant to represent a complex conflict within a man's soul. The most important use Shakespeare made of this heritage was in the situation of Pericles, who lost himself at sea. Although the play brings us to an understanding of Pericles' condition, it has been difficult to find the terminology to describe it. Helicanus, in the play, calls it "melancholy" (V.i.219), a traditional medieval term with precise meanings. Pericles had in fact suffered from "dull-ey'd melancholy" (I. ii.3) when he returned to Tyre from Antioch, and again at the banquet in Pentapolis where Simonides comments that his shipwrecked guest "doth sit too melancholy" (II.iii.54). In both cases, however, Pericles could talk, hear, see, remember the past and plan for the future; his melancholy was a long way from the depths of his later condition. It is also worth noting in passing that there was a tradition, persisting in England up until the twelfth century, of an eighth capital sin, *tristitia*, or sadness. It was later incorporated into the scheme of seven capital sins by making it (as in Gower) a sin of *acedia* —which meant spiritual as well as physical sloth, a drying up of the spirit. Both melancholy and sadness tell us something of Pericles' condition, but neither is a sufficient concept for a state which seems to me best described as despair, the sin pictured by Giotto's "Last Judgment" as a woman hanging herself, and by a capital on the Ducal Palace in Venice as a woman thrusting a dagger into her own throat (Bloomfield, pp. 103-4).

The apparent death of Marina breaks Pericles, and he responds to it with a kind of spiritual suicide. Even his appearance becomes that of a corpse: shut up in the mausoleum of his tent, speechless, sightless, his clothes unchanged, his hair and nails grown out to macabre lengths. John Arthos has described Pericles' state as "apathy," a state that he falls into "when, believing Marina dead, through some stubborness he grows dumb, rejecting in life everything but sorrow."[10] I would recommend instead that Pericles' apathy should be understood in the root sense of the word, that he is insensible to everything, *including* sorrow. Unable to bear any further blows, he has deliberately taken the extreme course of suicide; by inflicting upon himself a death of the spirit, he has isolated himself from further pain. Arthos' point of view does receive some support from Helicanus in the play, who says that Pericles eats only enough to "prorogue his grief" (V.i.26), but Helicanus, we have seen, is an unreliable diagnostician. To him, Pericles is simply undergoing another bout of melancholy, and he does not realize the accuracy of the corpse appearance that Pericles has assumed.

Although despair had been incorporated by the medievals into the scheme of the seven capital sins as another sin of *acedia*, it also belonged to another tradition, a group of sins known as the "unforgivable" sins against the Holy Spirit— "unforgivable" because these were sins that by their very nature put obstacles in the way of forgiveness. Pericles' spiritual suicide has erected the walls of a tomb about him, walls which, Lysimachus realizes, can only be breached by the artillery of Marina's "grace"—now understood in all the meanings of that word.

> She, questionless, with her sweet harmony
> And other chosen attractions, would allure,

Andrew Welsh

And make a batt'ry through his deafen'd ports,
Which now are midway stopp'd. (V.i.44-47)

In the Christian scale, despair was a sin even more serious than the incest of Antiochus or the murderous envy of Dionyza. In Middle English it was called *wanhope*; it sins against the virtue of hope by abandoning hope and rejecting the possibility of any help from within or without. How close Pericles was to the total and final isolation of despair is seen only as the walls that he had built around himself come down one by one. First to fall are the walls built around his senses, entombing them away from a world that had become an unbearable sequence of sorrows. The gift of music was another heritage that Pericles had passed on to his daughter, and in the recovery scene Marina first approaches him with a song. There is no immediate response, but when she approaches him again he breaks the long dumbness of his voice with bestial snarls and pushes her away: life returns first on the most primitive level, and like a provoked animal he snaps at the provoker and retreats back into his hole. She begins her story by telling of her parentage, and fragments of her voice break through the walls around his hearing. As he mumbles the fragments over, we see life stumbling and groping its incoherent way out of a long isolation:

> My fortunes—parentage—good parentage—
> To equal mine—was it not thus? what say you?

Sight returns next, and he looks at her. As he does, another wall begins to crack: "You're like something that—" But he breaks off. The strongest wall has been built around the painful memories in his own mind, and he pushes back this momentary resurgence of the past. When Marina speaks again, however, answering his question with her birth-riddle, the implications of the riddle, the beauty of her voice, and her

107

resemblance to his lost wife bring him to a full confrontation with the memories he has walled out of consciousness:

> I am great with woe
> And shall deliver weeping. My dearest wife
> Was like this maid, and such a one
> My daughter might have been: my queen's square brows;
> Her stature to an inch; as wand-like straight;
> As silver-voic'd. . . .

After her story is told and Pericles realizes that she is his daughter, he recognizes Helicanus and cries out,

> O Helicanus, strike me, honour'd sir!
> Give me a gash, put me to present pain,
> Lest this great sea of joys rushing upon me
> O'erbear the shores of my mortality,
> And drown me with their sweetness.

He can feel pain again, and even invites it—both to convince himself that she is not a dream of his "dull'd sleep" and to remind himself that pain and sorrow alloy the human life to which he has returned. The sensation of "present pain" marks the falling of the final wall as the corpse emerges from the tomb, revived by a power of Marina's that has reached even deeper than Cerimon's recovery of Thaisa.

All of the heritages of the old tale that crop up at different points in the play—the telling of the tale, the riddles, the tradition of the capital sins—are fused in the magnificent recognition scene between a father and a daughter, a scene about heritages. This is true of the newest heritage in the tale as well, a heritage from the flourishing emblem book tradition of Renaissance Europe. Images derived from emblems have been found throughout Shakespeare's work, and in this play Simonides praises the knights at his banquet with an explicit

reference to the emblems and heroic devices that appeared
on the title pages of books:

> To place upon the volume of your deeds,
> As in a title-page, your worth in arms,
> Were more than you expect, or more than's fit.
>   (II.iii.3-5)

It has been known for a century that the devices of the knights
in the tournament scene of Act II, a scene not in either of the
play's sources, were drawn from emblem books. Henry
Green showed that three of the six devices that the knights
presented to Thaisa were adapted from Claude Paradin's *De-
vises Heroïques* (1551; English translation, 1591), two of them
appearing also in Geoffrey Whitney's popular *A Choice of
Emblemes* (1586), and that sources for two more can be found
in other emblem books.[11] Only for the device of the sixth
knight, Pericles, has no source been found. The devices con-
sist of an emblematic image and a motto, or "moral," and
they are presented to Thaisa in this order (II.ii):

First Knight: the device is "a black Ethiop reaching at the sun,"
   and the motto is *Lux tua vita mihi* ("Thy light is life to me")
Second Knight: the device is "an arm'd knight that's conquer'd
   by a lady," and the motto *Piùe per dolcezza che per forza*
   ("More by gentleness than by force")
Third Knight: the device is "a wreath of chivalry," the motto
   Me pompae provexit apex ("The crown of the triumph has
   led me on")
Fourth Knight: the device is "A burning torch that's turned up-
   side down," the motto *Qui me alit, me extinguit* ("Who feeds
   me extinguishes me")
Fifth Knight: the device is "an hand environed with clouds,
   Holding out gold that's by the touchstone tried," and the
   motto is *Sic spectanda fides* ("Thus is faithfulness to be
   tried")
Sixth Knight: the device is "A wither'd branch, that's only

green at top," the motto *In hac spe vivo* ("In this hope I live")

These are not heraldic coats of arms representing the noble lineages of the knights, but devices which each knight designed himself to express his purpose. Mario Praz reminds us that the device does not look back to the past of family glories, but to the knight's own future: the device, or *impresa*, "is nothing else than a symbolical representation of a purpose, a wish, a line of conduct (*impresa* is what one intends to *imprendere*, i.e. to undertake) by means of a motto and a picture which reciprocally interpret each other."[12] Thus Thaisa, asked by her father "to entertain The labour of each knight in his device" (II.ii.15), is reading in the devices not only the knight's artistic accomplishments but also the various lines of conduct each knight sees himself following in the attempt to win her hand. All of the knights are suitors for Thaisa's love: the tournament is part of the labor they have undertaken to win that love, and the devices show their conceptions of that love.

The first knight's device of life dependent on the sun is an emblem of (in the modern sense) necessity; it expresses to Thaisa his view that love is essential to life. The second knight's device, a knight conquered by a lady, views love as conquest, while the third knight's device, the wreath of chivalry, views love as honor. The device of the fourth knight is a torch extinguished by the wax that fed it (cf. the dying fire in Sonnet 73, "Consum'd with that which it was nourish'd by"), and it sees love as paradox. The fifth knight's device is an emblem of faith, expressing this knight's view of love as faith. The device presented by the sixth knight, Pericles, is of course an emblem of hope. Earlier in the play Pericles, the prince of Tyre, had referred to his position as the head of a state as

> no more but as the tops of trees
> Which fence the roots they grow by and defend them.
> (I.ii.31-32)

Now his roots and support have withered and he is nothing but a shipwrecked man, his only heritage the rusty armor that he wears. His only experience with love also withered at the court of Antiochus. Of all the knights, he in particular can only look forward. The device he presents, a withered branch green only at the top, expresses love as hope. His hope does blossom, we see, for he wins the tournament and he wins Thaisa, but fourteen years later, when Pericles again needs this device, he has lost it. His despair (*wanhope*) is an abandonment of hope and an abandonment of any purpose directed toward the future, yet he is recovered by his future, the fruit of his past hope, in the figure of Marina. Emerging from his self-made tomb, Pericles sees Marina as an emblematic statue, the figure of Patience on a king's tomb—an image, it has been shown, that is also a heritage from the emblem books (Hoeniger, p. 147n):

> yet thou dost look
> Like Patience gazing on kings' graves, and smiling
> Extremity out of act. (V.i.137-39)

Even over a tomb Patience will wait, refusing to believe that time brings only loss and annihilation to human life. The extremities of despair and suicide, the smiling figure shows, are shortsighted acts that forget the future, that forget the emblem of hope and the promise of rebirth in the withered branch. The figure is his daughter, Pericles learns, and she has recovered him with the gifts—"graces"—of word, music, and hope that are her heritages from him.

In the epilogue spoken by Gower at the end of the play, Shakespeare brings together the first and the last heritages of

111

the tale. Gower had begun the play with an emblematic motto for the tale itself, keeping it in another language as the emblematists always felt the motto should be: *Et bonum quo antiquius eo melius* ("And the older a good thing is, the better it is"—I.Cho.10). Now the story-teller steps forward one last time and turns his whole story into an emblem:

> In Antiochus and his daughter you have heard
> Of monstrous lust the due and just reward.
> In Pericles, his queen and daughter, seen,
> Although assail'd with fortune fierce and keen,
> Virtue preserv'd from fell destruction's blast,
> Led on by heaven, and crown'd with joy at last.
> In Helicanus may you well descry
> A figure of truth, of faith, of loyalty.
> In reverend Cerimon there well appears
> The worth that learned charity aye wears.

We are reminded that it is an old tale, that it all happened long ago. The long temporal narrative is seen at the last transformed into Gower's emblematic tableau, complete with figures of the Virtues and Vices. As Charles Olson said of Melville's great sea tale, time is here pushed back so far it turns into space,[13] and the space waits for the next story-teller and his audience to enter. In this last flourish, the dramatist has transformed Gower himself into an emblem as well, the figure of the scholar-poet as an emblem of the old tale, its many heritages, and its triumphs over time by the human imagination laboring in faith and hope and love to engender a future.

---

1. Peter Goolden, ed., *The Old English* Apollonius of Tyre (London: Oxford Univ. Press, 1958), p. xii; Elizabeth Hazelton Haight, *More Essays on Greek Romances* (New York: Longmans-Green, 1945), p. 178. Ben Edwin Perry, however, argues in *The Ancient Romances* (Berkeley and Los Angeles: Univ. of California Press, 1967), pp. 294-324, that this romance is unique in being the creation of a Latin author.

Andrew Welsh

2. R. H. Dawkins, "Modern Greek Oral Versions of Apollonius of Tyre," *MLR*, 37 (1942), 169-84.

3. F. D. Hoeniger, ed., *Pericles*, New Arden Shakespeare (London: Methuen, 1963), pp. xxiii-lii.

4. G. Wilson Knight, *The Crown of Life: Essays in Interpretation of Shakespeare's Final Plays* (1947; rpt. London: University Paperbacks, 1965); Derek Traversi, *Shakespeare: The Last Phase* (Stanford, Calif.: Stanford Univ. Press, 1955); Northrop Frye, *A Natural Perspective: The Development of Shakespearean Comedy and Romance* (New York: Columbia Univ. Press, 1965).

5. II.i.122; all citations from *Pericles* are taken from the New Arden edition by F. D. Hoeniger.

6. *CA* VIII.271-72, 1152; citations from Gower are taken from *The English Works of John Gower*, ed. G. C. Macaulay, E.E.T.S., Nos. 81-82, 2 vols. (London: Kegan Paul-Trench-Trübner, 1901).

7. Gower, *CA* VIII.1864-67; Twine, *The Patterne of painefull Adventures*, in *Narrative and Dramatic Sources of Shakespeare*, ed. Geoffrey Bullough, VI (London: Routledge and Kegan Paul, 1966), 474.

8. P. Goolden, "Antiochus's Riddle in Gower and Shakespeare," *RES*, NS 6 (1955), 246-47, quotes the riddle and works it out ingeniously.

9. For the background of the tradition and its appearances in medieval English literature see Morton W. Bloomfield, *The Seven Deadly Sins* (Michigan State Univ. Press, 1952).

10. *"Pericles, Prince of Tyre*: A Study in the Dramatic Use of Romantic Narrative," *SQ*, 4 (1953), 266.

11. *Shakespeare and the Emblem Writers* (1870; rpt. New York: Burt Franklin, n.d.), pp. 156-86.

12. *Studies in Seventeenth-Century Imagery*, 2nd ed., Sussidi Eruditi, 16 (Rome: Edizioni di Storia e Letteratura, 1964), p. 58.

13. *Call Me Ishmael* (San Francisco: City Lights, 1947), p. 14.

7

CORIOLANUS AND THE EPIC GENRE

Richard C. Crowley

Coriolanus HAS NOT BEEN THE OBJECT OF A GREAT DEAL OF critical commentary.[1] Furthermore, what little criticism it has elicited in recent years has often been hostile toward the work, denigrating the play on the ground that it is not another *Hamlet* or *Macbeth*.[2] Caius Marcius himself has come in for a great deal of unfavorable appraisal—he is neither imaginative enough, nor sympathetic enough, nor "grand" enough to qualify as tragic hero. Maurice Charney, for example, typifies the tone of many commentaries:

> Coriolanus himself is the least inward of Shakespeare's tragic protagonists, he is literally isolated and uncomfortable in soliloquy, and he does not have a rich and pregnant consciousness of what is happening to him.[3]

Similarly, D. J. Enright, in his essay, "Coriolanus: Tragedy or Debate?" takes a dim view of Marcius' qualities as tragic hero:

> The first thing we notice is that the witnesses in this judgment [of Marcius' character] are many—as if Shakespeare felt

114

little confidence in his character's ability to emerge from his own words (he is, indeed, so little introspective) in the way that Macbeth or Othello emerges; as if Coriolanus can only display himself in active battle, and even in ancient Rome there cannot be perpetual war.[4]

And it is, of course, but a single step from disapproval of Marcius as hero to misgivings about the play in general:

> As a Shakespearean tragedy, it lacks just those elements that seem to us most characteristic: self-awareness, inner torment and doubt, an agonizing process of recognition, and a calm and self-willed reconciliation with the forces of one's destiny.[5]

Without entering into the question of the accuracy of the preceding judgments (how "calm" for example are Hamlet and Macbeth at the end of their respective tragedies?) we can say that the above passage typifies much criticism toward *Coriolanus*. Time and again, one notes a general tendency among scholars to approach the play with a copy of the *Poetics* in one hand, as it were, and the play itself in the other, ticking off those "characteristics" of the ideal Aristotelian tragedy which we here find missing: "self-awareness," for example, as well as "inner torment" and "agonizing" recognition.

I would suggest an alternate approach toward the work. Instead of asserting what the play is not, might it not be more profitable to ask what it is? If *Coriolanus* is not another *Hamlet* or *Macbeth*, and if the central figure in this particular work fails to live up to the ideals set forth by Aristotle, might we not ask ourselves whether, in fact, Shakespeare was not working within the framework of a deliberately mixed or hybrid genre—one which, like Marlowe's *Tamburlaine*, owes a great deal to the epic form as well as to the dramatic? If we approach this late play of Shakespeare's—following as it does upon the heels of *Antony and Cleopatra*—as one in which the author was attempting to amalgamate certain traits peculiar to both "tragic" and "epic" heroes, then our appreciation of the work might be increased. It would suggest that Coriolanus owes as much to Odysseus, Achilles, and other men of heroic might as to Oedipus Rex, and that the play itself, with its emphasis upon wrath, military virtuosity and "o'erweening pride," presents a mixture of the heroic and the dramatic within its five acts. *Coriolanus* is not the story of an introspective, intellectual type, well-meaning and articulate, whose indecision leads to fatal errors, but of a bustling soldier, the "mightiest warrior" of his time, who, like Achilles, bears the defects of his virtues—impatience with the limitations of others, a disdain for protocol, and a childish tendency toward petulance and sulkiness when not given his own way. Like Achilles, too, Marcius is eventually stung and roused into something like human compassion by the plight of those he holds dear; Patroclus' death is to Achilles what the sight of his family on bended knee before him is to Coriolanus—the source of a moment of truth that brings the errant hero back to his senses and causes him to place concern for others before wounded vanity. But these moments, moving and edifying though they are, occur too late to prevent damage, mortal and profound, to the central figure.[6]

II

In an attempt to show the relationship between *Coriolanus* —both the play and the individual—and the epic, I should like to examine three aspects of the work: first, the imagery of the play, which invites comparison between Marcius and mythic heroes; secondly, certain tendencies of literary theory in the sixteenth century which pointed the way toward bringing the drama and epic more closely together as genres; and, finally, the nature of the central conflict within the play, which, I think bears a certain resemblance to the type of *agon* we often find confronting a central figure in myths of heroic legend.

116

First of all, we might bear in mind that the text of *Coriolanus* constantly invites comparison between Marcius and figures of legendary lore. Early in the play, for example, a comparison is made between Marcius and Hector by Volumnia; chastizing Virgilia for expressing concern over her husband's military fate, Volumnia says, concerning the possible spilling of blood:

> Away you fool! It more becomes a man
> Than gilt his trophy. The breasts of Hecuba
> When she did suckle Hector, look'd not lovelier
> Than Hector's forehead when it spit forth blood
> At Grecian sword, contemning. (I.iii.36-40)[7]

In this same scene, Valeria compares Virgilia to Penelope, and Marcius to Ulysses:

> You would be another Penelope. Yet, they say, all the yarn she
> spun in Ulysses' absence did but fill Ithaca full of moths.
> (I.iii.79-81)

It is only natural, of course, that in a play whose setting is pagan Rome, Shakespeare would choose to have his characters express themselves in tropes of classical lore. By the same token, it seems quite natural, perhaps, that the chief character bear some comparison, in his own right, to the greatest heroes of the Graeco-Roman age. Certainly, in battle, for example, the comparisons between Coriolanus and Homeric and Vergilian warriors occur quite frequently. Thus, in his first foray, Marcius invokes the Roman god of war:

> Now, Mars, I prithee make us quick in work,
> That we with smoking swords may march from hence
> To help our fielded friends! (I.iv.10-12)

And, when it is feared that he has perished in battle, Marcius' deeds are eulogized by his friend Titus Lartius in the following manner:

> Thou wast a soldier
> Even to Cato's wish, not fierce and terrible
> Only in strokes, but with thy grim looks and
> The thunder-like percussion of thy sounds
> Thou mad'st thine enemies shake, as if the world
> Were feverous and did tremble. (I.iv.56-61)

Even Marcius' arch-enemy Aufidius goes back to classical lore when confronting Coriolanus:

> Wert thou the Hector
> That was the whip of your bragg'd progeny,
> Thou shouldst not scape me here. (I.viii.11-13)

One or two other examples might be given of the frequent occasions on which, explicitly or by implication, Marcius and his deeds of valor invite comparison to classical figures. Achilles comes to mind, perhaps, when reading Cominius' description of Marcius' prowess in battle:

> He stopp'd the fliers
> And by his rare example made the coward
> Turn terror into sport. As weeds before
> A vessel under sail, so men obey'd
> And fell below his stem. His sword, death's stamp,
> Where it did mark, it took. From face to foot
> He was a thing of blood, whose every motion
> Was tim'd with dying cries. (II.ii.100-107)

And Cominius had begun this tribute by citing Marcius' "valor," a quality held in the highest esteem by the Romans:

> It is held
> That valor is the chiefest virtue and
> Most dignifies the haver: if it be,
> The man I speak of cannot in the world
> Be singly counterpoised. (II.ii.80-84)

Valor, then, is Coriolanus' strong suit; indeed, he cannot be "singly counterpoised" (that is, matched by any other single person) in this regard. And when we remember that such valor was not only "honoured in Rome above all other virtues,"[8] but that the conflict between this *virtus* and love forms the basis of many heroic dramas, we can, I think, begin to appreciate the extent to which Marcius fits into this heroic pattern. At any rate, even if we allow for the element of hyperbole possibly contained in Cominius' tribute, the fact still remains that Coriolanus was, with little doubt, the mightiest warrior in the world, and that such an accolade entitled him to rank with the epic greats of the heroic past.

Indeed, we might say that even Marcius' misdeeds and errors are of the epic kind, since they are due, in no small measure, to that kind of hubristic pride which distinguished mythic warriors of the past. Achilles and Ajax, for example, often erred by having the defects of their virtues; their bravery and valiant spirit occasionally veered off into the immoderate direction of foolhardiness and arrogance. It might be remembered, in this regard, that when Cominius, early in the play, praised his own soldiers for the conduct in battle, he remarked,

> Breath you, my friends. Well fought!
> We are come off
> Like Romans, neither foolish in our stands
> Nor cowardly in retire . . . (I.vi.1-3)

a tribute to moderation and prudence which might be taken, at the same time, as casting a certain amount of disapprobation upon the somewhat excessive military virtuosity of Marcius. For, two brief scenes earlier, we had watched Marcius attacking the gates of Corioli single-handedly; and his subsequent disappearance inside the enemy gates had brought forth the words, "Fool-hardiness! Not I" (I.iv.46), from a witnessing soldier. When we remember, in this connection, that Aristotle had cited "foolhardiness" and "cowardice" as equal offenses against the golden mean of courage,[9] we begin to wonder whether Coriolanus is not guilty of some degree of imprudence, however nobly motivated.

Indeed, we might go one step further and suggest that the pride and disregard of personal restraint that Marcius exhibits in battle have their civic corollary in the kind of contempt for procedural policy that he later displays toward the populace. Whether attacking a city single-handedly, or refusing to show his wounds to the Citizens, Marcius demonstrates a good deal of pride as well as courage. In war, Coriolanus, like Achilles, has the strength and magnificence to justify his pride; later, however, in attempting to relate to others in a social way, when shrewdness and deference are called for, he shall be found wanting.

The canny Aufidius puts his finger on this weakness of character when, in speaking of his foe, he observes that Marcius is "Bolder" than, though "not so subtle," (I.x.17) as the devil. And boldness, of course, as well as a concomitant lack of prudence, often characterizes the epic hero, whether he be an Achilles from legendary lore or an Almanzor from heroic drama. One further instance of Marcius' great pride comes to mind—his admission to his mother that he would rather be the servant of the people in his own way "Than sway with them in theirs" (II.i.191), calling to mind Satan's famous challenge in *Paradise Lost* that it is "Better to reign in hell than serve in heaven." One would not wish, necessarily, to make a Satanic or Byronic hero of Coriolanus, but it is true, nonetheless, that he contains within his personality elements of that kind of overbearing pride and defiance of custom that is the mark not only of epic heroes but of romantic rebels. In any event, much of the imagery within the play, we suggest, invites comparison between Coriolanus and epic greats; and secondly, in temperamental gifts and defects, and by dint of physical and military prowess, Shakespeare's protagonist deserves a place among the legendary greats of the past.

III

If the imagery of the play invites comparison between Coriolanus and ancient epic heroes, so too do certain theories of the Renaissance—particularly literary theories of sixteenth-century Italy—in which a movement is begun to bring more closely together the drama and epic as genres, and to unite the dramatic and heroic protagonist; we find suggestions, among critics, that the *Poetics* is not infallible as a guide to critical theory, and that someone like Achilles, perhaps, as well as Oedipus Rex, might serve as prototype for the "ideal" dramatic hero. We find such notions as tragic "flaws," and passive suffering for one's hubristic errors, being replaced by the idea of a swashbuckling, military personality, a man committed to action rather than reflection, a "doer" rather than a thinker, whose faults, while certainly present, instill in us a sense, almost, of awe and wonder rather than pity and fear. Jacopo Mazzoni, for example, begins to draw away from Aristotle:

> As to the authority of Aristotle . . . I say first of all that Aristotle has not spoken fully of all things pertaining to the poetic art, and that we can see this clearly whenever we read the splendid *Decades* of Patricius, in which everyone can easily see how far from perfect is the little book by Aristotle called the *Poetics*.[10]

Another critic, Minturno, begins to stress the idea of the romantic hero as the ideal dramatic protagonist. In speaking of figures who have inspired poets throughout the ages, Mazzoni mentions in particular such legendary heroes as Achilles, Ulysses, Aeneas, and their medieval successors, Orlando and

Rinaldo. Furthermore, he lays heavy emphasis upon the "marvelous" as a quality particularly suited to tragedy and the tragic hero; the matter of tragedy, he suggests,

> . . . should be magnificent and serious, dealing with great and famous persons and marvelous and notable actions.[11]

This stress upon the "marvelous" and "magnificent" represents, of course, a shift away from Aristotle, who had observed, more mildly, that a tragedy need simply be "serious and complete" in its action. Again, while Aristotle had maintained, with customary moderation, that a tragic hero is "the intermediate kind of personage, a man not preeminently virtuous and just, whose misfortune, however, is brought upon him not by vice and depravity but by some error of judgment,"[12] a later, Italian critic—Castelvetro—presents the ideal tragic protagonist in a far more exaggerated light:

> Those persons of tragedy are royal and have greater souls and are proud and have a strong desire for what they desire, and, if injury is done to them or they think it is going to be done to them, they do not run to the magistrate to make complaint of that injury nor do they bear it patiently, but they make a law for themselves according as their passions speak to them and kill for vengeance those who are distant and those united to them by blood, and in their desperation not merely those united to them by blood but sometimes themselves.[13]

Time and again one notices on the part of these critics a tendency to tinge their writings with romantic flavor. Words like "magnificent" and "marvelous" occur frequently, whether in discussing the nature of dramatic tragedy itself or the character and temperament of the ideal hero. Thus, Castelvetro tells us that the plot of a tragedy should "contain action not human alone but also magnificent and royal,"[14] and adds:

There is presented here the sixth thing required of the plot that it be beautiful, namely that it should be marvelous, since it is said in the definition of tragedy that it should be not merely an imitation of an action that is magnificent, perfect, etc., but also an imitation of things terrible and worthy of compassion. And because these things are terrible and excite compassion chiefly by means of the marvelous, it is not well to omit speaking of the marvelous, which generates and increases terror and compassion, in order that there may be full knowledge of terror and compassion as principal parts of the action or of the fable of the tragedy.[15]

The notion of the "marvelous" or unusual as fit fare for tragedy is echoed by Minturno, as the more modest claims of Aristotle grow dimmer; supporting Castelvetro, Minturno says,

... we may widen the range of subjects suitable to tragedy and define it in such a way that whoever suffers a marvelous thing, if it is horrifying or causes compassion, will not be outside the scope of tragedy, whether he be good or whether he be evil.[16]

Gone is Aristotle's notion that the tragic hero be an "intermediate kind of personage," so far as virtue is concerned; with Minturno, our hero may be "evil," so long as what he suffers and undergoes is a "marvelous thing," "horrifying," and capable of causing "compassion." One can detect, perhaps, the increasing influence of Longinus' notions of the "sublime," the awe-inducing element at work here, as well as the medieval tendency to pull away from "reality," and head toward the allegorical and the ideal in its depictions of fable and character. The Senecan influence is, of course, another factor, as we note the increasing critical stress upon heroic retaliation and revenge rather than upon the passive expiation for one's misdeeds that had characterized "classical" Greek tragedy and the reflections of the *Poetics.* As Castelvetro suggests, the new tragic protagonist, wounded and out-raged by alien and hostile forces, takes matters into his own hands, often in a martial or military way, and goes down fighting.

I would not claim that each of the above observations and critical citations has, necessarily, a direct, one-to-one relation-ship with such a character as Coriolanus. Nevertheless, it seems reasonable to suggest that the general tendency here outlined among Italian critics to opt for a more vigorous, ro-bust, and "marvelous" type of protagonist in drama than the passive sufferers of many a Greek tragedy had portrayed—together with the fact that the movement itself can be traced, I would suggest, to such a more proximate work as Sidney's *Defense of Poesy* with its exalted claims for the creator of fiction and his artifact—might well have contributed to an over-all effect upon Shakespeare (and Marlowe, and others as well) in their attempts to depict not simply "flawed" heroes, but men of might, faults, and sublime heroic strength as well.

IV

One final notion that might be touched on, in suggesting that *Coriolanus* is within the epic tradition, and that is the fact that the basic dilemma or *agon* within the play centers around the conflict between love and honor. In writing of his own heroic plays, Dryden had said that such a work should be "an imitation, in little of an heroic poem,"[17] and that "love and valor"[18] should be their central concern. We find that Shake-speare's play anticipates such a thesis. Like Dryden's Alman-zor, Coriolanus, a military man of awesome power and tre-mendous pride, finds himself caught between the demands of his concept of honor on the one hand and his emotional affin-ities on the other. Volumnia is to Marcius what Almahide is to Almanzor, Patroclus to Achilles, Dido to Aeneas, and Cleo-patra to Antony. There are, of course, not only subtle but major differences and refinements within these groupings; nevertheless, in each instance, we find the central figure—usually martial and authoritarian—torn between duty and desire, principles and flesh, "la gloire" and human needs.

It would seem unnecessary, in this connection, to dwell in tedious fashion upon the mere fact, in itself, that Volumnia exerts a tremendous—and, often, tremendously harmful—influence upon her son and causes conflicts within him that lead to his death. It is Marcius' love for his mother—or, at least his psychological dependency upon her—that provides the play with its central tension, and provides the "love/honor" *agon* that informs the drama.

Quite early in the play, in fact, before we have even met Marcius or his mother, one of the Citizens sums up the view toward Coriolanus that is shared by most of the people of Rome:

> I say unto you, what he hath done famously, he did it to that end; though soft-conscienced men can be content to say it was for this country, he did it partly to please his mother and to be proud, which he is, even to the altitude of this virtue.
> (I.i.35-39)

These lines, occurring so early in the play, provide us with one of our first, and deepest impressions of the hero. Here the twin forces of his life are adumbrated: his love of his mother and his own deep sense of pride. Later in the play, Volumnia herself echoes, to some extent, the Citizen's earlier comments, when she tells her son:

> Thy valiantness was mine, thou suck'st it from me;
> But owe thy pride thyself. (III.ii.129-30)

Time and again, Marcius gives in to his mother—temporarily at least—in order to placate her and keep her good will. She urges him, for example, against his better judgment and instincts, to proceed in mild fashion toward the Tribunes and Citizens, in his quest for the Consulship:

> I prithee now, my son,
> Go to them, with this bonnet in thy hand;
> And thus far having stretch'd it (here be with them),
> Thy knee bussing the stones (for in such business
> Action is eloquence, and the eyes of th' ignorant
> More learned than the ears), waving thy head,
> Which often, thus, correcting thy stout heart,
> Now humble as the ripest mulberry
> That will not hold the handling—say to them
> Thou art their soldier, and, being bred in broils,
> Hast not the soft way which, thou dost confess,
> Were fit for thee to use, as they to claim,
> In asking their good loves; but thou wilt frame
> Thyself (forsooth) hereafter theirs, so far
> As thou hast power and person. (III.ii.72-86)

Obviously, a man like Coriolanus is going to have a great deal of difficulty in attempting to follow such advice; nevertheless, despite his pride and contempt for the Citizens, he gives in:

> Must I go show them my unbarbed sconce? Must I
> With my base tongue give to my noble heart
> A lie that it must bear? Well, I will do't. (III.ii.98-100)

But when he does, in fact, confront the Consuls and Tribunes he finds himself unable to conduct himself in the demeaning and self-deprecatory manner advocated by his mother; and we find here, at the end of Act Three, the first serious clash between Marcius' love and devotion toward his mother and his own sense of honor and self-esteem. For, despite his promise that he would conduct himself becomingly, the taunts and jibes of the Plebians, urged on by Sicinius and

Brutus, prove too much for him; we soon find him cursing the crowd, and replying to their cries that he be banished:

> You common cry of curs, whose breath I hate
> As reek o' th' rotten fens, whose loves I prize
> As the dead carcasses of unburied men
> That do corrupt my air, I banish you!
> . . . Despising
> For you the city, thus I turn my back.
> There is a world elsewhere. (III.iii.120ff.)

In this confrontation, his own sense of valor and honor takes precedence over his vows to his mother; later, of course, in the play's climactic scene between himself and family, love shall triumph—at the cost of Marcius' own life:

> O mother, mother!
> What have you done? Behold, the heavens do ope,
> The gods look down, and this unnatural scene
> They laugh at. O my mother, mother! O!
> You have won a happy victory to Rome;
> But for your son—believe it, O believe it!—
> Most dangerously you have with him prevailed,
> If not most mortal to him. (V.iii.182-188)

In fact, most of the play's *scene à faire* is devoted to an exploration by Shakespeare of the dramatic tension imposed upon Coriolanus by virtue of his being torn between love and duty. Having just dismissed Menenius, sending his old friend back to Rome "with a crack'd heart," Marcius is startled to find his wife, mother, and young son before him. "My wife comes foremost; then the honour'd mould/ Wherein this trunk was fram'd, and in her hand/ The grandchild to her blood" (V.iii.22-24) But, feeling himself beginning to waver, Marcius tries to cast all feeling from consideration: "But out, affection!/ All bond and privilege of nature, break! Let it be virtuous to be obstinate" (V.iii.24-26). A moment later, however, his humanity begins to assert itself once more:

> What is that curtsy worth? or those dove's eyes,
> Which can make gods forsworn? I melt and am not
> Of stronger earth than others. (V.iii.26-28)

The agonizing vacillation continues, as the hero approaches the breaking point. His mother bows, his young son simply looks at him with "an aspect of intercession which/ Great Nature cries 'Deny not'" (V.iii.32-33); Marcius again tries to summon his reserves of authoritarian protocol:

> Let the Volsces
> Plough Rome and harrow Italy! I'll never
> Be such a gosling to obey instinct, but stand
> As if a man were author of himself
> And knew no other kin. (V.iii.33-37)

Even Aufidius—or, perhaps, especially Aufidius—is not blind to the possibly mortal dilemma which confronts his archenemy:

> I am glad thou hast set thy mercy and thy honour
> At difference in thee. Out of that I'll work
> Myself a former fortune. (V.iii.200-202)

What Aufidius here calls "mercy and honor," is the dramatic equivalent of Dryden's "love and valor," forming, as it does, the central conflict in the majority of epics and heroic plays; it is at the heart of Shakespeare's study of Caius Marcius, and gives a further reason for placing Coriolanus within the tradition of epic, rather than Aristotelian, drama.

V

One final, concluding note, by way of postscript, might be made, and that is that, if the play is "epical" in tone, it seems

Richard C. Crowley

to fall, generically, somewhere between the history plays and "pure" tragedies of Shakespeare in terms of emphasis. Fredson Bowers and L. A. Beaurline have suggested that not enough has been done on the relationship between the history plays of the Renaissance and later Restoration tragedy.[19] I would imagine that the allusion, partially at least, stems from the fact that in both these dramatic forms the central figure is a great military man attempting to operate against a background of involved and complex political maneuverings, while, at the same time, beset by nearly insoluble problems of personal and national loyalties. The Bolingbrokes, Edward II, Marc Antony of the Renaissance emerge later, temperamentally at least, as Almanzor, El Cid, Horatius and Dryden's Maximillian. It has been my purpose in this paper to suggest that Coriolanus might be admitted to such company, and that one might do worse, perhaps, than to include that unhappy figure in any such study as that proposed by Beaurline and Bowers.

1. The most recent PMLA Bibliography, for example, shows 37 entries for *Hamlet*, 27 for *Othello*, and six for *Coriolanus*; in 1967, there were 25 listings for *Hamlet*, 25 for *King Lear*, and, again, six for *Coriolanus*. These proportions seem fairly representative of ratios produced during recent years.
2. Much written criticism revolving around the play has centered upon the question: "How sympathetic, or reflective, or imaginatively grand is (or isn't) Coriolanus, compared to the Shakespearean major tragic figures?" Maurice Charney, in *Shakespeare's Roman Plays* (Harvard: Harvard U. Press, 1961) finds Marcius rather wanting along these lines, as does D. J. Enright, in "*Coriolanus*: Tragedy or Debate?" in *Essays in Criticism*, IV (1954), 1-19; John Palmer, in *Political Characters of Shakespeare* (London: Macmillan, 1945), p. 297, compares Marcius to "the splendid oaf who has never come to maturity . . . more characteristic of an adolescent than a grown man," while O. J. Campbell, in his now-famous analysis, speaks of Coriolanus' "completely infantile" attitude toward his mother, a relationship which reminds the critic of "the frightened obedience of a whimpering urchin." See O. J. Campbell, *Shakespeare's Satire* (New York: Oxford U. Press, 1943), p. 211.
3. Maurice Charney, ed., *An Introduction to Shakespeare's Roman Plays* (Boston: D. C. Heath, 1964), p. ix.

4. *Ibid.*, p. 156.

5. *Ibid.*, p. ix.

6. I should like, at this point, to pay tribute to Eugene M. Waith's seminal work, *The Herculean Hero* (New York: Columbia University Press, 1962). This study, a milestone in critical approaches to "heroic" plays, should be read in its entirety as an antidote to the "Aristotelian" rigorists who insist on examining all tragedies from the point of view of "tragic flaws" and "recognitions." My own ideas, presented throughout this paper, cover much of the terrain first staked out by Professor Waith; but *The Herculean Hero* is both broader and narrower than my own thesis, covering, as it does, seven plays (*Tambourlaine, Coriolanus, Antony and Cleopatra, Bussy d'Ambois, The Conquest of Granada, Aureng-Zebe* and *All for Love*), while, at the same time, limiting its study to a consideration of Hercules as the ideal dramatic hero.

7. All references to the text of *Coriolanus* are taken from J. Dover Wilson's edition (Cambridge: Cambridge University Press, 1969).

8. Wilson's gloss on these lines notes: "Cf. North, p. 144: 'Now in those days, valiantness was honoured in Rome above all other vertues: which they called *Virtus*, by the name of vertue self, as including in that generall name, all other speciall vertues besides'." (Wilson, pp. 183-84).

9. Aristotle, *Ethica Nicomachea*, ed. by W. D. Ross (Oxford, 1915), Bk. III.6.1115^b, 24ff.

10. In Allan H. Gilbert, ed., *Literary Criticism from Plato to Dryden* (New York: American Book Co., 1940), p. 359.

11. Gilbert, p. 291.

12. W. D. Ross, ed., *The Works of Aristotle* (Oxford: Oxford U. Press, 1966), XI, 1452-53.

13. Gilbert, pp. 329-30.

14. Gilbert, p. 319.

15. *Ibid.*, p. 328.

16. *Ibid.*, p. 293.

17. Dryden's central notions concerning style and matter in relation to heroic plays are to be found, of course, in his essay "Of Heroic Plays," printed as Preface to the initial publication of *The Conquest of Granada* in 1672. For the notion that "an heroic play ought to be an imitation, in little, of an heroic poem," see, among other editions, *John Dryden*, ed. by George Saintsbury (London: Mermaid Series, n. c.d.), p. 30.

18. *Ibid.*

19. L. A. Beaurline and Fredson Bowers, ed., *John Dryden: Four Tragedies* (Chicago, 1967), p. 10.

8

CYMBELINE AND THE COMEDY OF ANTICLIMAX

Leonard Powlick

FOR THE MORE THAN THREE HUNDRED YEARS SINCE ITS FIRST publication critics have debated where among the other plays of Shakespeare to place *Cymbeline*. The first fault, of course, lay with Hemminge and Condell who included it with the tragedies in the first folio edition, and it is obvious that *Cymbeline* is no tragedy. The usual tendency of critics to say definitely that if it is not fish, then it must perforce be fowl has in this case been scrupulously avoided, and the result has been that some combined form—tragicomedy or romance—has been used to describe the play. The popularity of the Beaumont and Fletcher tragicomedies, which came out at roughly the same time as *Cymbeline*, apparently justifies placement of *Cymbeline* in the same generic bag with *Philaster* and *A King and No King*. Yet the difference in tone between these and *Cymbeline* is enormous. What distinguishes *A King and No King*, for instance, from Beaumont and Fletcher's *The Maid's Tragedy* is simply the ending: through clever plotting, the former is given a happy ending; in tone,

131

the two are equally tragic. Neither is Fletcher's famous definition—"A tragie-comedie is not so called in respect of mirth and killing, but in respects it wants deaths, which is enough to make it no tragedie, yet brings some neere it, which is inough to make it no comedie. . ."[1]—a sufficient measure. In addition to the fact that Fletcher's own tragicomedies are not adequately defined by this description, it is sufficiently broad to describe such diverse plays as Aeschylus' *The Eumenides* and Labiche's *A Trip Abroad.* If we follow Fletcher's practice, however, we find that in his tragicomedies the tone is not that of comedy, but of tragedy. Such is not the case in *Cymbeline.*

When we look at *Cymbeline,* we find that it contains all the elements necessary for a comedy, even if it does meet the definition of tragicomedy as put forth by Fletcher. In the matter of tone alone, for instance, the serious inevitably gives way to the comic. This comic tone is shown in the very opening lines of the play which, as Una Ellis-Fermor points out for other plays,[2] set the tone for what is to come after:

> You do not meet a man but frowns. Our bloods
> No more obey the heavens than our courtiers
> Still seem as does the King's. (I, i, 1-3)[3]

What starts out as serious exposition degenerates into double talk. The effect of the speech is to draw us up short, to deflate the pompous atmosphere hinted by the sound of the words. In the same manner, Twain's Duke and Dauphin are shown up. To produce the same result, a Chaplin or a Keaton would, in the most serious of scenes, fall on his face. In Beaumont's own *The Knight of the Burning Pestle,* the citizen and his wife are ridiculed because they admire just such pompous lines spoken by Master Humphrey.

Thus there is set up in *Cymbeline* a comic tone which, for

Shakespeare, is unique to this play. What gives *Cymbeline* its special quality is this technique of deflation, of the frustration of expectations, of anticlimax. In his *The Foundation of Aesthetics*, Theodor Lipps describes this technique:

> The comical is the insignificant, less impressive, less significant, less important—i.e., not sublime—which takes the place of something relatively great, impressive, significant, important, sublime. . . . Something great or relatively great is expected and something rather insignificant occurs which appears to be the fulfillment of expectation, but yet, on the contrary, cannot appear as such on account of its insignificance.[4]

Lipps calls this a mountain laboring to produce—*a mouse.* Just such a pattern dominates *Cymbeline.*

The distinct echoes of Shakespeare's tragedies to be found in *Cymbeline* have frequently been noted, but their purpose has only been guessed at ("lack of inspiration" is one of the more extreme guesses); and yet they fit perfectly into the comic structure outlined by Lipps. In *Cymbeline* Shakespeare has used these echoes, aware that the audience would be familiar with tragic situations, in order to set up an expectancy, then proceeds to frustrate that expectation. Given the circumstances of a particular situation, the audience would be led to expect certain events, perhaps not Lipps' "sublime" ones, but certainly important ones. These events, in each and every case, do not occur.

In a tragedy most of the larger events are predictable. Once the chain of circumstances is set in motion we know fairly well what the hero will (or at least *should*) do in his given situation. Shakespeare, in *Cymbeline*, takes great pains to build just such expectations, only to undercut them. One such instance occurs when Posthumus arrives in Philario's house. We are told in great detail about his adventure in France:

. . . Twas a contention in public, which may without contradiction suffer the report. It was much like an argument that fell out last night, where each of us fell in praise of our country mistresses; this gentleman at that time vouching—and upon warrant of bloody affirmation—his to be more fair, virtuous, wise, chaste, constant, qualified, and less attemptable than any the rarest of our ladies in France. (I, iv, 48-55)

This matter was the cause of a near-mortal combat between Posthumus and the anonymous Frenchman, a combat that ". . . would by all likelihood have confounded one the other or have fall'n both." To the rest of the men in the room, the dispute seemed to have been over a triviality. Yet we are told that Posthumus did not, and still does not consider the matter trivial: "But upon my mended judgement, if I offend not to say that it is mended, my quarrel was not altogether slight" (I, iv, 42-43). Thus, when Iachimo taunts him about Imogen's fidelity, we expect—and have been led to expect—that there will be another mortal combat, this time with Iachimo. After all, even considering Posthumus' faith in Imogen, what Iachimo says of her is outrageously insulting as well as false:

With five times so much conversation I should get ground of your fair mistress, make her go back even to the yielding, had I admittance, and opportunity to friend. (I, iv, 96-98)

The sexual innuendoes in these lines, applied to Imogen, are far from the trivial matter in France, and if Posthumus was moved to violence then, these references to his wife should be sufficient to send him into a rage and reaching for his sword. Instead, he makes a wager that Iachimo cannot seduce Imogen. Posthumus' certainty of her fidelity is not sufficient to explain this action, for the tone of Iachimo's words is insult enough—and provocation enough. Thus, we are led to expect some violent scene and some great action from Posthumus (if a duel can be considered great), and we get some-

thing far less than great. The seriousness of the scene is total-
ly undercut by the triviality of the result. To use Lipps' metaphor, the mountain has labored greatly only to produce a
mouse.

This technique of frustrating expectations through the use
of anticlimax occurs repeatedly in the sections of the play
dealing specifically with the travails of Imogen and Posthumus. We again find it in the scene of Iachimo's attempted
seduction of Imogen. As he plants the idea of Posthumus'
infidelities (shades of Iago, even to the similarity of their
names), we are given the distinct impression that he is succeeding:

> *Imogen:*   Revenged?
> How should I be revenged? If this be true—
> As I have a heart that both mine ears
> Must not in haste abuse—if it be true,
> How should I be revenged? (I, vi, 128-32)

Iachimo's answer is a model of the urbane, continental lover's:

> *Iachimo:*   Should he make me
> Live like Diana's priest betwixt cold sheets,
> Whiles he is vaulting variable ramps,
> In your despite, upon your purse? Revenge it.
> I dedicate myself to your sweet pleasure,
> More noble than that runagate to your bed,
> And will continue fast in your affection,
> Still close as sure. (I, vi, 132-38)

And what is Imogen's response? This paragon of womanhood,
whose intelligence has been much praised, whose resource-
fulness has been noted—calls for help.

Expectations reach new heights later in Imogen's bed
chamber. We see her asleep, with Iachimo rising from the
trunk. It is late at night and the entire household is fast asleep.

Iachimo has already indicated his violent attraction for her. The stage is set for a very dramatic scene. And Shakespeare makes certain that our expectations are aroused when Iachimo points out a resemblance between himself and Tarquin, calling *The Rape of Lucrece* to mind. The intensity of the scene builds as we watch him skulking about the chamber noting the details. He comes close to her, extolling her beauty, but then moves off. He comes back, describing the mole on her breast. When he notes that she has been reading the tale of Tereus and Philomel, the possibility of rape again arises. Then with a curt "I have enough" he returns to the trunk. His words and his action destroy the carefully constructed atmosphere wherein the expectancy of something violent has been deliberately nurtured. There will be no "great" action here either.

The same sort of action occurs when Iachimo reports his "success" to Posthumus. Posthumus, from all we learned of him before, is an impetuous, passionate man. Yet he readily accepts Iachimo's word. He is reassured by Philario, but he is convinced that Imogen has been unfaithful to him. He is certain that Iachimo could not possibly have the information he does except by having seduced her. To the suggestion that perhaps one of her women had been suborned, his immediate answer is that it was not possible since they were all "sworn and honorable." Thus, he completely undercuts his dramatic soliloquy in the next scene, and the only impression we now have of Posthumus is of his overwhelming gullibility. He rushes out muttering horrible threats:

> O that I had her here, to tear her limb-meal!
> I will go there and do't i' th' court, before
> Her father. I'll do something. (II, iv, 147-49)

Yet what is that something that he does? Like an Othello does he confront her and strangle her? Of course not. He sends a message to his servant to kill her. If we have been expecting Posthumus to act like Othello (and the implications are powerfully there that we should), our expectation is frustrated. The ultimate use of anticlimax occurs fairly late in the play. In fact, it must occur late because Shakespeare goes to great lengths to set up the situation, employing much of the plotting in the second half of the play for this purpose. The situation in outline is this:

1.   Imogen is on her way to Milford Haven to meet Posthumus. She is dressed as a boy, wearing clothes given her by Pisanio who was unable to obey his master's command. In addition, she carries a potion that Pisanio and she think is medicine, the queen thinks is poison, and we know to be a sleeping draught.

2.   She arrives at Belarius' cave and is immediately taken in and adopted as a brother.

3.   Cloten, the wicked queen's evil son, has learned that Imogen is on her way to Milford Haven and determines that he will follow her and rape her. To aid himself in this purpose, he dons the clothes that Posthumus was wearing when Imogen last saw him.

4.   He stumbles onto Belarius' cave (while Imogen is out of sight, of course), fights with Guiderius, is slain and beheaded.

5.   In the meantime, Imogen, feeling indisposed, has taken a dose of the elixir and falls into a death-like sleep. Belarius and her two unknowing brothers find her, think she is dead, and lay her out in the clearing, chanting over her the lovely dirge "Feel No More the Heat of the Sun."

6.   Belarius and the boys reconsider their decision to cast Cloten's body into the river and resolve that, since he was a nobleman, to bury him. While they go off to prepare the graves for him and Imogen, they lay his headless corpse next to her. Given this situation, so carefully contrived, we know exactly

what will happen. We know that Imogen will awake, discover the body and think that it is Posthumus. We know that the situation is exactly the same (in its externals) as that in the monument in *Romeo and Juliet*, and we will assume—although by this time we should know better—that Imogen will attempt some violence upon herself. We are correct, but only up to a point. Imogen does awake and think that the corpse is that of Posthumus. In fact, she is absolutely certain of it:

> I know the shape of's leg; this is his hand,
> His foot Mercurial, his Martial thigh,
> The Brawns of Hercules . . . (IV, ii, 309-11)

And with a cry she throws herself upon the body. But does she attempt to join him in death, as Juliet and Cleopatra do in similar circumstances? No, she instead becomes the servant of the first person who comes along, Lucius, the leader of the invading Roman army. Here, of all places, we could have expected a "great" action, but instead the trivial action undercuts our expectation.

The conclusion of *Cymbeline* is also built upon an anticlimax. In the famous masque in which Jupiter descends seated upon an eagle, we are led to expect that the threads of this most complicated plot will be unravelled by an actual *deus ex machina*. And with the tablet left upon the breast of Posthumus, we think that it is provided. The language, certainly, is obscure enough to be the key which will solve everything. Yet when the unravelling does occur, this paper has nothing to do with it. The human characters have already worked out their own solutions before Jupiter's riddle is even remembered. Whatever expectations have been aroused by this little piece of supernatural literature are dashed, and the promised *deus ex machina* becomes anticlimactic.

Northrop Frye says that" . . . comedy contains a potential

tragedy within itself,"[5] and in *Cymbeline* we can see the truth of this statement many times over, for here we find the potential for many tragedies. At any one of a dozen points in the play a different course of action could have turned the play into a tragedy. If the doctor had not substituted a sleeping potion for the poison that the queen had ordered; if Posthumus had allowed his temper to carry him into a duel with Iachimo; if Imogen had allowed herself to be seduced; if Iachimo had given free reign to his passion and ravished Imogen; if Pisanio had carried out his master's orders; if Cloten had found Imogen in the mountains; if Imogen had killed herself when she supposed that Posthumus was dead: any one of these alternative actions would have made *Cymbeline* into a Jacobean tragedy of the first rank. The implications of all these alternative—and expected—actions are obvious, because they had already been explored by Shakespeare and his contemporaries in their tragedies. But here the situations are never allowed to become tragic; they are continually being undercut by anticlimaxes. At each point in the play where there is a danger that something will become too serious, the anticlimax deflates the situation, making it laughable. Even the grief of Imogen when she thinks that she has discovered the body of Posthumus is less than serious when we take into consideration her absolute assurance in describing his characteristics. Just as in farce violence loses its repugnant and fearsome characteristics by being made unreal, so here the death of Cloten becomes less than horrible.

In *Cymbeline* Shakespeare posits situations identical with those found in his tragedies, but gives them different—comic —resolutions. Wylie Sypher has written:

> Unlike comedy, tragedy is a "closed" form of art, with a single, fixed, and contained meaning (by contrast to the disorderly relaxed meanings in comedy). Tragedy demands a law of necessity or destiny, and a finality that can be gained only by

stressing a logic of "plot" or "unified action" with a beginning, middle, and end. Within the confines of this action the hero is given to sacrifice or death. That is, tragedy performs the sacrificial rite without the festival—which means that it is a less complex, less ambiguous form of drama than comedy. Retaining its double action of penance and revel, comedy remains an "improvisation" with a loose structure and a precarious logic that can tolerate every kind of "improbability."[6]

We see this quality of "improvisation" and open-endedness in *Cymbeline*'s potentially tragic situations which are never allowed to become tragic, no matter how strongly the logic—or illogic—of the plot demands it. The characters are always in control of their own fates; they are not driven forward by a tragic destiny. In *Cymbeline*, each character has certain options open to him: he can perform the "great" action and become a tragic hero; or else he can perform the insignificant, unheroic action, showing that he is an ordinary mortal. The great action is never performed. By choosing the lesser, unheroic action, the character enables other possibilities of action to take place, and these actions accumulate until we end with a resolution. The great action reduces the possibilities of the plot; it would create an inexorable chain of events that the human characters would be powerless to affect. The insignificant action, on the other hand, shows the way to all sorts of possibilities, and the plot opens out to allow the characters to order their world. In the process, the pompous and the pretentious have been deflated.

Some critics comment that Shakespeare had written himself out by the time he came to write *Cymbeline*. They complain of the lack of any "great" actions or heroic characters in the play; what they fail to see is that their absence is to a great extent what the play is all about. In a sense, *Cymbeline* illustrates the constricting nature of tragedy. Shakespeare had mellowed with age, and here was no longer showing men as gods. Now, in effect, he is saying that to be a man is enough, that man, error-prone and unheroic, is still capable of making his own decisions and controlling his fate. Thus, the resolution of *Cymbeline* comes about by means of the characters themselves. Jupiter's cryptic letter does nothing but confirm a *fait accompli*. In *Cymbeline*, Shakespeare's vision has broadened rather than narrowed. The narrow confines of tragedy have given way to the broad possibilities of comedy. Susanne Langer has said:

> Comedy . . . expresses the elementary strains and resolutions of animate nature . . . , the delight man takes in his special mental gifts that make him the lord of creation; it is an image of human vitality holding its own in the world amid the surprises of unplanned coincidence.[7]

It is this delight in man's ability to order his existence that we find in *Cymbeline*. The play shows not a diminishing of Shakespeare's dramatic powers, but a reaffirmation of his faith in men and in life.

1.   Quoted in Una Ellis-Fermor; *The Jacobean Drama* (New York: Vintage Books, 1964), p. 204.
2.   *Ibid.*, p. 33.
3.   All references to the text are taken from the Cambridge edition of *Cymbeline*, ed. J. C. Maxwell (London and New York: Cambridge University Press, 1968).
4.   In *Theories of Comedy*, ed. Paul Lauter (Garden City, N.Y.: Doubleday & Co., 1964,) p. 393.
5.   Northrop Frye, "The Argument of Comedy," in *Theories of Comedy*, p. 455.
6.   Wylie Sypher, "The Meanings of Comedy," in *Comedy* (Garden City, N.Y.: Doubleday & Co., 1956), pp. 218-19.
7.   Susanne Langer, *Feeling and Form* (New York: Charles Scribner's Sons, 1953), p. 331.

9

SHAKESPEARE'S EXISTENTIAL COMEDY

Mike Frank

WHEN, IN *King Lear*, THE OLD KING VIOLATES THE DIVINE and social order of things the entire universe is thrown into upheaval, reminding us of one of the conventional ideas of Shakespearean criticism, namely that there is a moral order in the universe, and that any human violation of that order must lead to a more general chaos; nature itself is disturbed by human malice or folly. Similarly, in *Macbeth* the agonies of the tragic protagonist are reflected by the world around him, while in *Hamlet* the prince's dilemma is seen as an expression of the time itself being out of joint. But it is hard to see how this same bit of conventional Shakespearean wisdom, so appropriate to the great tragedies, relates to *The Tempest*. The striking differences between the world of the tragedies and the world of *The Tempest* is perhaps best seen in a comparison of the situations out of which *Hamlet* and *The Tempest* grow. In both cases there has been a usurpation of power, a transgression against the proper order of things. In *Hamlet* a force outside of the lives of the characters themselves, the ghost, appears and instigates the dramatic action; it is as though nature—the universe itself—is not content to rest until matters have been set right. But a similar usurpation in *The Tempest* elicits no comparable response from external forces. In the twelve years that have elapsed between the treachery of Antonio and the opening of the play nothing of especial note has happened either to Antonio himself or to the Milan which he now rules. And when a storm at sea leads to the righting of old wrongs the very storm itself is the handiwork of human agency.

The crucial difference between these two sets of circumstances is in the extent to which nature has ceased playing a providential role in the later play. Nature—by which I mean everything in the universe except human action and human will, everything except what we might call the human spirit —nature, which in the tragedies is an active agent bent on correcting the general disorder resulting from human folly, is in *The Tempest* quite neutral. The view of nature in *The Tempest* is, then, not very different from the modern view: it is an inescapable force which can be exploited for human good—Prospero *does* use the storm as a way of reestablishing a disrupted moral order—but which in and of itself is neither good nor evil. In a curious essay—wonderfully perceptive in many ways and yet based on a fundamental misconception of the world of the play—Robert Langbaum argues that the "profoundest statement" of *The Tempest* is "that life, when we see through it, is tragicomically gay—that the evil, the violence, the tragedy are all part of a providential design."[1] He is surely right in insisting on the tragicomical gaiety. But surely he makes what must be a fundamental mistake in seeing that gaiety as the result of providence. For isn't the point of Prospero's actions that there is no providential design, that man must forge his own moral order? Jan Kott, I think, is much closer to the truth when he speaks of the world of *The Tempest* as one "in which nature and history, royal power and morality, have for the first time been deprived of theological meaning."[2]

Indeed if one may speak of *The Tempest* as having a thematic nexus, as being about—and thus defining—a particular idea, that idea is nature, and the way nature must be dealt with in a world deprived of theological meaning. The word *nature*, and the idea it represents, is as central to the play as *nothing* is to the opening of *King Lear*. Miranda sees Ferdinand as unnatural (I, ii, 420-422); Prospero calls Antonio "unnatural" (V, i, 79); and Alonso realizes that the events on the island involve "more than nature" (V, i, 243). Behind these specific references, of course, is the question of art—or magic—versus nature and, most important, the setting of the action on an apparently natural island, a setting which allows for the reexploration of the notion of a pastoral utopia and the relative advantages of nature and civilization. In a brilliant essay Leo Marx relates *The Tempest* to the explorations of the new world with which it was contemporary, and shows that early reports from the West Indies alternately extolled the virtues of the islands as arcadian paradises and condemned them as hideous, fearful, and barbaric.[3] Clearly these early reports influenced the writing of the play—the opening of Act II is a comic rehearsal of the debate about the virtues of unspoiled nature; and one of the underlying purposes of the play is to deal with this problem, to arrive at a coherent view of nature.[4]

The vision of nature in *The Tempest* is likely best suggested—in very different ways—by Gonzalo and by Caliban; the former holds a persistently myopic view of nature, while the latter seems an incarnation of nature's real potential and its role in human affairs. It is generally agreed that Shakespeare mocks Gonzalo's notion of the island as a pastoral utopia, and it is often felt that the cynical comments of Sebastian and Antonio which surround Gonzalo's observations fatally undermine them. As Marx says, "It is impossible to miss the skepticism that Shakespeare places, like a frame, around the old man's speech" (p. 49). But surely there are other elements in the play which show the fatuousness of Gonzalo's views; after all, the comments of Sebastian and Antonio are surely not reliable guides. As it happens, in Act II, scene 1, we do realize that Gonzalo is wrong and the evil courtiers right, but this is only because Shakespeare has carefully led up to this scene by showing, first, that nature is not benevolent, and second, that Gonzalo is a somewhat dotty old man. Both of these purposes are accomplished in the very opening scene where we see the awesome power of nature and Gonzalo's inability to come to terms with it. In that scene we immediately encounter the insolent meanness of Antonio and Sebastian, but even they seem more aware of the need to defer to the boatswain than is Gonzalo, who, while the storm is raging, urges the boatswain to "be patient" (I, i, 15). Gonzalo is clearly a "good" man, his heart is in the right place, as Prospero makes very clear in Acts Four and Five. But in the face of the fury of nature, goodness is not enough. In his excessive benevolence Gonzalo is a first cousin to Polonius and perhaps even to Gloucester, all of whom deserve affection, perhaps, but surely not respect.

There are any number of obvious fallacies involved in Gonzalo's utopian vision, the most evident being the one pointed out by Sebastian, that he would be king of a commonwealth without sovereignty. We must also keep in mind that Gonzalo is so enthusiastic about the virtues of unspoiled nature not more than a few moments after he has faced a storm which seemed for the time to promise death to him and his party. But there is one further feature of Gonzalo's utopian dream that is less immediately striking and yet may be of even more fundamental importance. Gonzalo would abolish not only government, poverty, labor, treason, and impurity, but "letters" as well (II, i, 146); that is to say Gonzalo would dispense with learning, or, to take a somewhat broader view, with civilization itself. In short, Gonzalo seems to favor a reversion to a state of noble savagery. Now, whatever credence one gives to such an idea, it must be extremely suspect in a play whose very meaning depends on the learning of the protagonist. Prospero's original mistake may have been one of excessive devotion to learning—and the concomitant handing over of the reins of government to his brother—but it is only that learning itself—Prospero's wisdom, art, and magic—which is able to overcome the forces of nature and restore the moral order.

Gonzalo is, as I have said, good. But his goodness untempered by wisdom is so ineffectual in dealing with the real world that in some ways he presents a danger greater than that of Antonio and Sebastian, although his very ineffectuality makes it highly unlikely that this danger will ever become a practical one. The inadequacy of his perception of the world is made clearest in the character of Caliban. Some critics, Langbaum among them, seem not entirely sure what to make of Caliban, and are apparently troubled by their inability to determine from the play whether or not Caliban is human. That seems to me a not very important question; perhaps a stage director might have to face the question of the proper way to have Caliban appear, but in terms of the meaning of the play it is, I think, quite clear what Caliban is. To put it simply, he is the principle of nature itself. At one point Trinculo observes with some wonder "That a monster should be such a natural!" (III, ii, 30-31). Critics are quick to point out that "natural" means idiot, and surely this is the surface meaning. But equally surely Shakespeare's use of the word here is loaded. In his annotations to The Arden Shakespeare edition of the play[5] Frank Kermode glosses the word *natural* as follows: "A monster is by definition unnatural; yet this one is a natural (an idiot)." But isn't the point precisely that the conventional definition held by European civilization is inaccurate? Caliban *is* natural, and he *is* a monster, and he *is* also an idiot. Shakespeare's use of the word *natural* makes it very clear that in the world of the play raw nature is monstrous—remember the storm which introduces us to the world of the play by presenting nature in its most malevolent aspect—and is also to be equated with idiocy in that it is only learning and art—in short, civilization—that can counteract the force of nature.

The first time Prospero speaks to Caliban he addresses him as "Thou earth" (I, ii, 316), thus emphasizing not only his baseness but also his identity with natural forces, the kind of identity implicit in our use of such terms as *mother earth* and *mother nature*. Some critics see Caliban as representing the natural element earth, while Ariel represents the element of air, nature in a more benevolent aspect. To schematize the play in such a way is, I believe, to miss its thematic focus. The matter is a crucial one, and since Langbaum's view is a representative one which raises many significant questions it is worth quoting in full:

> Caliban is natural in that he is earthy and earthbound, low, material. But Ariel is just as natural in that he represents the fluid elements of water and air and also those bodiless energies of nature that strike us as "spiritual." Caliban, whose name may derive from "cannibal," is the natural man seen in one aspect. But Miranda is also natural, and the two are contrasted throughout. Both were brought up in a state of nature; and if Miranda never saw a man other than her father, Caliban never saw a woman other than his mother. Caliban is natural in the sense that nature is rudimentary and mindless; he cannot be educated. Miranda is natural in the sense that we take the Golden Age or the Garden of Eden to be our natural condition. (pp. 189-190)

Langbaum sees Ariel as a two-sided symbol, representing both the fluid elements and the spiritual qualities of nature.

No doubt Ariel does represent the "spiritual," but to include spirit as part of nature is to miss the crucial dichotomy of—and antagonism between—nature and spirit, nature and education, nature and art, nature and civilization. Curiously this is a dichotomy that Langbaum himself alludes to just a few lines earlier in saying that the play raises "the question whether nature is not superior to art." Certainly art must be closely identified with spirit, and the very terms of his question suggest, rightly I think, that spirit is not to be identified with nature at all, except to the extent that man's nature allows for the development of spiritual faculties. By insisting that Ariel is natural, Langbaum is able to argue that Miranda too is natural, and that this is her great virtue. He admits shortly afterward that Miranda has indeed been very carefully educated by her father, but this apparently doesn't make her in any significant way unnatural as far as he is concerned. But it is precisely the extent to which she has been educated that she is good, and had she not been subject to Prospero's tutelage she would certainly have been very different. This difference is defined, and the fundamental dichotomy underlying the play made most explicit when Prospero, speaking of Caliban, refers to him as

> A devil, a born devil, on whose nature
> Nurture can never stick; on whom my pains,
> Humanely taken, all, all lost, quite lost. (IV, i, 188-190)

The word *nurture* as used here includes all those other categories—art, magic, learning, civilization—which the play repeatedly opposes to nature. To see spirit itself—that human faculty out of which all these redemptive qualities grow—as part of nature is surely to overlook the play's thematic pivot.

The main problem with Langbaum's interpretation—the fundamental misconception to which I referred much earlier —is his acceptance of the idea that "the Golden Age or the

Garden of Eden [is] our natural condition." To believe that is to make the same mistake made by Gonzalo, to believe in the nobility of the natural man. *The Tempest* makes it quite clear that the Golden Age, and any other similar pastoral ideals, are merely that—ideals, creations of the human imagination. It is important to remember that to whatever extent life on the island is attractive, it is so as a result of the art of Prospero. And since it is learning which can overcome the forces of nature, it is crucially important that Miranda has been educated whereas Caliban has not.

Caliban, then, is the principle of nature itself, the incarnation of the external natural world, or—to put the issue more abstractly—matter. Ariel, on the other hand, represents not the element of air, as Langbaum suggests, but of the human spirit itself. Caliban and Ariel become symbolic incarnations of the principles that define the play. Significantly Ariel is freed by Prospero's magic, and it is Prospero's magical art that obtains for him the services of Ariel. In terms of the scheme I am defining, it is Prospero's spiritual achievements which enable him to utilize the pure spirit that is Ariel. There is, then, a double meaning when Prospero refers to Ariel as "My brave spirit." On the level of plot he is talking to Ariel, defined by the *dramatis personae* as "a spirit." But on a symbolic—which is to say thematic—level he is addressing the spiritual forces that have made him what he is; in a sense he is addressing his soul.

And yet, in spite of his spiritual accomplishments, Prospero does not release Caliban. It might appear at first that given his magical powers and the services of Ariel Prospero would be able to dispense with Caliban. But one of the very important aspects of Prospero's wisdom is his realization that he cannot do without Caliban, which is another way of saying that he cannot give up his control of the material world. For one thing, to free Caliban would be to lose some things that he cannot do without. When Miranda hesitates to visit Caliban because of his villainous ugliness her father explains his importance to their lives:

> But, as 'tis,
> We cannot miss him; he does make our fire,
> Fetch in our wood, and serves in offices
> That profit us. (I, ii, 312-314)

Man cannot live by spirit alone, as it were. The unique, and implicitly tragic, feature of man is that he is neither pure spirit, like Ariel, nor pure matter, like Caliban, but is caught in an uneasy tension between the two. He strives to be like Ariel but cannot dispense with the services of Caliban.

Prospero, furthermore, cannot free Caliban so long as he is on the island, because to do so would be to unleash the full force of untrammeled nature, a point made strikingly clear by the account of Caliban's original enslavement by Prospero. When Prospero comes to the island he treats Caliban "with human care" (I, ii, 348), until Caliban attempts to rape Miranda. In doing so he is not being evil in the way that the conspirators are evil; unlike them, he is not immoral, only amoral, and in attempting to rape Miranda he is merely following the imperatives of his own nature. The results of amoral action may be as detrimental to human society as those of immorality; but Prospero realizes that on a philosophical—as opposed to practical—level they must be viewed differently. This difference Shakespeare makes quite clear in the presentation of Caliban. Although Caliban is surely as potentially dangerous as Antonio and Sebastian, he is not presented as a villain. From the start we are made actively to dislike the conspirators, but the play elicits no such response to Caliban. Which of course is as it should be, for to hate Caliban would be as silly as hating the rain or the wind of a storm. But it would be equally foolish to ignore Caliban and the forces he represents, thereby letting them interfere with the pursuit of human goals. This is what Prospero very quickly realizes, which leads to the subjugation of Caliban. "This island's mine, by Sycorax my mother,/ Which thou tak'st from me," Caliban says in one of his complaints to Prospero (I, ii, 333-334), and in one way he is very right. In citing his inherited claim to the island, Caliban suggests the curious fact that Prospero, like his brother, is something of a usurper. But there can be no doubt that in this case, for Prospero, for Shakespeare, and for us, the usurpation is justified. When Prospero arrives on the island it might be the memory of his own exile that makes him attempt to treat Caliban "humanely," which means *kindly* but no doubt also suggests that Prospero tries to treat Caliban as a human. In doing so, however, Prospero makes the same mistake which Gonzalo is to make a dozen years later, that of taking the pastoral dream as fact, of not recognizing the eternal antagonism between the processes of nature and human aspiration. But Caliban's attempted rape of Miranda enables Prospero to recognize the truth very quickly. He learns that nature, while not evil, is indifferent to human values and aspirations, and that the success of the human endeavor requires constant vigilance and the domination of natural force by the arts of human civilization.

And this is the crucial difference between the world of the tragedies and the world of *The Tempest*. In the earlier plays there is, apparently, some moral order external to man, an order which imposes a system of values that man must follow; in such a world moral behavior is probably best understood in terms of a commitment to the proper order of things, a commitment that might well be called religious. But in *The Tempest* there is no such external order to which man must commit himself; there is simply an indifferent and impersonal nature which will follow its own imperatives regardless of what man does. In such a world—a world very much like that of modern existentialism—moral behavior is best understood not in terms of religious commitment but in terms of art, that is in terms of all those uniquely human powers which can be used to control the forces of nature and work toward the preservation of human civilization. It is significant that Prospero is not a priest—of whatever kind—but a magician, and that the text continually refers to his special abilities not as supernatural power but as his art.

II

There is one other important difference between the world of the tragedies and that of *The Tempest*. Implicit in the former, as in all theologically oriented views of the universe, is the idea that once the thorns in the side of the moral order are eliminated and the evil extirpated, man is once again at peace with his environment. Men may die, but the fundamental coherence of the universe remains intact. No such assurances are to be found on Prospero's island. His world makes sense only to the extent that man—and man's art—is able to impose some order and meaning upon it. Even more important, in Prospero's world, a world deprived of theological meaning, there can be no final victory against the forces of nature: mortality, which in a theocentric universe is mitigated by the transcendent, is here man's ultimate and insurmountable fate. Nature may be coped with, and some of its disruptive visitations avoided, but in the final analysis nature is implacable, and its final inescapable trump card is death.

All of this necessitates a radically new view of the function of art. Until now I have used the term *art* indiscriminately to refer both to what we would today call art and to what we would now tend to call science. The two are related in that they are both manifestations of man's ability to make sense and order out of his world, but there are important differences between the two. Science, we might say, is man's way of controlling the external world; art, his way of coming to imaginative terms with it. The former deals with material reality, the latter with human attitude. The former consists of ways of dealing with the threats imposed by nature, and at times of avoiding their danger, the latter consists of ways of coming to terms with the final and unavoidable victory of nature over the human organism. To put it in terms of the dramatic structure of the play, the former deals with ways of controlling Caliban, the latter with the best ways of making use of Ariel.

Of these two ways of dealing with the world the former, the scientific, is the more consistent in its purposes. In general one fights a storm much the same way regardless of one's philosophical outlook; although the meaning of a natural disaster may be conceived in different terms, the actual practical process of coping with it will remain largely the same. Thus Prospero's—and Shakespeare's—emphasis on dominating nature, on not assisting the storm, while interesting in its implications, is hardly of decisive importance. But *The Tempest* is about more than the need to use all available human resources to fight the vagaries of nature in order to shore up walls against the inroads of chaos, a need which forms the informing principle of many of the works of Joseph Conrad. The centrality of that need for Conrad leads him to depict a universe in which a dogged perseverance is the highest good, and in which, finally, bitter resignation is the only legitimate way of relating to the inevitable victory of chaos. Shakespeare is able to move far beyond this kind of existential despair, even in a world deprived of theological meaning, by asserting that art is not only a way of fighting against nature—a fight that man always must lose in the last analysis—but is also a way of coming to imaginative terms with the world. Prospero's art, that is to say, involves not only what we would call science, but also what *we* would call art. Even while he is insisting on the need not to give an inch to Caliban, Prospero is demonstrating how man may best use the prerogatives of Ariel, the prerogatives of his own spirit. And Prospero's greatest wisdom is his realization of the limits of the power of the spirit, his recognition that while art can work miracles there is a point at which it must stop, at which its powers cease.

I have been working toward a definition of Prospero's wisdom, which is also the theme and "message" of the play. Let me stop, at this point, and present what I take to be the most important elements of that theme, after which I will return to the text to support my hypothesis. Prospero, it seems to me, realizes that man is finite although his spirit recognizes the infinite and therefore has infinite aspirations; that man's unique curse—and blessing—is that he is neither all spirit like Ariel nor all matter like Caliban: he is matter and subject to the laws of nature, and yet he has awareness of spirit which makes him dissatisfied with the limitations of his corporeal being; that man must leaven his animal nature with his spiritual powers, just as in the outside world he must impose his artifice on the natural material world; that the pastoral myth is not literally true, but that man nonetheless must have such a myth to live by; that the pastoral myth, like all other visions of human perfection, is a wish that grows out of the limitations of the human condition—that the imagination is a way of coping with the unbridgeable gap between the human condition and human aspiration—but that without the double nature of human consciousness even the notion of perfection would not exist; that the glory of the human condition lies precisely in the achievements of the human imagination, and that, as a result, any fundamental change in the human condition is not only impossible but inconceivable in that it would eliminate the very circumstances which led to it; that any attempt to resolve the fundamental ambivalence of the human condition—the split between matter and spirit—must either deny the spirit thus making man no better than Caliban or must deny the body thus alienating man from the physical world in which he lives and without which he would have no existence; that, finally and fundamentally, man's greatness is in his spirit, but that spirit can exist only in man's corporeal being, and that to deny the body in favor of the spirit would be to eliminate the spirit as well.

The passage in which most of these themes are first made manifest occurs in the first scene of Act IV and will repay close attention. While Caliban, Stephano, and Trinculo plot their revenge upon him, Prospero decides that he must bestow upon the betrothed Miranda and Ferdinand "some vanity of mine Art" (1. 41). The word *art* is striking. It suggests, as do any number of other references in the play, that Prospero's magic may be identified with art. But here the nature of that identity is made extremely clear: what Prospero's art creates is a play. The means at his disposal may exceed those of most directors, but the end result is largely the same, a fiction, a projection of the human imagination.

The masque itself relates to the themes of *The Tempest* in two important ways. First, Venus and Cupid are explicitly excluded from the celebration lest they exercise "some wanton charm upon this man and maid" (1. 95). This exclusion reminds both the young lovers, who are the masque's primary audience, and viewers or readers of *The Tempest*, who are the masque's audience once removed, of the importance of Prospero's oft-repeated prohibition against submitting to sexual passion. It is not merely chastity itself that so concerns Prospero. But giving in to sexual desire becomes, as a result of Caliban's attempted rape, a symbol of the forces of natural impulse that must be restrained. This feature of the masque and Prospero's seemingly obsessive insistence on Ferdinand's continence are then directly related to, and expressive of, the view of nature which the play presents.

The second thematically focal feature of the masque is Ceres' final speech (ll. 110-117). In it she repeats in modified form what Gonzalo had said upon first seeing the island; it too is a vision of the pastoral ideal. Now while this ideal may have no place in the attempts of real people to deal with the real world, it surely does have a place in art, as is suggested by Prospero's choice to include it, for Prospero stands in relationship to the masque much as Shakespeare does to *The Tempest*: he is the artist, the magician who simulates reality. As part of a pastoral masque Ceres' speech is hardly worth comment. But Ferdinand's reaction to it is.

> *Fer.* This is a most majestic vision, and
> Harmonious charmingly. May I be bold
> To think these spirits?
> *Pros.* Spirits, which by mine Art
> I have from their confines call'd to enact
> My present fancies.
> *Fer.* Let me live here ever;
> So rare a wonder'd father and a wise
> Makes this place Paradise. (IV, i, 118-124)

The conversation takes place on two different levels. Ferdinand sees the spirits as having an independent existence. In answering Ferdinand's question Prospero explains that they are merely the spirit of his art, projections or enactments of his imagination. But he answers in such a way as to leave Ferdinand's naiveté intact, and as a result Ferdinand, himself taken in by a vision of pastoral utopia, wishes to remain on the island permanently. Like Gonzalo, he mistakes the world of the imagination for the world of reality. Prospero, not yet ready to undermine Ferdinand's illusions or his innocence, recalls his attention to the masque.

But barely a moment later Prospero himself interrupts the masque when he remembers that Caliban is plotting against his life. In fact what he is doing—at least on a symbolic or thematic level—is waking from the dream of perfection that his imaginative art has created, recalled to the world of material reality by the immediacy of the danger that faces him from Caliban, that is from nature. Gonzalo would live in the dream —and Caliban would kill him; Prospero knows that to live in the dream is to invite death. One might well say that Prospero recognizes the necessity of what Freud called the reality principle.

In dismissing the spirits who have presented the masque, Prospero is not symbolically dispensing with the services of spirit entirely. Here the distinction between art and science becomes important: Prospero must interrupt an imaginative endeavor in order to undertake a very practical one. But before doing so he makes what is surely the most famous and most important speech in the play, in which the relationships between the real world and the world of imaginative perception are explored:

> Our revels now are ended. These our actors,
> As I foretold you, were all spirits, and
> Are melted into air, into thin air:
> And, like the baseless fabric of this vision,
> The cloud-capp'd towers, the gorgeous palaces,
> The solemn temples, the great globe itself,
> Yea, all which it inherit, shall dissolve,
> And, like this insubstantial pageant faded,
> Leave not a rack behind. We are such stuff
> As dreams are made on; and our little life
> Is rounded with a sleep. Sir, I am vex'd;
> Bear with my weakness; my old brain is troubled:
> Be not disturb'd with my infirmity:
> If you be pleas'd, retire into my cell,
> And there repose: a turn or two I'll walk,
> To still my beating mind. (IV, i, 148-163)

Perhaps the first thing to be noted is that the tone of the speech is certainly not accounted for by Prospero's awareness of the plot against him, a plot that he can deal with without any difficulty. But although he may have no trouble with this particular Caliban at this particular time, he recognizes that the principle of Caliban, earth, will eventually overwhelm the principle of the play, spirit. The recollection of the specific fact of Caliban's plot startles him into an awareness of the more general fact underlying that plot, the fact of mortality. For surely mortality is the theme of the speech that follows.[6] Prospero notes that the vision—that is, the masque —is baseless, which, in this context, means unfounded. But it also suggests that the vision is unfounded because it disregards Caliban, who is best described by the word *base*, Similarly when a few lines later he calls it an insubstantial pageant, he indicates that it lacks substance, matter, material reality—it is entirely an expression of spirit. But as an expression of pure spirit it is untrue to the human experience.

The multiple levels of the speech are clear enough. Prospero uses the evanescence of the masque as a paradigm for the evanescence of the society he has established on the island, of the theater in which the play *The Tempest* is being presented, and of life in general. The word *globe* refers to the masque, the island, the theater of the same name, and finally to the world itself, the globe that is the earth. The stoical acceptance of mutability as essential to the human condition that informs Prospero's speech hardly requires further comment. But the inclusion of a self-conscious reference to the Globe Theater, to the play as play, does. It is not enough, I think, to say that since the Globe Theater is part of the real world, it too will fade. That is obvious. Moreover it ignores the idea of art and illusion which the theater represents, which is so important a theme in *The Tempest*, and which in some ways makes the theater—that is the experience of art—significantly different from the real world outside it. To put it more simply, the speech comments not only on the inescapable limitations of the human situation but also on the role of art and imagination in coping with that situation, and finally on the limits of art.

Long before the Globe Theater as a physical entity ceases to exist, Shakespeare—through Prospero—seems to be saying, the world that currently occupies the Globe, the world of the play called *The Tempest*, will come to an end. The audience, which has interrupted its "real" concerns for an afternoon in order to share the common dream of art, will return to the real world. The speech—like the extraordinary time scheme adopted by Shakespeare for this play in which dramatic time is almost identical with real time, Shakespeare's plays generally being presented between three and six while the action of the play takes place between two and six—points to the parallel between Prospero's art and Shakespeare's. The masque is interrupted twice, first when Ferdinand mistakes art for reality, second when Prospero's recollection of a real danger forces an impatience with his dreams of perfection. *The Tempest*, however, requires no interruption because, unlike the masque, it is perfectly candid about its own limitations. It is, in a sense, about its own limitations, and about the limits of art in general.

But Shakespeare's creation and manipulation of the world of *The Tempest*, if superficially similar to Prospero's presentation of the masque, is, on a more profound level, analogous to Prospero's manipulation of life on his island. Prospero's impatience with the masque when he is reminded of Caliban's plot—that is of mortality—may be seen as a dissatisfaction with the workings of the imagination when they lead one away from a coming to terms with the real world and the moral responsibilities it imposes on man. The masque, the representation of an idealized pastoral utopia, leads to irresponsibility; it brings Ferdinand to the point of repeating Gonzalo's mistake. The island itself, on the other hand, though as much the product of Prospero's art as the masque, does not misrepresent the truth about human life. At first Gonzalo is fooled, but the progress of later developments will open his eyes. Shakespeare is then akin to Prospero. Both men present a pastoral world for our satisfaction. But both—Prospero by manipulating nature and finally by admitting that the island is his work of art, and Shakespeare by presenting us with Prospero and by making his play about the limits of art—give us the truth and make it quite clear that the pastoral situation is not a natural one but one that exists only by virtue of man's efforts to impose his imagination on the indifference of the natural world. By this reading Prospero is a model of the artist, and his manipulation of nature on his island a model for the role of the artist in human society: to impose his imaginative ideals on recalcitrant nature to whatever extent possible, but to recognize the limitations of the human spirit in overcoming nature; to live as much as possible with Ariel while remembering that man is partly Caliban.

It is only if we understand the play in this way that Prospero's final abjuration of his magic and his decision to leave his pastoral paradise make sense. When Prospero is ready to leave his island he announces that he will "retire me to my Milan, where / Every third thought shall be my grave" (V, i, 310-311). There is apparently some dispute over the precise meaning of "every third thought," but whatever we take the other two thoughts to be the third one is clearly mortality, and Prospero's return to Milan is, in a sense, a coming to terms with his inevitable end as a human being. Just as the play *The Tempest* is over, and the audience must return to their real world, so Prospero's island paradise is over, and he too must return to the real world.[7] Shakespeare sees the pastoral ideal as a manifestation of the paradox of the imagination: the desire for perfection which can exist only in imperfect beings, the desire to be free of our material limitations which would not exist if we were not matter. Prospero's rejection of the island is therefore a rejection of the world of pastoral fancy, a world which disregards "every third thought" and which, as a result, leads to an inability to come to moral terms with the real world. When Miranda first sees the royal party she is led to marvel at the "goodly creatures" and is convinced that they must come from a "brave new world" (V, i, 182, 183). Because of the limitations on her education resulting from her isolation on the island she mistakes a group of scoundrels, usurpers, drunks, fools, and would be assassins for the cream of mankind. Despite Prospero's efforts, her education by art is incomplete, and a fuller appreciation of what is involved in the human situation will depend on her living in society. This certainly must be one of the reasons why Prospero decides to remove to Milan.

And yet, on a somewhat different level, Miranda is absolutely right in her naive expression of wonder. For the world of human society is in many respects a brave new world when compared with the isolation of the island; it may not be perfect, but perfection is not the human condition, and it may well be that faced with the choice between the perfection of art and the limitations of life Miranda chooses the latter. Significantly, though, when Ferdinand first sees Miranda he is as struck with awe as Miranda herself will be later on. For Ferdinand, who has known only the real world, the spirituality that Miranda embodies is as marvelous as the reality of human society is for Miranda. This is not merely a fanciful way of saying that the grass is always greener on the other side. It is Shakespeare's way of pointing out the perpetual dilemma of the human condition; half matter and half spirit, man strives for a wholeness, attempts to rise above the paradox of his consciousness, but cannot do without the element he attempts to rise above. Caliban is perfect—which is why he is not evil—and Ariel is perfect, but man is not capable of either kind of perfection. And any attempt to reach such perfection involves a misconception of the nature of human life and an abdication of moral responsibility. Prospero, who understands both Miranda and Ferdinand and the limitations of their views, thus chooses to renounce his magic and return to the world of social reality. But his magic, like the magic of any artist, has worked to sharpen his auditors' awareness of the place of man in the world and the nature of human responsibility. Langbaum puts this very well indeed:

> Art is just such an experience of enchantment. The speech in which Prospero breaks his magic wand . . . is his comment on the relation between art and life. For in breaking his wand and taking himself and the others back to Italy, Prospero seems to be saying that the enchanted island is no abiding place, but rather a place through which we pass in order to renew and strengthen our sense of reality. (p. 199)

III

There remains the matter of the tone of the play. I have, in my title, referred to the play as a comedy, and the mood of forgiveness and conciliation which dominates its denouement reinforces one's sense that it is, as does the marriage of Ferdinand and Miranda, of course. Yet it seems odd that a comedy should end with the protagonist clearly looking forward to his own death. And the single most important speech in the work—the one Prospero makes after interrupting the masque—comes awfully close to despair.

It should be noted, though, that Prospero's speech does not end on a desperate note. He seems to come to his senses, as it were, and immediately apologizes to Ferdinand for carrying on as he has; indeed, he refers to his previous statements as the products of infirmity, of a "beating mind." In part, of course, Prospero is merely being tactful. Ferdinand is yet young, on the verge of being married, and Prospero hardly wants to burden him with a kind of existential angst. But

Prospero's very tact is an act of kindness which epitomizes the nature of the play's comic resolution, as does Prospero's even greater kindness in forgiving the conspirators.

No doubt every human being is caught in an inescapable existential trap; no doubt "we are such stuff as dreams are made on." But what *The Tempest* seems to imply is that once we have realized this fact we can act accordingly; more specifically, since nature is indifferent to man it is a matter of some importance that men are not indifferent to each other. It is for this reason that Prospero refuses to burden the innocent Ferdinand with his problem. And if Ferdinand's innocence makes him less than fully ready to deal with the real world, the resolution of the play and life in Milan under Prospero's guidance will take care of that in due time. The important thing is that a realization of the truth about life and nature lead not to cynicism, as it has for Antonio and Sebastian, but to an increased benevolence, as it does for Prospero. And that is precisely the comic affirmation of the play: though the universe may be devoid of theological principle, and though nature may be indifferent, cynicism is a mean and an immoral response, for it can only make matters worse; benevolence and human cooperation are the only sensible and moral alternatives. This idea, like so many others in the play, is reinforced in the epilogue when the speaker explains that the only thing standing between him and despair is the indulgence of the audience. The spirit of charity, which alone keeps Prospero from despair, similarly is the only thing that can preserve the actor playing his role from an analogous fate. The play is a comedy because it affirms positive human values, and it affirms them not in spite of but because of the inherent flaws of human existence and the imperfection that is man.

There is, finally, one more reason for the affirmation with which the play concludes. One of the things *The Tempest* deals with is the importance of art. Now whatever else one may want to say about art, it should be clear that it is what Freud calls a substitute gratification; it satisfies needs that cannot be satisfied more directly in the world of immediate experience. In other words art could not exist in a world of perfect creatures leading perfect lives: neither Swift's Houyhnhnms nor the inhabitants of Huxley's Brave New World have any art at all.[8] Art is something people create because their lives are imperfect, and one of the functions of art is to make life as perfect as possible, and to imaginatively explore what perfection would really be like. But obviously art must be all process, and never, in any final sense, product. For the achievement of perfection would eliminate the art which made it possible. Thus Shakespeare, in celebrating man's art, is by implication also celebrating the imperfection of man, his mortality and the double nature of his consciousness, without all of which art would not exist. What Prospero has understood, and what his art—and Shakespeare's—attempts to make clear, is that man's imperfection is inseparable from his glory.

1. Robert Langbaum, "The Tempest and Tragicomic Vision," *The Modern Spirit* (New York: Oxford University Press Paperback, 1970), p. 187.
2. Jan Kott, "Prospero's Staff," *Shakespeare Our Contemporary* (London: Methuen, 1964), p. 180.
3. Leo Marx, "Shakespeare's American Fable," *The Machine in the Garden: Technology and the Pastoral Ideal in America* (New York: Oxford University Press Paperback, 1967), pp. 34-72. See especially pp. 46-57.
4. Throughout my essay I will have recourse to such expressions as "the purpose of the play," "the vision of the play," "intention," "meaning," and so on. I hope it is superfluous of me to add that in none of these cases do I mean to indicate that Shakespeare consciously held the views I attribute to the play, or that he consciously intended the play to mean what I claim it means. I am, rather, talking more about that element in the work which can be defined as the intention of the play—as opposed to that of the author—or, alternatively, the meanings intended by the author's second self. It seems to me that one of the most important achievements of recent literary criticism—if not the most important—has been the redemption of the "meaning" of a text from the rigidities of historical intentionality on the one hand, and, on the other, from the aleatory Empsonisms of granting equal status to any and all

Mike Frank

"meanings" which may be inferred from the text by an ingenious critical methodology. I trust that my reading of *The Tempest* occupies that safe ground cleared by these critical theories and is neither mechanical nor anarchic. In calling the play "existential" I certainly don't mean that Shakespeare was an existentialist, consciously or unconsciously. Merely that the perception of and attitudes to the world expressed in the play are largely those of modern existentialism; and that these perceptions and attitudes—although perhaps very far from Shakespeare's actual purpose in writing the play—are demonstrably there in the work and not merely the creation of critical sophistry.

5. All my line references are to the 6th edition (1958) of the Arden text.

6. Kermode suggests that Prospero's perturbation is the result of his sense of ingratitude: "Caliban's ingratitude recalls that of Antonio—to the one he gave the use of reason, to the other ducal power. The conspiracy afoot reminds him of the trials of the past twelve years, which are now being rapidly re-enacted." I find this reading very unacceptable for two reasons. First it assumes that Prospero really believes that Caliban should have become civilized, when it is quite clear that he knows that his attempts to give reason to Caliban were not only futile but meaningless and silly as well. More important, it hardly accounts for the philosophical force of Prospero's speech. A man faced with ingratitude may get angry, but he normally does not find that ingratitude sufficient reason for stoical speculation on the human condition.

7. Shakespeare elaborates upon this idea and reinforces the analogy between magician and playwright in the wonderful epilogue to the play. When the actor who has played Prospero says, "Now my charms are all o'erthrown," he is clearly referring both to his charms as Prospero the magician—that is, his charms *within* the fiction—and to his charms as an actor—that is, his charms as the presenter *of* the fiction. Both magic and drama are artifice; and just as Prospero has given up his wand, so the actor has given up his persona. In each case the character is left to face the real world without the benefit of his art. The parallels between artificer and artist in the rest of the epilogue are clear enough.

8. I hasten to add that neither the land of the Houyhnhnms nor the Brave New World seem to me perfect. But they are perfect in terms of their internal structures and the needs of their inhabitants, who are so satisfied with their lives that they need no substitute gratification at all. Indeed, in Swift's work the very idea of art, which is always to some extent a fabrication and thus a "lie," is unthinkable. The point of all of which is, of course, that for creatures such as we are perfection is not only impossible, it is inconceivable, a point that Samuel Johnson recognized some two centuries ago when, in *Rasselas*, he devoted a chapter to a consideration of "The Wants of Him Who Wants Nothing."

10

APPROACHING THE GENRE OF
THE TEMPEST

Gerald Schorin

S CHOLARS HAVE VENTURED SUFFICIENT HYPOTHESES ABOUT
the meaning of *The Tempest* to appease all but the most
demanding student; nevertheless, as Frank Kermode points
out, "There is disappointingly little memorable criticism of
The Tempest, although the play has always been held in high
esteem."[1] Perhaps one reason for this apparent lack of inci-
sive criticism concerns the genre of *The Tempest*. The terms
"romance" and "comic romance" are most often used as dramatic base camps from which scholars explore the more
glamorous and daring peaks of theme and characterization.
Very seldom, though, are these terms discussed or defined
with reference to the play. And the resulting generic assumptions foster a spectrum of critical opinion that ranges from
simple character study to a complex allegory which argues
for *The Tempest* as a history of the church.[2] A discussion,
therefore, of *The Tempest*'s genre may not only account for
this broad range of critical opinion, but also help focus attempts that deal with the comic, tragic, and romantic elements in the play.

Gerald Schorin

The Tempest, perhaps foremost among Shakespeare's plays, offers the student an opportunity to examine the underlying structures, myth and ritual, that function to define drama. Northrop Frye claims that "drama appears when the myth encloses and contains the ritual. . . . The ritual acts are now performed for the sake of representing the myth rather than primarily for affecting the order of nature."[3] In our play, the plot in general and the actions of Prospero in particular enable us to discover many of the ritualistic and mythic devices that Frye alludes to. Most critics seem to be, however, more or less unconcerned with *The Tempest's* deep structure, preferring to translate the play's underlying elements into the term "romance"—some even going so far as to see the drama as a fantasia. E. E. Stoll, for example, warns against imparting too much meaning to the play because, for Shakespeare, *The Tempest* is "a rather simpler story of his than usual, a sort of glorified fairy-tale."[4] While most of us do not share Professor Stoll's view, in one way his point is valid. The largest portion of *The Tempest*, excluding only sections of the first and fifth acts, is very like a fairy-tale; here the drama comes closest to its meaning of game or play (*ludus*). All of the action of the play occurs on the island and "observes the unity of time so rigidly that the time seems to keep shortening as the play proceeds."[5] An equally important segment of the play, verbally referred to but not physically represented on stage, is necessary for us to understand the action on the island. This portion of the drama is comprised of two distinct parts: the history of Prospero's banishment, related in a long speech to Miranda (I.ii. 65-106),[6] and the implied comedic ending wherein Prospero will regain his duchy, Ferdinand and Miranda will wed, and all parties will be released and forgiven. Such a division of the play is not a novel suggestion; E. M. W. Tillyard has previously argued that *The Tempest* is composed of different "planes of reality." Tillyard's use of this term, however, sheds more light on thematic questions than on structural ones. This essay will attempt to enlarge upon Tillyard's original use of *The Tempest's* planes of reality in order to lead us to a generic reassessment of the play. For our purpose, the play has three different planes of reality. In Prospero's speech to Miranda he explains their presence on the island; this level of reality, the narration of what has happened in Milan, establishes the concept of usurpation as a precedent for action in *The Tempest*. The second plane of reality, and the prevailing one, includes the play's contemporaneous action; in other words, this plane deals in what we as audience see acted on stage. The third plane of reality includes all the implications of the unresolved conclusion of *The Tempest*: the marriage of Ferdinand and Miranda, the future of Prospero, and the future of Antonio. Isolating these separate planes of reality into the time sequences of what has happened in Milan, what happens on the island, and what will happen back in Milan and Naples is only partially satisfactory. In order to arrive at the dramatic skeleton of the play, from which we can establish its generic category, we must also examine the basic elements of the plot—the myth and ritual already mentioned—first pointed out in the early twentieth-century research of Colin Still.[7]

It is not difficult to see why Still's interpretation of *The Tempest, Shakespeare's Mystery Play*, has not found much favor since its publication. Relying largely on textual evidence and data from, among other sources, Eleusinian initiation rite, Still sought to prove:

(a) That the play belongs to the same class of religious drama as the Mediaeval Mysteries, Miracles, and Moralities;

(b) That it is an allegorical account of those psychological experiences which constitute . . . Initiation;

(c) That its main features must, therefore, of necessity resemble those of every ritual or ceremonial initiation which is based upon authentic mystical tradition; and

168

(d) That actually the resemblance to initiatory rites . . . is
so consistent and exact that, if we do not accept the foregoing
three propositions . . . we must assume either the occurrence
of an incredible series of coincidences or the perpetration by
the poet of an equally incredible literary freak.[8]

Whether or not we subscribe to Still's interpretation of *The
Tempest*, the research he undertook is, even today, impressive, especially since his conclusions about initiation, from
pagan, near eastern, cabalistic, and classical lore, were derived
without recourse to Frazer's anthropological data. For our
discussion, the combined scholarship of both Colin Still and
Sir James Frazer may enable us to focus clearly on the primitive structure of *The Tempest*'s plot.

Any view of the plot structures which support *The Tempest*'s action must center on Prospero, who functions as a mythical archetype, much like the Frazerian priest-king:

In this sacred grove (*Diana Nemorensis*) there grew a certain
tree round which at any time of the day, and probably far into
the night, a grim figure might be seen to prowl. In his hand he
carried a drawn sword, and he kept peering warily about him
as if at every instant he expected to be set upon by the enemy.
He was a priest and a murderer; and the man for whom he
looked was sooner or later to murder him and hold the priest-
hood in his stead. The post which he held by this precarious
tenure carried with it the title of king; but surely no crowned
head ever lay uneasier, or was visited by more evil dreams,
than his.[9]

Not an exact analogy, Prospero's situation is, nevertheless,
strikingly similar to that of Frazer's mythical priest-king. Because of his interest in white magic, Prospero neglects the
rule of his duchy, forfeiting its administration to Antonio:

The government I cast upon my brother
And to my state grew stranger, being transported
And rapt in secret studies. (I.ii. 75-7)

Such neglect of royal duty will obviously lead to usurpation, and in this respect Prospero is in the priest-king's position. Now the notion of a cyclical chain of usurpation, revolving around Prospero, becomes apparent. Antonio, aided by Alonso, overthrows Prospero, who in turn arrives on the island and overthrows Caliban. Usurpation has also affected, or will affect, most other characters in the play: Ariel was usurped by Sycorax, Sycorax by the citizens of Argier, Alonso by Ferdinand (when the latter assumes himself to be king of Naples by reason of his father's alleged drowning), Alonso by Sebastian (only an attempt, but still the usurping act), Caliban by Stephano and Trinculo, and Prospero (attempted) by Stephano.

Frazer also states that the mythical priest-king may often be surrounded by slaves and virgins, and this is apparent in *The Tempest* where Prospero is attended by his virgin daughter, Miranda, and by the servants, Ariel and Caliban. In the archetypal example, the aging and physical dependence of the king is heralded by a desertion of his slaves and virgins. Again, the same general procedure is followed in *The Tempest*; desertion is not the analogous term for what happens to Prospero, but the result will be the same when Miranda marries Ferdinand, Ariel and Caliban are released, and Prospero drowns his book and thereby relinquishes the powers it represents (note that this action does *not* occur on the island, but is left for some future time).

The courtship of Ferdinand and Miranda perhaps offers the most exact parallels between *The Tempest* and the archetypes described by Frazer and Still. The first meeting of these two people, fostering love-at-first-sight, begins actions that recapitulate primitive custom. We notice that Miranda recalls the tribal taboo, demanded by her father, of not mentioning her name—or in Frazer's terms:

Unable to discriminate clearly between words and things, the savage commonly fancies that a link between a name and the person or thing denominated for it is not a mere arbitrary and ideal association, but a real and substantial bond which enters the two in such a way that magic may be wrought on a man.[10]

Miranda, of course, is hardly a savage, but the surprise and guilt that she seems to convey when breaking this taboo is mindful of this primitive belief.

> *Ferd.*:   I do beseech you—
> Chiefly that I might set it in my prayers—
> What is your name?
> *Mir.*:   Miranda. O my father,
> I have broke your hest to say so! (III.i. 34-38)

Miranda's *faux pas*, if it is that and not an intentional taboo-breaking, bespeaks a growing intimacy between her and Ferdinand that must inevitably lead to marriage. Shakespeare makes Prospero seem well aware of this burgeoning relationship, which may help explain why Prospero is so hard on his prospective son-in-law. In the archetypal ceremony,

the novices are initiated by their fathers-in-law. Broadly speaking, the initiation ceremony comprises the following phases: first, the preparation of the 'sacred ground' where the man will remain in isolation . . . second, the separation of the novices from their mothers and, in general, all women; third, their segregation in the bush . . . fourth, certain operations performed upon the novice. . . . Throughout the period of initiation, the novices must behave in a special way; they undergo a number of ordeals, and are subject to various dietary taboos and prohibitions.[11]

This archetypal situation corresponds analogously with Ferdinand's situation. He is initiated by his prospective father-in-law; the island of *The Tempest* corresponds to the "sacred ground"; Ferdinand is separated from women, with the exception of Miranda, who sees him secretively; and he is put through several operations, much milder, however, than typical subincision rite:

> *Pros.*:   I'll manacle thy neck and feet together (I.ii. 860.)

In addition, Ferdinand is charmed by Prospero and unable to draw his sword; this, too, is a kind of operation. He must endure the ordeal of log-carrying in order to win Miranda, which in itself is a demeaning chore, but especially so for one who assumes that he is King of Naples. Lastly, the dietary taboos correspond exactly with the archetypal version:

> *Pros.*: Sea water shalt thou drink: thy food shall be
> fresh-brook mussels, withered roots, and husks
> Wherein the acorn cradled. (I,ii)

Ferdinand succeeds in his initiation and is promised Miranda, and to mark the successful completion of this rite of passage, Prospero arranges for the masque of the goddesses. Enough has already been written about the masque (and antimasque). It might be noted, however, that the heavenly joys of Juno are equated with the earthly joys of Ceres or, as in the archetypal wedding, personal fertility is equated with natural fertility.

It should be apparent now that *The Tempest*'s plot is composed of various archetypal elements, ones dealing with usurpation in general and the killing of the king in particular (Ferdinand himself poses a threat to Prospero, which helps account for Prospero's harsh treatment of him—the priest-king can be certain of no one, not even a son-in-law). The question that now arises concerns the import of this archetypal deep structure and how it affects a generic definition of the play. One way of isolating genre from this mythical type

Gerald Schorin

is to trace back the history of individual genres. F. M. Cornford, in discussing Attic comedy, states that

> The general formula of progress for comedy is a steady drift from mystery to mime. We see how the original group of stock masks were the characters required for a certain unvarying ritual action. They were at first serious, and even awful, figures in a religious mystery: the God who every year is born and dies again, his Mother and his Bride, the Antagonist who kills him, the Medicine-man who restores him to life. When the drama lost its serious magical intent, probably the Antagonist and the Doctor were the first to become grotesque.[12]

In Shakespeare, Prospero is the controlling magus who, because of his status as priest-king, is representative of the God, and because of his magical and healing powers, the Medicine-man. These abilities or roles assure that the audience sees Prospero as fantastic, and in this sense, he is grotesque. There is no one antagonist in *The Tempest*; instead, two separate character groups function in this role: the first consists of Antonio and Sebastian, whose acts are unnatural (the killing of the king, as in *Macbeth*, must offend the natural order) and hence grotesque; the second group consists of Stephano and Trinculo, and perhaps Caliban, all of whom are grotesque in the sense of being absurd. There cannot be much doubt that these characters drift toward the comic rather than the tragic spectrum. No murder or other violent act has been committed on the island, and all characters with malevolent dispositions are intentional, not actual, villains. The fact that this villainy is never successfully practiced establishes a tendency toward the comic because "The mythical or primitive basis of comedy is a movement toward the rebirth and renewal of the powers of nature, this aspect of literary comedy being expressed in the imagery more directly than in the structure."[13] We might, however, question this statement and ask how comedy differs from tragedy: is not the killing of the king one valid and often-practiced means of power renewal and regeneration? One solution may be that both comic and tragic actions spring from one source, or as Wylie Sypher argues:

> It is now accepted that art is born of rites and that the comic and tragic masks are themselves archetypal symbols for characters in a tribal 'semantics of ritual.' Behind tragedy and comedy is a prehistoric death-and-resurrection ceremonial, the rite of killing the old year (the aged king) and bringing in the new season (the resurrection or initiation of the adolescent king).[14]

The theme of usurpation, the killing of the king, is, as we see, neither comic nor tragic in itself, but gives rise to both comic and tragic actions. In *The Tempest*, although the play is obviously not considered a tragedy, scholars have pointed out certain tragic elements. G. Wilson Knight notes that "Prospero is a matured and fully self-conscious embodiment of those moments of fifth-act transcendental speculation to which earlier tragic heroes, including Macbeth, were unwillingly forced."[15] And E. M. W. Tillyard observes that tragic elements are to be found in the play, elements typical of Elizabethan revenge tragedy, yet "*The Tempest*, by keeping this destruction portion largely in the background and dealing mainly with regeneration, avoids the juxtaposition of the two themes."[16]

We have seen, then, that critics of *The Tempest* do recognize a tragic pattern as well as a comic pattern in the play, although the regenerative comic elements are paramount. Moreover, examination of the mythical and ritual basis of the comic and tragic masks isolates, in *The Tempest*, the archetypal act of the killing of the king from which the divergent forms of comedy and tragedy spring. Although we may accept the plot of *The Tempest* as a comedy with tragic overtones, it still remains for us to consider the term most often used to describe this play: romance.

Frank Kermode, in the introduction to his edition of the
play, speaks for most critics in saying that *"The Tempest* has
always been recognized as a romance."[17] Yet few critics have
agreed upon what constitutes a Shakespearean romance. Professor Stoll, quoted above, considers a romance, at least one
of this sort, to be of fairy-tale quality; and while this exact
term is not often used in describing the play, many scholars
seem to accept Stoll's idea that the fantastic and the other-
worldly constitute a romance. Lawrence Bowling separates
the semblance of reality from the romantic world, and in this
sense he shares Stoll's approach:

> The temptation to see *The Tempest* as a romance is almost ir-
> resistible. The surface appearance of *The Tempest* does point
> in the direction of romance; but a close examination of the play
> reveals that it is not at all devoid of meaning and common
> sense, that it is in no way the "poetical dream" of a man bored
> with real people and real life.[18]

If a romance cannot at all be concerned with real meaning
and common sense, then this criticism is just, but must we
deny any semblance of real life to romance? Kermode attempts to arrive specifically at the nature of Shakespearean
romance without making these assumptions:

> Romance could be defined as a mode of exhibiting the action
> of magical and moral laws in a version of human life so selec-
> tive as to obscure, for the special purpose of concentrating at-
> tention on these laws, the fact that in reality their force is in-
> termittent and only fitfully glimpsed. Thus, although we may
> believe that in the end the forces of fertility, or of plenty,
> triumph, and that it is a law of human life that they should do
> so, we would not hold it as a rational conviction that this must
> be so in every single case, of every individual; yet comedy, by
> a formal law, proved by a few suggestions, ends in a feast or
> wedding. In the same way we accept even more arbitrary de-
> vices, such as that of the crucial "recognition" of tragedy and

comedy, as formal laws corresponding to, and in some valuable way illuminating, diurnal forces which are intermittent and rarely visible. In the realm of what we agree to call romance these conventions are both more frequent and more arbitrary.[19]

In this definition romance selectively intensifies aspects of human life, thus allowing for fantasy without denying the presence of plausible and realistic actions. Kermode claims that romance differs from comedy and tragedy in that its conventions are "both more frequent and more arbitrary," but perhaps there is an even more specific differentiation.

The primal act on which *The Tempest's* plot is based can be considered neither comic nor tragic in itself, but can give rise to one or both of these attitudes; also Kermode's definition of romance has sufficient latitude to include the realistic as well as the fantastic elements of the play. It remains for us to determine the predominant genre of *The Tempest* and to account, in this determination, not only for the action on the island, but also for the pre-island and post-island ramifications.

Many critics, including some quoted above, feel that *The Tempest* is a romance simply because the major character deals, at least physically, in magic. From the play's inception to its conclusion Prospero is the controlling magus—utilizing, through his magical art, the service of Ariel to create the storm, to prevent the wedding party from coming to harm, to charm or harass them, and finally, to make them confess their guilt and then reunite them. This action is typical of romance, and to understand the play, even on the simplest literal level, we must accept the arbitrary convention of Prospero's magic. When we accept this convention, we must also reject or temporarily displace our knowledge about the real workings of nature, because "comedy's appeal, no matter how contrived the plot may be, is the audience's sense of solid values in a real world."[20] The world of *The Tempest* is not based on these solid, real values; it cannot be predominantly comedic. Romance, therefore, must be its generic mode.

No matter how many realistic elements the definition of romance includes, however, it cannot account for the pre-island and post-island segments of the play. Before his usurpation in Milan, Prospero was guilty of a preoccupation with white magic, but the preoccupation and not the magic itself was responsible for his downfall. At the play's conclusion, Prospero says that:

> I'll break my staff
> Bury it certain fathoms in the earth,
> And deeper than did ever plummet sound
> I'll drown my book. (V.i. 54-57)

Thence he will retire to Milan where every third thought shall be his grave. Both the past action in Milan and the implied future action seem to be non-romantic in that no fantasy is apparent, there are no arbitrary conventions that we must accept, and no special cases of human experience are mentioned or suggested. It is necessary for us to improve on our romantic definition of *The Tempest*. Northrop Frye places *The Tempest*

> In the fifth phase of comedy . . . [where] we move into a world that is still more romantic, less Utopian and more Arcadian, less festive and more pensive, where the comic ending is less a matter of the way the plot turns out than of the perspective of the audience. When we compare the Shakespearean fourth-phase comedies with the late fifth-phase "romances," we notice how much more serious an action is appropriate to the latter: they do not avoid tragedies but contain them.[21]

Professor Frye is here arguing for *The Tempest* as a romantic comedy rather than a comic romance, yet it is noteworthy that he allows for the tragic implications of this play. Surely any generic definition of *The Tempest* must consider the tragic as well as the comic implications. A number of other critics have also recognized the tragic side of the play, a perception that does much to counteract a view of *The Tempest* as a simple romance. D. G. James, one such critic, states that

> Shakespeare, in *The Tempest*, does not at all exhibit human life as no longer tragic. The tragic sense of life is not something which can be put away, or an illness of which one may be cured; and the "promised end" is not to be put off. It is true to say of *The Tempest* that all ends happily. Antonio and Sebastian will not reign in Milan and Naples: Ferdinand and Miranda will do that. But we shall not, if we are wise . . . take this to signify mankind's release from days few and evil.[22]

Whether or not we agree with James' assessment of the characters' futures, his warning about denying the tragic aspects of *The Tempest* is a timely one.

One way to account for the tragic and comic, as well as the romantic, elements of the play is to return to the division of the play into pre-island, island, and post-island planes of reality. Prospero's original usurpation in Milan with his resultant exile to the island seems to be considerably more tragic than either comic or romantic. All the action on the island (which means all the action in the play) is romantic because it is always under the magical control of Prospero; and because most of the characters successfully advance toward the new society of the play's final scene, we must consider the island sequences to be comic romance. But what of the post-island society: who will rule back in Milan and Naples? The play's comic conclusion is not a conclusion at all, since we never see the characters leaving the island, nor the freeing of Ariel and Caliban, nor the marriage of Ferdinand and Miranda, nor the celebrative journey back to Italy where, we assume, a restored society will commence. Our knowledge of the comic conclusion must be based, and correctly so, on extrapolated evidence from the unresolved romantic world of the play. And surely, if we extrapolate this knowledge, we must also consider less obvious but equally important possibilities. Both James and Kermode address themselves to this problem:

> There is penitence enough in Alonso; and there is, perhaps, penitence in Caliban. There is little enough of it in Sebastian; there appears to be none in Antonio. Sebastian indeed exclaims, on seeing Ferdinand and Miranda: "A most high miracle!" But Antonio then and later shows signs of neither wonder nor regret. "This thing of darkness I acknowledge mine," says Prospero of Caliban; but Antonio was a thing of far greater darkness, and was his own brother.[23]

> . . . Antonio is, none the less, one of Prospero's failures; as far as can be deduced from the closing passages, in which Antonio is silent, he will not choose the good; unlike Sebastian he is unimpressed by it, and refuses to close the circuit of noble virtue which excludes only Caliban. Prospero must acknowledge another thing of darkness. A world without Antonio is a world without freedom; Prospero's shipwreck cannot restore him if he desires not to be restored, to life. The gods chalk out a tragicomic way, but enforce only disaster. The rest is voluntary.[24]

These articulate statements about Antonio are not intended to suggest a tragic reading of the play, which would be an obvious misreading. On the other hand, never do we see a truly comic conclusion; the characters only *tell* us what will happen back in Italy. If we take Prospero's word (as we must) that Ariel and Caliban will be freed, that Ferdinand and Miranda will marry, and that he will return to rule Milan, then we must take him at his word when he claims that every third thought will be his death. Prospero is returning, not only an old man, but an old man without any magical art—an art that has already saved two rulers, himself and Alonso. Most importantly, we must accept Antonio's *non serviam*. It is indeed a legitimate question to ask what will happen to Prospero back in Milan, and there are tragic possibilities. The tragedy of a renewed usurpation is possible, perhaps even likely. Knowing this, it seems difficult to understand James' desire to see a comic ending where "it is clear that all that will happen will lead to the restoration of Prospero to his throne,"[25] when that restoration may be extremely tenuous. If a valid case can be made for tragic overtones in *The Tempest*, then we have a mixed-mode categorization problem, with comedy, tragedy, and romance present in the same work.

One way out of this generic miasma is by analogy to the wheel of fortune. Generally speaking, most critics agree with Frye that "The wheel of fortune is a tragic conception: it is never a genuinely comic one, though a history play may achieve a technically comic conclusion by stopping the wheel turning halfway."[26] Ordinarily we would not expect to apply this concept to *The Tempest*, but Frye's application of the wheel of fortune concept to a history play also is valid for it. For we are seeing a history play in a larger than usual sense. Our archetypal examination reveals that the basic plot of *The Tempest*, much like Freud's analysis of *Oedipus the King*, concerns the struggle for power (the desire to become king) and the danger of attaining a position of power (the imminent usurpation). Freud sees this conflict in father-son terms; Frazer finds it to be a tribal-wide concept; and Shakespeare makes it largely a fraternal conflict. Because of its almost universal prevalence, some critics have argued that Prospero, as unrealistic as he is, represents Shakespeare himself; in so far as Shakespeare partakes of humanity he, like all of us, is Prospero. Jan Kott, using other terms, sees *The Tempest* as ". . . a morality play that is being performed upon the island."[27] Kott, however, is only partly correct. We are seeing *the* morality play upon the island, an extant version of the Frazerian priest-king's situation, which is one of the major plots comprising the dramatic experience.

The wheel of fortune lies at rest, for most of the play, in the position of comic romance, wherein Prospero, who has been king (*regnavi*) is moving comedically toward a regaining of the kingship. But although he has not technically attained his former position, he is no doubt the king of the island, and therefore in the precarious midwheel position on the *fortuna rota* (*regno*). *The Tempest* concludes its action with the wheel of fortune in the position of romance, leaning toward the promised comic society of the future, but at the same time threatening a backward revolution into the tragic society of the past. In Frye's terms, the wheel of fortune is in the summer or romance position, turning between the spring and fall, or comic and tragic, positions.

The concept of the *fortuna rota* serves more as a model of *The Tempest's* tripartite structure than as a thematic analog for the play. There are only three positions on the wheel: *regnavi*—I have been king; *regno*—I am king; and *regnabo*—I shall be king. These positions correspond quite closely with Prospero's changing status within the play. At the beginning we learn, from his speech to Miranda, that he has ruled Milan but was usurped by his brother, Antonio; during the course of the play Prospero rules the island; and at the conclusion he states that he will return to rule in Milan. Thus the wheel runs through a full circle. Additionally, there is the implicit threat, already discussed, that Antonio will reinstitute the whole process of usurpation. This final suggestion, which never becomes more than a suggestion, keeps the wheel of fortune ever turning.

Now we can finally generically redefine *The Tempest*. All of the play's action takes place on the island and we know, due to Prospero or Miranda, that Antonio and Sebastian cannot kill Alonso, and Stephano and Trinculo cannot usurp Prospero. Also, Prospero's magic metaphorizes the fantastic experience of the island. Romance, therefore, is the controlling genre for *The Tempest*. Additionally, the play is a comic romance because of the buffoonery of Stephano and Trinculo, the *idiotes* figure of Caliban, the love and impending marriage of Ferdinand and Miranda, and most importantly, the assumed regeneration and restoration. This assumption leads us to one other: the play is also tragicomic romance because of Antonio's unrepentant evil and its threat to Prospero. The drama ends without telling us what exactly will happen in the future, and if everything looks rosy there remains the dark cloud of Antonio's malevolence. The logical expectations that this ending sets up help account for the *The Tempest*'s ability to elicit a broad critical range. Whatever the critic seeks—comedy, tragedy, romance, even allegory—surely can be discovered by focusing on one segment of the wheel of fortune (or on one plane of reality) and ignoring the rest. Unresolved endings of this nature also force us, as audience, to look outside the world of the play (which differs considerably, in this play, from counting Lady Macbeth's children); in doing so we become manipulated by the richness of the Shakespearean universe, which also may tend to lead us away from the play and into abstruse critical realms.

Although he never uses the term *tragicomic romance*, Kermode is the only scholar to observe the interaction of these genres in the play, and to hypothesize on Shakespeare's reasons for choosing this form:

> The pastoral romance gave him the opportunity for a very complex comparison between the worlds of Art and Nature; and the tragicomic form enabled him to concentrate the whole story of apparent disaster, penitence, and forgiveness into one happy misfortune, controlled by a divine Art.[28]

Gerald Schorin

I have only touched on the complexities of form and structure of *The Tempest*. What defies analysis is the incredible dramatic unity and economy of statement with which Shakespeare, in this second shortest of his plays, suggests these complexities.

1. William Shakespeare, *The Tempest*, ed. Frank Kermode (Cambridge: Cambridge Univ. Press, 1954), p. lxxxi. All future references to the Introduction will be cited as Kermode.
2. Emma Brockway Wagner, *Shakespeare's "The Tempest"* (Yellow Springs, Ohio: Antioch Press, 1933).
3. Northrop Frye, *A Natural Perspective* (New York: Columbia Univ. Press, 1965), p. 59.
4. E. E. Stoll, "The Tempest," *PMLA*, 47 (1932), 699.
5. Frye, p. 57.
6. This and all subsequent references to the play are to Kermode's Arden edition, cited above.
7. Colin Still, *Shakespeare's Mystery Play* (London: Cecil Palmer, 1921).
8. *Ibid.*, pp. 8-9.
9. Sir James Frazer, *The Golden Bough* (New York: Macmillan, 1927), p. 1.
10. *Ibid.*, p. 244.
11. Mircea Eliade, *Birth and Rebirth* (New York: Harpers, 1958), pp. 4-5.
12. F. M. Cornford, *The Origin of Attic Comedy* (Cambridge: Cambridge Univ. Press, 1934), pp. 201-02.
13. Frye, p. 119.
14. Wylie Sypher, "The Meanings of Comedy," from *Comedy: Meaning and Form*, ed. Robert Corrigan (San Francisco: Chandler, 1965), p. 34.
15. G. Wilson Knight, *The Crown of Life* (London: Methuen, 1961), p. 208.
16. Lawrence Bowling, "The Theme of Natural Order in *The Tempest*," *College English*, 12 (1951), 203.
17. Kermode, p. lv.
18. Bowling, p. 203.
19. Kermode, pp. liv-lv.
20. Bernard Knox, "*The Tempest* and the Ancient Comic Tradition," *Virginia Quarterly Review*, 31 (1955) 74.
21. Northrop Frye, *Anatomy of Criticism: Four Essays* (Princeton: Princeton Univ. Press, 1957), p. 184.
22. D. G. James, *The Dream of Prospero* (Oxford: Oxford Univ. Press, 1967).
23. *Ibid.*, pp. 140-41.
24. Kermode, p. lxii.
25. James, p. 141.

26. Frye, *A Natural Perspective*, p. 120.
27. Jan Kott, *Shakespeare Our Contemporary*, trans. Boleslaw Taborski (New York: Doubleday, 1966), p. 256.
28. Kermode, p. lix.

11

MUSIC AND *THE TEMPEST*

Theresa Coletti

THE VITAL CENTER OF *The Tempest* IS ITS MUSIC. PERVAD-
ing and informing the action of the play, music is always
sounding, always affecting and shaping the lives of the characters. Often directionless and ambiguous in its meaning, the
music of *The Tempest* provides a context for Prospero's magical machinations and becomes, through the course of the
play, a powerfully evocative symbol of this magic. In *The
Tempest* music is the medium through which order emerges
from chaos; it is the agent of suffering, learning, growth, and
freedom.

Critics who have noted the pervasiveness of music, songs,
and musical allusions in Shakespeare's drama[1] have often attempted to extrapolate from the canon of his work and posit
a distinct philosophy of music which they insist he was trying
to communicate in his plays. This is most easily accomplished
by rather vague references to Renaissance ideas of divine
harmony and the "music of the spheres," that macrocosmic
heavenly order of which this worldly microcosm was thought
to be a reflection. It has also been pointed out that during the

Renaissance, music came more and more to be associated with a "rhetoric of emotion," a kind of language of the heart in which man could express his inmost feelings and communicate them to others.[2] Though neither of these notions can account for our experience of a play as musically rich as *The Tempest*, together they can provide us with helpful tools for understanding how Shakespeare employed music in his drama. For from ideas of order we can derive principles of structure, and if there is a providential design in *The Tempest*, it is certainly an artistic and a musical one. Furthermore, this design manifests itself in the manner in which it speaks to deep human feelings; it is meaningful in the extent to which it can express the "language of the heart." In *The Tempest* these two modes of interpretation form a unity from which music emerges as an emotional and philosophical idea. Embodying its own conceptual integrity, music becomes a force that transcends its power as *melos*, or in the case of song, as *melos* and *lexos*, to achieve its status as the play's presiding symbol of both feeling and form.[3]

This explanation will account, I hope, for what may appear to be my subsequent neglect of the *melos* of *The Tempest*'s music. From contemporary song books of the period one is able to conclude with a certain amount of assurance that some of the play's actual music still survives. Peter Seng points out the existence of possible original melodies for two of the songs, "Full fathom five" (I, ii, 397) and "Where the bee sucks, there suck I" (V, i, 88).[4] That the evidence for the remaining body of the play's music is sparse gives us, I think, license to employ our "imaginative" ears to evoke in our own minds the presence of those "strange and solemn airs" that pervade *The Tempest*. The absence of considerations of melody in my discussion of the songs will not, I hope, be perceived as an oversight, but rather as a methodological step necessitated by my thesis that the ontology of music in *The Tempest* is an ideational as well as a melodic one.

If we want to examine music as an informing idea in *The Tempest*, we can begin by looking at a play with which it has many affinities, *As You Like It.* One can view *The Tempest* and *As You Like It* as companion plays in more than one sense. In terms of plot they share many common elements. Each begins *in medias res*; Duke Senior and Prospero have both been deposed before the plays' actions begin. Each drama presents a principal figure whose machinations orchestrate events to bring about a desired end; Rosalind wishes to win Orlando and Prospero to recover his dukedom. Both plays juxtapose groups of good and bad characters; there are the evil-doers and the victims of evil. The primary actions of *The Tempest* and *As You Like It* unfold in artificial worlds where the old exigencies of court life do not obtain. Prospero's island and the Forest of Arden become places of self-discovery where new standards of behavior are learned. Each play's deepest concern is with the process of recognition of error and regeneration, and finally, each abundantly employs music as a vehicle for commenting upon this process or for helping to bring it into being.

As You Like It is richer in music than the plays that preceded it. From his experience with the earliest comedies Shakespeare had probably learned the value of music as an important dramatic device. Here the songs are more carefully integrated, reinforcing and illuminating the themes of the play. The first song, "Under the greenwood tree" (II, v. 1), portrays the life of the exiles in the Forest of Arden and focuses their dramatic situation. Cast from their position of security at court, the new inhabitants of Arden are learning that nature supplies a home that is in many ways far superior to the one they have left behind: "Here shall he see no enemy / But winter and rough weather" (II, v. 6-7).[5] A musical statement of one of the themes of the play, the beneficent effect of nature on man, the song also reveals the character of its two singers, Amiens, the cheerful exile, and Jaques, the melancholy cynic. This is a fine instance of music as dramatic economy. Simultaneously fulfilling two functions, the song delineates the import of the play's action and displays antithetical responses to it.

The placement of the songs in *As You Like It* also intensifies the play's dramatic movement. "Blow, blow, thou winter wind" (II, vii, 174) repeats the theme of the first song, but it is more caustic, more explicit in its comment. The implications of this song, which contrasts winter's natural violence with the violence that human beings inflict upon each other, are undercut by its dramatic position. Coming directly after Orlando carries in his faithful but debilitated servant Adam, the song becomes an ironic comment upon itself, for we have just seen an example of friendship that is not "feigning," of loving that is not mere "folly." We have also discovered that Duke Senior's attachment to Orlando's father survives in his kindness to the son. Like Jaques' misanthropic speech on the ultimate insignificance of human life, the song makes a point which the events of the play qualify, and the agent of this qualification is the very benignity of nature itself.

One final instance of the use of music in *As You Like It* is worth noting. While perhaps bearing no explicit relationship to the progress of the plot or the nature of character, the song "It was a lover and his lass" (V, iii, 5) has an evocative power that imbues the entire conclusion of the play. Celebrating a life of love and springtime, the song by contrast reminds us of the winter of exile and misfortune that has just passed. It looks ahead to the marriages that are about to take place and brings a sense of freshness to inform the repentance that Duke Frederick and Oliver experience. More atmospheric than thematic, this song suggests a new order of living and being; it transcends the events of the play to provide a context that expresses their fullest meaning. In this sense it comes closer than any other song in the play to the use of music that Shakespeare employs in *The Tempest*.

This brief discussion of *As You Like It* illustrates how important to a drama music and song can be. Taken together, the songs of *As You Like It* form more than a decorative enhancement of the action. Amiens' simplicity and energetic gaiety are so closely connected to its progress that it is very difficult to imagine the play without him or his songs. The music of *As You Like It* moves with the play as an analogous structure of mood and motive. It does not, however, become the structural principle of the play itself. This is where *The Tempest* takes its crucial departure from a play with which it otherwise shares many similarities.

The difference between the two plays is, of course, the chronological fact of twelve or thirteen years. Historical considerations of dramatic presentation—the acquisition by the King's Men of the Blackfriars Theatre—can, in part, account for the unique use to which music was put in *The Tempest*. But the deepest distinctions between *The Tempest* and *As You Like It* are those that point to profounder questions of ethics and the nature of freedom and responsibility. The answers supplied by *As You Like It* are essentially those of the comic vision—that human nature is susceptible to goodness and that man, if not perfectible, is at least reformable. But Shakespeare's romances follow the writing of the tragedies, and they are caught in a delicate balance between the affirmation of the earlier plays and the dark and ponderous probings of *Macbeth* and *King Lear*. And if they are able to sustain or even suggest a positive vision, it is only after an excess of suffering and the painful passage of time.

The divergent attitudes toward time that *As You Like It* and *The Tempest* reveal are perhaps a key to understanding the very different roles that music takes in each of these plays. In one sense, time seems to be of little significance in *As You Like It*. Duke Senior and his company regret their unfortunate exile, but the Forest of Arden has a medicinal effect that tempers the burden of the past and makes the present livable, even enjoyable. The future, too, looms in their consciousness as neither a promise nor a threat. There is in the play, however, the repeated appearance of what I call "the salutary moment," those unique instants when men and women fall in love and when wrong-doers recognize their errors and seek forgiveness. This is the "love at first sight" of Rosalind and Orlando, of Celia and Oliver. It is also the instantaneous conversion of Duke Frederick by his encounter with a religious hermit and the quick reformation of Oliver when saved from the devouring jaws of a lion by the intervention of his brother. Time, then, in *As You Like It* is fragmented and dispersed; it is important insofar as it coincides with certain significant incidents. Helen Gardner, speaking of the "unmeasured time" of this play, points out that comedy by its very nature makes use of changes and chances which are not really events but "happenings."[6] Comedy exploits adaptability; it tests a character's willingness to grasp the proper moment and fashion it to his own end. Briefly, it dramatizes Rosalind's advice to Phoebe: "Sell when you can, you are not for all markets" (III, v, 60). This *carpe diem* attitude toward living, which depends on the coincidence of situation and desire, posits a sense of time that locates value in the particular moment. Time's effect, then, is not cumulative but instantaneous; it is not the fulfillment of destiny but life lived "as you like it."

I stated earlier that the music of *As You Like It* formed a structure analogous to the movement of the play, and I think my point is reinforced if we notice that the songs tend to embody this special "momentary" quality as well. They either occur in relatively short scenes devoted to the consciousness of "having a song" (II, v; IV, ii; V, iii), or they exploit a significant moment by providing an ironic or thematic comment (II, vii; V, iv). The possible exception is "It was a lover and his lass" (V, iii), the import of which has already been discussed.

Theresa Coletti

If the musical instances in *As You Like It* parallel in theme and tone the movement of the play, the music of *The Tempest* orchestrates its developing action at every point. The songs of *As You Like It* are largely situational; for the most part, they do not require a comprehensive view of the drama to render them meaningful. They do not depend upon time as a moving force that brings events and feelings to a certain issue. Time, however, is of utmost importance in *The Tempest*. Prospero has four hours to complete his magic revels; this sense of time (and timing) thus makes *every* moment meaningful. An intuition of urgency, a recognition of catastrophe just barely avoided, imbues our experience of *The Tempest*. Our perception of time in the play includes both a sense of the "proper moment" and a feeling of necessary duration. Ariel saves Gonzalo and Alonso from the swords of Antonio and Sebastian in "the nick of time," but Alonso saves himself by enduring a period of suffering. And I think, too, we can see how the shape of time in *The Tempest* is largely coextensive with its music. For music informs the play not only as an agent of the "proper moment"; it also directs and integrates all of the play's moments into the total vision that is the play. *The Tempest* could not exist without its music, whether it is the strange and solemn airs that accompany the magic banquet, the sprightly singing of Ariel, or the drunken cavorting of Caliban, Stephano, and Trinculo. All of these bear an intimate relationship to each other; all relate to Prospero's one significant action—his effort to recover his dukedom and to bring his enemies to a recognition of their past and their errors.

Ultimately one's view of the importance of music in *The Tempest* will depend upon what one thinks the play's dramatic import finally is. If one believes that Prospero's island is an harmonious one where redemptive grace allays and triumphs over evil, one is apt to find its music symbolic of a celes-

191

tial concord which will eventually obtain on earth. It is true
that *The Tempest*'s music revolves around the opposition of
concord and discord and that the agents of these two modes
of being respond (or do not respond) to it in their respective
ways. But rather than seeing the play as the victory of harmony over disorder, I think *The Tempest* suggests how very
difficult it is to bring order into being and that order, once
achieved, is indeed a fragile thing, precariously balanced between the violent past from which it has emerged and the
threatening future which may consume it. Music, then, as-
sists at the birth of this tentative order, and Prospero's music
must be considered in terms of both the extensions and limitations of his art.[7]

The first song of the play is Ariel's "Come unto these yellow
sands" (I, ii, 375), which he sings to a grieving Ferdinand.
The tempest has finally subsided, and Ariel's song celebrates
the simplicity of the calm earth into which Ferdinand has
been transported. As an invitation to the dance, "then take
hands," the song looks ahead to that moment at the end of
the play when all of its characters are joined inside Prospero's magic circle. The magic which Prospero had used to
invoke the tempest now enchants Ferdinand, drawing him
further into the island and toward Miranda. This is the first
crucial step toward their marriage, which will in part resolve
the parental strife that had been Prospero's cause for raising
the tempest. One critic has suggested that this song is the musical counterpart of the sweet-singing Sirens' invitation.
"The island has all the magical charms of Circe's island:
strangers from afar have been lured to it and Prospero provides a magical banquet and charms his visitors by music's
powers, so that they are no longer able to obey their reason-
ing powers."[8] Here Prospero's more benevolent powers re-
place the lust and destruction of the Sirens, and the music
leads Ferdinand, not to an easy satisfaction, but to a test of

discipline and faithfulness. Ferdinand's response to the song, "Where should this music be? I' th' air or th' earth?" (I, ii, 388), establishes the magical quality of this island, where the very air is music. W. H. Auden has written that "the song comes to him as an utter surprise, and its effect is not to feed or please his grief, not to encourage him to sit brooding, but to allay his passion, so that he gets to his feet and follows the music. The song opens his present to expectation at a moment when he is in danger of closing it to all but recollection."[9]

As Ferdinand follows this elusive music, Ariel begins his second song, "Full fathom five thy father lies" (I, ii, 397). Probably no song of *The Tempest* is so well remembered and perhaps no other is thematically so important. Ferdinand is made to believe that his father is dead; similarly, Alonso will believe that Ferdinand is dead, and in that belief he will undergo the madness, the "sea change" of grief and humility, from which he will emerge transformed. The poetry of the song transports Alonso from the world of mutability and flux to a kind of permanence. His bones and eyes become coral and pearls; the "sea" gives form to what was subject to decay.[10] Thus the song reminds us that the life of Milan—the disordered world of usurpation and potential tyranny—is now under the shaping influence of Prospero's art. Ferdinand reacts to the song not with grief but with awe: "This is no mortal business, nor no sound / That the earth owes" (I, ii, 407-408). The music, in the play's first triumph over history, moves Ferdinand to accept his past and leads him to the future—and Miranda.

The swift agent of Prospero's well-timed music, Ariel plays a "solemn strain" (II, i, 178) that lulls the Milan travelers to sleep. Gonzalo, in his simplicity and warm-heartedness, submits most easily, but Alonso soon follows. Sebastian and Antonio, however, are significantly exempted from the effect of the music. Prospero's magic has no power over them. Their own imperviousness to this music, their inability to hear it, contrasts sharply with Caliban, who, even in his vile earthiness, is subject to the music's seduction. "The isle is full of noises," he tells Stephano and Trinculo, "Sounds and sweet airs that give delight and hurt not" (III, ii, 132-133). When Sebastian and Antonio plot to take the lives of Alonso and Gonzalo, Prospero's music urgently intervenes. Ariel sings a warning song, "While you here do snoring lie" (II, i, 290), into Gonzalo's ear, and the sleepers awake. The music that had induced their slumber becomes the agent of their deliverance; Alonso and Gonzalo escape catastrophe.

One of the primary distinctions to be made about music in *The Tempest* is, of course, that there is Ariel's music and there is Caliban's music. And while there is that moment when Caliban seems to come close to understanding both of these musical languages, he remains, for the most part, on the side of the raucous and the bawdy. This is the music of Stephano and Trinculo as well. Stephano's first two songs, "I shall no more to sea" (II, ii, 41) and "The master, the swabber, the boatswain, and I" (II, ii, 45), are indeed the "scurvy tunes" that he calls them. The songs are a kind of comic diversion and an introduction to the buffoonery of the three that is to follow. Their lustiness and earthiness offers a clear antithesis to the obedient chastity of Ferdinand and Miranda, who are learning that fulfillment must be by desert and not demand.

Caliban, now under the influence of his new god "sack," raises his own voice in song. His "Farewell master" (II, ii, 173) and "No more dams I'll make for fish" (II, ii, 175) signalize his revolt from Prospero. The latter song ends with a call for freedom, reminding us, perhaps, of Ariel's behest early in the play that Prospero release him. Ariel must work for his freedom; Caliban expects his to fall into his lap. It is important, too, I think, and perhaps ironically significant that the only two characters in the play who *ask* for freedom are the non-human ones, while all the other characters are very much involved in a struggle to be free from history, from each other, and from themselves. Caliban's "scurvy song" heralds the delusion he is about to come under in thinking Stephano and Trinculo the vehicle through which his freedom may be realized. Together the comrades plot to kill Prospero and take the island, and they seal their bargain with their song "Flout 'em and scout 'em" (III, ii, 118). Caliban remarks, "That's not the tune" (121), and Ariel enters with his tabor and pipe and a wholly different kind of music. This evokes different responses from the three; Stephano thinks it the devil, Trinculo expresses penitence, but Caliban counsels them not to fear this intervention. Curiously, the two scenes of the drunken songs frame the scene of log-bearing Ferdinand, engaged in his trial to prove to Prospero his fitness for Miranda. Ferdinand's sobriety in performing his task and his willingness to accept control and responsibility—his efforts to bring about his own freedom—are thrown into relief by this contrast with desire run wild. This reminds us that Prospero's attempt to bring a new order into being is threatened on all sides by strongly motivated self-satisfaction and potential anarchy.

Ariel's music, then, has intervened a second time to hinder the enactment of a plot hatched to assassinate a ruler. Similarly, shortly after the maneuvers of Stephano, Trinculo, and Caliban to do away with Prospero, we see Antonio and Sebastian once again involved in machinations to kill their king. Again Ariel interrupts, this time with "solemn and strange music" (III, iii, 18), and he produces the dance of the strange shapes and their banquet. Alonso and Gonzalo admire the apparition, calling it "harmony" and "sweet music." Antonio and Sebastian, still beyond the pale of the island's music, can only relate the phenomenon to mundanities of geography and travelers' tales. Gonzalo thinks the shapes' "manners" more gentle than human kind, while Sebastian wants to eat the food they have placed in front of him. Like Stephano, Trinculo, and Caliban, his earthly-mindedness has no access to the beauty that affects Gonzalo and Alonso.

Ariel enters again, this time disguised as a harpy, and the banquet disappears. He explains to them the initial effect and purpose of his music: "you 'mongst men / Being most unfit to live, I have made you mad" (III, iii, 57-58). Ariel reminds them of their deposition of Prospero and promises them "lingering perdition" unless they are able to experience "heart's sorrow / And a clear life ensuing" (82). Ariel is telling the representatives of Milan that they must submit to the music of the island and endure the pain that the achievement of freedom involves or continue to be agents of chaos and evil. This is the point where the powers and limitations of Prospero's art merge. While it is true that the play has revealed that there are those amenable to order and those that are not, Prospero can only use his music to bring his captives to a consciousness of their own disordered, threatening behavior. His music cannot perform that transformation by itself. As Ferdinand had to choose whether or not he would undergo the ordeal of log-bearing, Alonso must choose whether or not he will repent. In doing so he must experience a depth of despair as a necessary prelude to his recovery: "My son i' th' ooze is bedded; and / I'll seek him deeper than e'er plummet sounded / And with him there lie mudded" (III, iii, 100-102).

Perhaps the most magnificent use of music in *The Tempest* is that which introduces and informs the masque that Prospero produces as a wedding blessing for Ferdinand and Miranda. The song "Honour, riches, marriage, blessing" (IV, i, 106) looks forward to the happy union of the couple. Yet while the song of Juno and Ceres bespeaks a life of plenty, this is not the same kind of richness that Gonzalo had envisioned when he dreamed of his ideal commonwealth: "Bourn, bound of land, tilth, vineyard, none; / . . . all men idle, all" (II, i, 148, 150). Juno and Ceres sing of the bounty that is the result of cultivation: "Barns and garners never empty, / Vines with clust'ring bunches growing" (111-112). This copiousness is the result of dedicated work, of nature and nurture, and the dance which concludes the masque is one of nymphs and "August-weary" reapers. We should remember, too, that Prospero's magic is also the outcome of his hard "labours." If we would chide Gonzalo for his innocent simplicity in imagining a golden world, the masque song balances his dream with one that must admit the necessity of the human work that brings fruitfulness and bounty.

This masque is perhaps revelatory of Prospero's imaginative desire to see order and goodness, but it expresses this goodness as the result of meaningful human effort. The frailty of this vision, however, shows itself by rapidly dissolving as Prospero remembers Caliban's "foul conspiracy" against his life.[11] Jan Kott has called this play "the great Renaissance tragedy of lost illusions,"[12] and while one may hesitate to see it as the dark and murky drama which he thinks it is, one must, I think, give credence to the sense of incompleteness that emerges as the play comes to a close. For there are gaps, empty spaces in our perception of the human lives we have seen portrayed, which we suspect even Prospero's finest magic and greatest music cannot touch. His famous "Our revels now are ended" speech (IV, i, 148) seems, in fact, to point to the limitations of the musically enchanted spectacle he has produced. Just how fragile it really is is evidenced by its ambiguous effect on Prospero himself. For he has yet to be reminded by Ariel that "the rarer action" is one of loving forgiveness, and there is that crucial moment when it seems as if his "nobler reason" will be as baseless as the fabric of his vision. When "the insubstantial pageant" fades, what is left is Prospero and his beating mind.

His labors, however, are not without positive issue. Prospero's music had made Alonso and his company mad, yet that madness was a necessary prelude to their recognition of guilt and repentance. If Prospero's music led the shipwrecked travelers to an awareness of their own history, it also provided a vehicle through which this awareness—this madness—could be healed. They enter Prospero's magic circle to a "solemn air . . . the best comforter / To an unsettled fancy . . ." (V, i, 58-59). Yet if they have attained a freedom from madness, it is a freedom that must accept the burden of responsibility for its past and future. In this context, Ariel's final song, "Where the bee sucks, there suck I" (V, i, 87), is significant. One critic has suggested that this song, which is about Ariel's freedom, is really a lyric coda to the entire play, celebrating the attainment of freedom on the part of all who have been involved.[13] I think the song has a different and greater function. As it suggests Ariel's approaching happiness, it points to the world beyond the play, the world which must remain that of our imaginings. And in going beyond the world of the play, we must inevitably consider not only the "cowslip's bell" and the merry summer that Ariel looks forward to with delight, but also Milan and the world to which the reinstated Prospero must return. Ariel's song most poignantly reminds us that his freedom is not the freedom of a Prospero or an Alonso, that only a spirit can be free to the four elements. For the court of Milan freedom must now reside in responsible action emerging from the recognition of the pain of history.

Throughout *The Tempest* Prospero's art—his music—had been the measure of the shaping influence he had on the lives of other people. Its power finally, I think, must be as tentative as the conclusion to which it brings us. It has united Ferdinand and Miranda and created a new future for Alonso, but Antonio is still trapped in vile self-seeking, and the cases of Sebastian and Caliban are questionable. Music has helped to bring about some order in what had been chaos, some concord from what had been discord.[14] But Prospero breaks his staff and drowns his book, and thus he abandons his music as well. There is the suggestion, I think, that from now on the attainment and preservation of freedom and forgiveness will be a thoroughly human effort in which music can no longer intervene.

1. Works often cited are: John Long, *Shakespeare's Use of Music: A Study of Music and Its Performance in the Original Production of Seven Comedies* (Gainesville: University of Florida Press, 1955); John Robert Moore, "The Function of the Songs in Shakespeare's Plays," *Shakespeare Studies by Members of the Department of English of the University of Wisconsin* (Madison, 1916), pp. 78-102; Richmond Noble, *Shakespeare's Use of Song with the Text of the Principal Songs* (London: Oxford University Press, 1923).

2. John Stevens, "Shakespeare and the Music of the Elizabethan Stage," *Shakespeare in Music*, ed. Phyllis Hartnoll (London: Macmillan & Co., 1964), p. 48.

3. I am grateful to Professor Jarold Ramsey of the University of Rochester for pointing out to me this distinction between *melos* and *lexos* and for his helpful advice throughout the preparation of this paper.

4. *The Vocal Songs in the Plays of Shakespeare* (Cambridge: Harvard University Press, 1967), pp. 256-57, 271.

5. All line citations are from *William Shakespeare: The Complete Works*, ed. Alfred Harbage (Baltimore: Penguin Books, 1969).

6. "As You Like It," *More Talking of Shakespeare*, ed. John Garrett (London: Longmans, Green & Co. Ltd., 1959), pp. 21-22.

7. Rose Zimbardo in her article "Form and Disorder in *The Tempest*," *Shakespeare Quarterly*, 14 (1963), 49-56, very capably notes that the opposition of order and disorder is the crucial tension set forth in the play and suggests that Prospero's art must be seen in terms of this opposition. My intention is to show how the play's use of music augments this tension dramatically and symbolically at every point of the action.

8. John Cutts, "Music and the Supernatural in *The Tempest*: A Study in Interpretation," *Music and Letters*, 39: 4 (October, 1958), p. 348.

9. "Music in Shakespeare: Its Dramatic Use in the Plays," *Encounter*, 9 (December, 1957), p. 43.

10. Zimbardo, p. 51.

11. Zimbardo, p. 56.

12. *Shakespeare Our Contemporary* (New York: Anchor Books, 1966), p. 271.

13. Seng, p. 271.

14. Zimbardo, p. 55.

12

POST-CREATION FREEDOM IN
THE TEMPEST

Elton D. Higgs

IT IS A MARK OF SHAKESPEARE'S MATURE POWERS AS AN ARTIST
that he is able to fit so many elements of life into a single
context. In no play did he succeed so eminently in illustrating
this ability as in his last full play, *The Tempest*. It is a play
for all seasons, having elements of romance, comedy, fantasy,
political intrigue, and tragedy. But even more remarkably,
this last of Shakespeare's plays embodies his profoundest comments on the Janus-like nature of new beginnings in the life
of man. As Prospero works everything toward the redemption of past evils through the purgation of his enemies and
the marriage of Miranda and Ferdinand, it becomes increasingly apparent that one may mitigate the past, but not forget it; that one may look optimistically toward the future,
but not without realizing that the very freedom to seek the
good carries with it the possibility of finding evil. And not
even the God-like power of Prospero can permanently suspend the ambiguous possibilities of a world where freedom is
exercised.

Elton D. Higgs

I

The working relationship between Prospero and Ariel in *The Tempest* creates the power that pervades the action of the play; indeed, nothing at all happens apart from their power. Yet, the climax of the action of the play involves ~~the severing of this relationship by~~ the freeing of Ariel from the service of Prospero. Ariel's eagerness for his freedom sets the tone of his relationship to Prospero from the very first time we see them together, when Ariel responds reluctantly to Prospero's orders:

> Is there more toil? Since thou dost give me pains,
> Let me remember thee what thou hast promis'd,
> Which is not yet perform'd me. / . . . My liberty.
> (I. ii. 242-244; 245)[1]

And Prospero, after teasing Ariel with reminders of the sprite's obligations to him, consents to release him "after two days" (I. ii. 298). Although Prospero originally gained Ariel's service by releasing him magically from an imprisonment imposed by the witch Sycorax, he has become increasingly dependent upon Ariel, so that freeing him becomes coincident with Prospero's relinquishing all his supernatural powers and returning once again to the outside world and to the status he occupied before he came to the island. It is this choice by Prospero which forms the core of the play, for it has implications even beyond the development of Prospero's character: the act of manipulating the world of experience, whether by God or by man, carries with it the decision as to whether one will maintain the security of absolute control, or release what he has helped to form so that it can test the uncertain potentials of freedom.

Prospero is the symbolic agent of creation on two levels, ~~apart from the literal events of the play.~~ Just as God created the world in six days through His Spirit, so Prospero uses Ariel to do work which he plans to have finished by "the sixth hour" (I. ii. 240-41; V. i. 4-5), at which time he must cease his labors and leave the people on the island to their freedom. At the same time, he serves as an image of the playwright, who creates an island of magic within a sea of reality.[2] The point of the play on both levels is that the suspended state of existence which accompanies an act of creation, whether literal or imaginary, cannot be sustained indefinitely, at least not in the world as human beings know it. In *Genesis*, God created the world, and He saw that it was good; but He had to leave man to his own choices: the tree of knowledge of good *and* evil had to be set before him. The created thing must have its freedom, for good or ill; else, both creator and created are in captivity, and the act of creation has not been consummated. On all levels, the post-creation choice is whether or not to permit some balance to be struck between perfectly controlled romance and ambiguously free reality.

It is in this context that Prospero must choose whether to relinquish the manipulative "art" which has enabled him to interrupt the unpredictable flow of normal life. We see him in the action of the play only as an eminent success, but his very presence on the island is a result of his refusal to face the difficulties of the real world of Milan. All he can do with his arts of magic, even on the island, is to suspend temporarily the results of evil and allow time for other elements to come into play. He must eventually allow to the same set of characters who cast him asea the opportunity (and the danger) of acting according to their own desires and receiving the consequences of their actions, whether all turns out well or not. The suspension of evil consequences, during which neither tempest nor plot can bring harm to those who walk upon the island, has a legitimate purpose, for both Prospero and Shakespeare; but that legitimacy is verified only when the spell is broken, and both magic and poetry are subordinated to the vicissitudes of freedom.

Elton D. Higgs

We are ushered into the play by a disturbance in the elements which immediately removes us from the normal flow of everyday life, with its ordinary distribution of good and ill. We are wrenched with the travelers out of the midst of the stormy sea and cast upon an island where their clothes are not even wet (II. i. 62-65). Death is suspended: everyone on the island except Caliban and Ariel, who are citizens of it, has been saved from death at sea, and the murder plots of Sebastian, Antonio, Caliban, Stephano, and Trinculo are foiled. Nothing is concluded in the play except the neutralizing of the past and the creation of new possibilities for the future.[3] Thus the events of the play are governed by the island and its spirit of magic; the normal course of life—specifically the return from the marriage of Alonso's daughter, Claribel—is interrupted by a suspended piece of action that looks both backward and forward. The storm has been raised by Prospero to redeem the past, but it cannot guarantee the future.

The progress of Prospero toward releasing both himself and those he temporarily controls from the artificiality of a perfect society is seen in both the major and the minor plots of the play. In the major plot—the retribution brought by Prospero on Alonso, Antonio, and Sebastian—the resolution comes with the betrothal of Miranda and Ferdinand. In the subplot—Ariel's espial and defeat of Caliban, Stephano, and Trinculo in their attempt to murder Prospero—we are concerned with Prospero's relationship to his two widely different servants on the island. The two plots are merged and the drama is skillfully brought to focus in the last scene, as Prospero gives up his magic, releases Ariel, forgives his enemies, and leaves in the hands of Ferdinand and Miranda the new world he has made possible.

II

Miranda is the hope of Prospero for a new start. He realizes from the first that only a union between her and the son of his

BEGINNING

203

enemy, Alonso, can bring about the reconciliation that he seeks. But he will not build his hopes on hiding the past or ignoring its possible effect on the future. He therefore tells Miranda the whole story of his being set adrift at sea by the very people who are now at his mercy on the island. Her reaction to their plight ("O, I have suffered / With those that I saw suffer." [I.ii. 5-6]) shows her tenderness, and throughout the play both she and Ferdinand show that they are untarnished by the feud between their fathers. Accordingly, they are safely put in the background soon after they meet (I. ii. 408ff), and the main action of the play is devoted to creating the kind of attitude on the part of the rest of the ship's party which will provide Ferdinand and Miranda with the best chance of making their new relationship work.

The older generation in the play has failed miserably; even the best of them are powerless (apart from Prospero's artificial powers) to turn their good intentions to much good. That "good old Lord Gonzalo" (V. i. 15), although he managed to save Prospero's life when he was set afloat with Miranda, is hopelessly naïve in his description of the commonwealth he would establish (II. i. 143-169), and he is mocked by the would-be villains, Antonio and Sebastian. Alonso, though he is repentant and somber at the loss of his son, would have been murdered had it not been for the intervention of Ariel. Even the marriage of Claribel, the King's daughter, is tinged with acrimony and regret (II. i. 102-135), and what should be an occasion of joy is overshadowed by the sins of Alonso and his confederates.

Since the union of Miranda and Ferdinand is presented in such idealized terms ("At the first sight / They have chang'd eyes."—I. ii. 443-44), it might at first be taken as a cure-all for the ills perpetrated by their fathers. But Prospero is not unaware of the dangers of a love which develops without any of the normal impediments of the world (I. ii. 452-454), which the two lovers will certainly have to face later. It is for this reason that he acts harshly toward Ferdinand and sets him to hard labor, with strict orders to Miranda not to speak with him. Prospero's sense of reality goes even further, however, for even when he has revealed his true feelings to Ferdinand, he is insistent on cautioning the lovers against being betrayed by their fleshly passions:

> Look thou be true. Do not give dalliance
> Too much the rein. The strongest oaths are straw
> To th' fire i' th' blood. Be more abstemious,
> Or else good night your vow! (IV. i. 51-54)

It is a mark of Prospero's development on the island that he accepts realistically, but without bitterness, the mixture of flesh and spirit in the world to which he must return. One may understand better how this development took place by examining Prospero's relationship to his two contrasting servants on the island, Ariel and Caliban.

III

The key to the difference between Ariel and Caliban, significantly enough, lies in their attitudes toward freedom. Both of them wish to have their freedom from Prospero, but Caliban, in contrast to Ariel, is incapable of being free. When he plots the death of Prospero and sings "Freedom, high-day, freedom" (II. ii. 186), it is in the shadow of his newly-formed, stupid servility to the drunken butler, Stephano. Ariel, on the other hand, must be free to fulfill his nature; he would not serve the base desires of Caliban's mother, the witch Sycorax (I. ii. 270-273), and he continually expects and anticipates his freedom from even so wise a master as Prospero. It is instructive, however, that both of these beings are employed by Prospero, and that the balance he must strike between their con-

trasting services on the island may have some correspondence
to forces he will have to deal with when he leaves the island.
Caliban has to do with things of the earth. When Prospero
and Miranda first came to the island, he showed them the
sources of food and water on it (I. ii. 332-338); later, after he
had brutishly tried to rape Miranda (I. ii. 348-350), he was set
to carrying wood and doing other basic tasks (I. ii. 313-315).
Ariel's tasks are all light, spiritual, and airy—"to fly, / To
swim, to dive into the fire, to ride / On the curl'd clouds" (I.
ii. 190-192).

It is important to note that, although he relies more on
Ariel, Prospero cannot ignore his relationship to Caliban.
When the plot of Caliban, Stephano, and Trinculo against
the life of Prospero has been thwarted, Prospero says to Alonso: "Two of these fellows you / Must know and own; this
thing of darkness I/ Acknowledge mine" (V. i. 274-276). Not
only does Prospero have to forgive his enemies, give up his
magic, and return to the world where he failed, but he must
also admit that the baser elements represented by Caliban
are something he cannot leave entirely behind. In fact, he
carries something of both Caliban and Ariel with him, sym-
bolizing the ambiguous potential of the world to which he is
returning. The unfettered, creative freedom of Ariel has to be
balanced by the earth-bound necessities represented by Caliban, for man is both spirit and body, transcendent and temporal; he exults in life, but he must acknowledge the certainty
of death.

Death, of course, is the last evil to which Prospero must
admit his (and his generation's) immediate vulnerability. In
The Tempest, it is seen in contrast not only to the suspended
state of existence on Prospero's island, but more importantly
to the youth and potential fruitfulness of Ferdinand and Miranda. The hope held out in *The Tempest* is not one of a paradise where evil has no power, but rather that of a new genera-

tion which may keep it in check. Ironically, however, it is
when Prospero is at the peak of his creative powers, in the
midst of the marriage masque he commands his spirits to perform for Ferdinand and Miranda, celebrating life and fruitfulness, that the immediacy of death breaks in upon him. He
is suddenly reminded of "that foul conspiracy / Of the beast
Caliban and his confederates" (IV. i. 139-140) against his life.
It is not merely the plot of Caliban that disturbs him, but the
whole spectrum of mortality that finds its focus in Caliban.[4]
Prospero has to face the necessity of dealing with an element
of baseness in his society (and in himself) which he would
gladly have covered over with the world of imagination that
his art has created. The world of imagination has its value, but
the influence of Caliban must be acknowledged and controlled. For all his nobility of mind, man and his works must
die. Prospero tells Ferdinand, as the masque vanishes:

> Our revels now are ended. These our actors,
> As I foretold you, were all spirits and
> Are melted into air, into thin air;
> And, like the baseless fabric of this vision,
> The cloud-capp'd towers, the gorgeous palaces,
> The solemn temples, the great globe itself,
> Yea, all which it inherit, shall dissolve,
> And, like this insubstantial pageant faded,
> Leave not a rack behind. We are such stuff
> As dreams are made on, and our little life
> Is rounded with a sleep. Sir, I am vex'd.
> Bear with my weakness; my old brain is troubled.
> Be not disturb'd with my infirmity.
> If you be pleas'd, retire into my cell
> And there repose. A turn or two I'll walk
> To still my beating mind. (IV. i. 148-163)

The reason that Caliban's plot raises a disturbance in Prospero's mind out of all proportion to the actual danger it poses
is that Prospero is faced once again with the same kind of situ-

ation that had toppled his dukedom in Milan; he runs the risk of refusing to exercise necessary power in the physical world because he is immersed in the private world of his learning. In this instance, however, he meets the test and exercises his supernatural power so thoroughly that he can afford to lay it aside and pick up those responsibilities which are his as a mere man. Neither power nor imagination, he has learned, are ends to be pursued for their own sake, apart from each other.

Thwarting his enemies on the island is almost too easy, and there are hints of a decision to be made by Prospero concerning what happens after he has broken his spells. Then, he must keep his promise to set Ariel free.

> At this hour
> Lie at my mercy all mine enemies.
> Shortly shall all my labours end, and thou
> Shalt have the air at freedom. (IV. i. 262-65)

Since Ariel has been the chief agent of his powers, Prospero realizes the implications of releasing him and is willing to accept them.[5] He says his farewell to the spirits who have served him, and concludes:

> But this rough magic
> I here adjure; and when I have requir'd
> Some heavenly music (which even now I do)
> To work mine end upon their senses that
> This airy charm is for, I'll break my staff,
> Bury it certain fathoms in the earth,
> And deeper than did ever plummet sound
> I'll drown my book. (V. i. 50-57)

"I will discase me," he says, "and myself present / As I was sometime Milan" (V. i. 85-86). He willingly consents to break the spell which disguises him and gives him supernatural control over the situation, and he becomes once again vulnerable to the ambiguous potential of normal human society.

IV

The Tempest is perhaps Shakespeare's most carefully constructed play, and all of the threads of the drama are subtly brought together in the last scene. The old sinners are brought to judgment and are forgiven, and the young people, who will start afresh, are dramatically revealed at their game of chess, oblivious to the rest of the world. Miranda's wide-eyed assessment of this new-born world has the spirit of pure romance about it:

> Oh wonder!
> How many goodly creatures are there here!
> How beauteous mankind is! O brave new world
> That has such people in't! (V. i. 181-184)

Here is the climax of the theme of new beginnings, and, as the development of the theme has led us to expect, it is tempered by Prospero's new-found worldly wisdom. There is a world of implication in his laconic response to Miranda's exclamation: " 'Tis new to thee" (V. i. 184). There is no sour sermon here, no crotchety self-righteousness, but merely a reminder that, although each generation should delight in the newness of its view of human society, each generation will have to yield to the next and retire, somewhat battered and less naive, to the earth whence they came.

In this last scene, every person is released from Prospero's power and is free to fulfill his own nature, good or bad. Of Alonso's party, Prospero says, "My charms I'll break, their senses I'll restore / And they shall be themselves" (V. i. 31-32). As Prospero doffs his magician's robes and dons the garments of his dukedom, he promises Ariel, "I shall miss thee, / But yet thou shalt have freedom" (V. i. 95-96). Even Caliban and his companions are commanded by Prospero to be set free (V. i. 252). The good old man Gonzalo sums up the effects of the action of the play on the characters involved:

> In one voyage
> Did Claribel her husband find at Tunis,
> And Ferdinand her brother found a wife
> Where he himself was lost; Prospero his dukedom
> In a poor isle; and all of us ourselves
> When no man was his own. (V. i. 208-213)

Note that each person found, not wisdom, not safety, not marital bliss, but himself, with all the ambiguous smell of mortality which that entails. For Ferdinand and Miranda, finding themselves was the discovery that temporary misfortune can temper and deepen the quality of ecstatic young love; for Alonso and Gonzalo, it was the realization that even in old age there can be opportunity to rejoice; for Prospero, it was that even his absolute power could not in this realm of man shield him from death.

Prospero clearly sees himself as having no defenses against mortality at the end of the play. He has faced death and accepted it as the ultimate mark of his finitude. He gives up not only his supernatural power, but the tenure of his generation in the positions of power in his world. His only desire is

> To see the nuptial
> Of these our dear-belov'd solemnized;
> And thence retire me to my Milan, where
> Every third thought shall be my grave. (V. i. 309-312)

Prospero's last display of power ("auspicious gales" for the trip home) is accompanied by a farewell to Ariel and the benediction, "To the elements / Be free" (V. i. 317-318). Prospero's creative manipulation of events has been completed, and all the characters have been freed to fulfill their own potential, whatever it may be. But the epilogue which Shakespeare puts into the mouth of Prospero makes it clear that there must be a post-creation release for both author and audience from the imaginative world which has brought them together. Neither must hold the other captive to that world: the author wishes to be thought of as more than the artistic god who created the world of the play, and the audience must return to the reality of the unpredictable world of their existence, in the midst of which the viewing of the play has been an island of constructive fantasy.

> Let me not,
> Since I have my dukedom got
> And pardon'd the deceiver, dwell
> In this bare island by your spell;
> But release me from my bands
> With the help of your good hands.
> Gentle breath of yours my sails
> Must fill, or else my project fails,
> Which was to please. Now I want
> Spirits to enforce, Art to enchant;
> And my ending is despair
> Unless I be reliev'd by prayer,
> Which pierces so that it assaults
> Mercy itself and frees all faults.
> As you from crimes would pardon'd be,
> Let your indulgence set me free. (Epilogue, 5-20)

The theme of creation has become the theme of rebirth; man cannot escape a world where there is potential for evil as well as good, but at least he can benefit from and imitate the creative power of God by making, from time to time, a new beginning. One way of tapping this power, as Shakespeare illustrates in *The Tempest*, is through the imaginative art of the theater. There, for a while, we are lifted above our mortal limitations and given, at least by an author of Shakespeare's

power, a chance to know ourselves better and return renewed
to face the exhilarating uncertainties of our freedom.[6]

1. All quotations from *The Tempest* are taken from the Arden Shakespeare edition of the play, ed. Frank Kermode (London: Methuen & Co., Ltd.; Cambridge: Harvard Univ. Press, 1958).

2. I wish to avoid any strictly autobiographical association of Shakespeare with Prospero, particularly the kind of criticism which has for the last one hundred and fifty years seen Shakespeare's retiring farewell to the theatre in Prospero's casting away his books and his magic staff. I am referring rather to the kind of reflection seen by John M. Murry, who finds in Prospero "an imaginative paradigm" of Shakespeare's poetic function (*Shakespeare* [London: Jonathan Cape, 1935], p. 391). Even closer to my purpose at some points is Norman Rabkin, who says that Shakespeare uses the role of Prospero to establish "an analogy between the imaginary world of his play and the art which creates the world" (*Shakespeare and the Common Understanding* [New York: The Free Press, 1967], pp. 225-26).

3. A viewpoint shared by Clifford Leech, "The Structure of the Last Plays," in *Shakespeare Survey* II (Cambridge, England: Cambridge Univ. Press, 1958), p. 26; and D. G. James, *The Dream of Prospero* (Oxford: Oxford Univ. Press, 1967), p. 171.

4. A similar view is expressed by Derek Traversi, *An Approach to Shakespeare*, 3rd ed. Vol. II (1938; rpt. Garden City, N.Y.: Anchor Books, 1969), p. 339.

5. In his poem on *The Tempest* entitled "The Sea and the Mirror" (in *For the Time Being* [London: Faber & Faber, 1945], p. 9), W. H. Auden has Prospero say to Ariel, "I am glad I have freed you, / So at last I can really believe I shall die."

6. Although I arrived at my conclusions on *The Tempest* independently of Professor Rabkin, I should acknowledge that my last paragraph is reinforced by his rich comments on pp. 228-29 of *Shakespeare and The Common Understanding*, where he stresses that as Prospero left the island, we must leave the mirror world of the theatre and relinquish our temporary privilege as mere spectators. The concluding paragraph of Rose Zimbardo, "Form and Disorder in *The Tempest*," *SQ*, *XIV* (1963), 56, is also relevant.

13

A READING OF *THE TEMPEST*

Andrew Solomon

If after every tempest come such calms,
May the winds blow till they have wakened death!

Othello

WHEN CALIBAN DRINKS STEPHANO'S WINE IN *The Tempest* and remarks, "The liquor is not earthly," he speaks truly, though the liquor might have been quite average in Naples. The wine is not of Caliban's world, for his world is Prospero's island, and, if we form no other conclusion about the island at first reading, we can be sure that it is far removed from our everyday experience. It is an island where an Ariel can make drunkards act as if they had "smelt music." Shakespeare has not withdrawn from everyday reality; he has gone beyond it in a search for truth told in finer tones. Hamlet had said:

There are more things in heaven and earth, Horatio,
Than are dreamt of in your philosophy.

Now Hamlet's creator examines the possibilities of his statement. Nor is this Shakespeare's first venture into the supernatural; *A Midsummer Night's Dream* at one level and the Weird Sisters at another foreshadow Prospero's island, as do the various ghosts and other glimpses of the spirit world. As Francois-Victor Hugo wrote, Shakespeare "did not question the existence of the invisible world; he rehabilitated it. He did not deny man's supernatural power; he consecrated it."[1]

The island is unreal and so are the events which take place on it. In Act III Gonzalo says, "If in Naples/I should report this now, would they believe me?" and in the last act he exclaims, "Whether this be/Or be not, I'll not swear." "These are not natural events," says Alonso, and fifteen lines later he adds:

> This is as strange a maze as e'er men trod.
> And there is in this business more than nature
> Was ever conduct of.

The Tempest holds riches only for those who have retained their sense of wonder. "Who will believe my verse in time to come," begins sonnet 17, and Shakespeare's concern for the fiction-like implausibility of poetic truth reappears many times: an unimaginative Theseus tells Hippolyta, "I never may believe these antique fables, nor these fairy toys," though one has just occurred; "If this were played upon a stage now, I could condemn it as an improbable fiction," remarks Fabian in *Twelfth Night*; in the play nearest *The Tempest* in time first a gentleman says, "This news which is call'd true is so like an old tale," and one scene later Paulina comments on the reappearance of Hermione, "That she is living/Were it but told you, should be hooted at/Like an old tale." In *The Tempest* Shakespeare goes beyond any pretense to realism. Real men alone will not suffice to convey Shakespeare's total meaning. Such earlier realistic abstractions as Iago and Desdemona must be replaced with fantastic abstractions—Caliban, Ariel and the island itself. But these are only devices. That they seem unreal does not matter, and Shakespeare tells us so from the mouth of Prospero:

> Do not infest your mind with beating on
> The strangeness of this business.

To transport us to so strange an island requires consummate artistry. The opening scene rises brilliantly to the challenge. On the one hand we are concerned with the very real danger to the men on the ship. They are panic-stricken. Their terror is immediate; they are alarmed for necessity of present life. Neither they nor we know that their safety has been insured by Ariel. While the strange ferocity of this tempest awes us, occurrences stranger still enter our minds simultaneously. Unsettling sounds have begun to transport us: the crashing thunder, the master's shrill whistle, the cry and "confused noise" below, and the constantly howling winds. In the New Cambridge edition the stage directions read, "Fireballs flame along the rigging and from beak to stern," and this is clearly true to Shakespeare's intent (and we recall Casca's words to Cicero in *Julius Caesar*, "Never till tonight, never till now,/ Did I go through a tempest dropping fire"). Years earlier *Macbeth* had begun with a violent storm for the same dramaturgic reason: to shock the audience out of their everyday world in preparation for the strange scenes to follow. The tempest is more even than a preparation. If we remember that at the dawn of Shakespeare's final period Thaisa asks Pericles, "Did you not name a tempest,/A birth and a death?" we glimpse the meaning of the present storm; the death opened *Macbeth*, the birth opens *The Tempest*.

Virtually every character in the play—except Miranda who in a sense is born and Ariel who is freed and needs no alteration—undergoes some sort of rebirth. Even the noble Ferdinand must be purified by Ariel's "Full Fathom Five" before he can meet Miranda. Prospero, too, is reborn. Though his rebirth has largely resulted from the effects on him of Miranda and Ariel, we cannot avoid the feeling that he was reborn earlier, in another play. In that most cosmic of tragedies, *King Lear*, we can detect the very promise of *The Tempest*. Though King Lear suffers the limits of human anguish, he clearly dies a far wiser and greater man. To some extent, in Prospero Lear has come back to us. John Dover Wilson writes, "[Prospero] is Lear all over again, Lear in another world, a better world,"[2] and, in a very moving essay on *The Tempest*, Harold C. Goddard has even remarked, with precise restrictions, that this final play could be retitled *King Lear In Heaven*.[3]

In *The Tempest* Shakespeare populates Prospero's island with characters from every place in the spectrum of good and evil. If we have no villain as impressive as an Iago it is because here evil has been apportioned among many characters, each villainous in his particular way and to his particular degree. The baseness of Caliban resides in his very nature. In the chain of being he falls below the human level. Yet there is a certain charm in Caliban equalled only perhaps by that of Ariel. What he does he has reason to do, and only an insensitive reading fails to sympathize with him to a degree. He is a monster, yet a monster who, as Quiller-Couch said, we feel like patting on the head.[4] Before we see him we learn that he has a human shape, but that Miranda does not like to look upon him. Though he is addressed, "Come, thou tortoise," the image has little credibility coming from the lips that had just snapped "malignant thing" to the spirit of fire and air. In fact, however harshly Prospero chastizes Caliban there is still a sense that he is not entirely serious in his threats. That Caliban has made improper advances toward Miranda rightfully disturbs Prospero; however, it seems hardly possible that

Caliban himself fully understands the moral seriousness of his offense. Most of the nobler human thoughts lie beyond Caliban's grasp; his only profit from learning language, he feels, is that he knows how to curse. Yet he is capable of great affection. The devotion which Prospero refused transfers itself to Stephano: "I'll show thee the best springs: I'll pluck thee berries:/I'll fish for thee, and get thee wood enough." And Caliban showers this affection upon Stephano because he will set the monster free; we do not condemn the same longing for freedom in Ariel. Similarly, Caliban shows a sincere appreciation of beauty. His description of Miranda almost equals Ferdinand's reaction to her in ardor, and his famous speech:

> the isle is full of noises,
> Sounds and sweet airs, that give delight and hurt not:
> Sometimes a thousand twangling instruments
> Will hum about mine ears; and sometimes voices,
> That, if I then had waked after long sleep,
> Will make me sleep again—and then, in dreaming,
> The clouds methought would open, and show riches
> Ready to drop upon me, that when I waked
> I cried to dream again.

far surpasses anything we might expect from Stephano and Trinculo. Even a monster raised on such an island must acquire some nobility. Prospero calls him "a born devil, on whose Nature/Nurture can never stick," and this is mostly true, for what hope is there for one whose only goal is to be Stephano's foot-licker. Some nurture, however, does stick on Caliban, and by the end of the play he has learned his lesson. "How fine my master!" he says honestly in the final scene as he shows he was not completely below learning after all:

> I'll be wise hereafter,
> And seek for grace. What a thrice-double ass
> Was I, to take this drunkard for a god!
> And worship this dull fool!

Perhaps at long last Caliban is being allowed to finish his dream and the riches have begun to drop from the clouds. Actually, the Stephano whose feet Caliban wished to lick seems a good deal more base than the monster, as does the jester Trinculo. Trinculo, to whom the clouds shed liquor, provides the play's comic relief (for it is needed in a romance, too) just as surely as does the gravedigger in *Hamlet*. How similar, in fact, are their jokes about England:

> *Ham.* Ay, marry, why was he sent into England?
> *Clown.* Why, because 'a was mad. 'A shall recover his wits there; or, if 'a do not, 'tis no great matter there.
> *Ham.* Why?
> *Clown.* 'Twill not be seen in him there. There the men are as mad as he.

> *Trin.* Were I in England now, as once I was, and had but this fish painted,—not a holiday fool there but would give a piece of silver: there would this monster make a man: any strange beast there makes a man.

Trinculo is the opposite of Prospero in that he fears the supernatural rather than masters it. Stephano, too, provides a contrast to Prospero, for he also has magic—though it is contained in a wine bottle. Stephano's songs, furthermore, with their crudeness recalling the songs of Iago, provide a standard by which to measure the sublimity of Ariel's music. If the plot of Stephano and company on Prospero's life is disturbing, it is never taken seriously as an immediate threat, for these characters are being held up to a mocking ridicule in the same manner as were Dogberry and Sir Andrew Aguecheek. The audience cannot miss the cowardice of Stephano, and even Caliban recognizes that Trinculo is "not valiant." Immediately after the log-carrying scene between Miranda and Ferdinand, Stephano contemplates ruling the island with Miranda as his queen; Shakespeare knew well how base Stephano would appear by this contrast with Ferdinand. The poet uses a similar contrast when, right after the richly poetic masque, Trinculo enters and remarks, "I do smell all horse-piss." Furthermore, in the fourth act while Caliban implores the other two to proceed swiftly with the plan which will free him from Prospero, they stop to quibble over Prospero's garments, and, by doing so, reveal a materialism and a triviality of mind quite impossible to Caliban. Yet even they attain their fitting level of self-awareness at the end, and, in this sense, are reborn. Confronted by Prospero's challenge, "You'ld be king o'th' isle, sirrah?" Stephano wisely puns, "I should have been a sore one then." Had Claudius or Macbeth, at the beginning of their plays, had the self-awareness that this drunken butler has at the end of his, many lives would have been saved.

The villainy of the mighty belongs to Antonio and Sebastian. In sonnet ninety-four Shakespeare had written, "They that have the power to hurt and will do none, . . . They rightly do inherit heaven's graces." Antonio and Sebastian are those who have the power to hurt and would use it. Both are characterized promptly in the first scene. Witness their initial curses directed at the boatswain who is trying to save their lives:

> *Seb.* A pox o' your throat, you bawling, blasphemous, incharitable dog!
> *Ant.* Hang, cur; hang, you whoreson, insolent noise-maker! we are less afraid to be drowned than thou art.

They are vile at all times, and our best opportunities to watch this vileness unfold come in Act II. Between them they make fifty-two aside comments in II.i while the others in their party evaluate their shipwrecked status. These aside comments are of a special kind, moreover, and represent a device used often before in Shakespeare. We are observing them observing others, and, in that respect, we are watching a play-within-a-play. Later, of course, with the masque we will see a play-within-a-play of a different sort, but here we get a chance to view Sebastian and Antonio in their role as audience. What we see are two corrupt villains brimming with derisiveness and selfishness. Late in the scene they re-enact the very villainy that caused Prospero to be banished from Milan. Here, though, we can at last differentiate between the two, and we see that Antonio is the worse. Antonio suggests the plan to murder Alonso. When asked if his conscience would trouble him he says, "I feel not/This deity in my bosom." Sebastian falters and hedges. Like Macbeth he is not above murder, but also like Macbeth the act requires some, if not much, hesitation. Even between such similar characterizations there are nuances to remind us of Shakespeare's penetrating vision. Sebastian is base enough; when the spirits bring the banquet before his party, he is blind to the wonders passing before him and thinks only of the food. When the banquet disappears Sebastian, again reminding us of Macbeth before Macduff, screams in absurd brashness, "But one fiend at a time/I'll fight their legions o'er." When Prospero refers to Sebastian as "a furtherer in the act" by which Antonio gained the dukedom, we can well believe it. However, it is Antonio whom Prospero finds "to call brother/Would even infect my mouth." It is Antonio who, when Ferdinand and Miranda are revealed at chess, cannot say with Sebastian, "A most high miracle." Of all the characters in the play, only Antonio gives us no reason to believe he can be saved.

Alonso, King of Naples, also has his faults, though they are far less than those of the other villains in the shipwrecked party. His chief fault lies in his inability to demonstrate a sense of judgment proportionate to his role as king. Prospero feels Alonso played an active part in stripping him of his dukedom, but from what we see of Antonio and Sebastian, including their intention to kill Alonso himself, it is not hard to imagine that Sebastian's contrivance with Antonio was far more instrumental than Alonso's. The king seems more obtuse than evil. Both Gonzalo's compassionate reassurances and Sebastian's petty recriminations in II.i evoke the same "Prithee peace," as though Alonso could not discriminate between them. Gonzalo speaks the only humane words Alonso hears in this part of the play, but the King of Naples cannot listen. Before the final scene we see nothing royal in Alonso's intellect; however, we do see a good deal that is commendable in his nature. Any comparison of the familial behavior of Alonso with that of Sebastian or Antonio shows how far he rises above them. Throughout the play Alonso sincerely mourns the supposed loss of his son. At the end of Act III he rushes off to join Ferdinand in the sea, and in the final scene he is overwhelmed both with happiness at having regained his son and with admiration for his new daughter. Nor can we forget that he has fathered and raised both the man who is worthy of Miranda and the "paragon" who had just become Queen of Tunis. Furthermore, as soon as he is embraced by Prospero he proves instantly worthy of his forgiveness. We have become accustomed to viewing Alonso as being as depraved as Sebastian and Antonio. He is not; only his combined power and susceptibility let him become their pawn. If not every inch a king, he is not, to any marked degree, evil.

Passing from evil to good, we come to the character who of all the humans in *The Tempest* is exceeded in sublimity only by Miranda, the faithful Gonzalo. Here is the last of the devoted friend-servants in Shakespeare. The strain that had included Juliet's nurse, Adam, Antonio of *Twelfth Night*, Horatio, Emilia of *Othello*, Kent, Menenius, Pisanio, Antigonus, Camillo, and Paulina ends with this "holy Gonzalo." Within him reside loyalty, reverence, optimism, and kindliness. Just as Antonio and Sebastian had been vividly characterized in the first scene, so too is Gonzalo. While everyone else flies about in panic it is Gonzalo who remains level-headed and optimistic: "Nay, good, be patient," he implores. When the ship's destruction seems unavoidable and others curse at being "cheated of our lives," Gonzalo stoically and faithfully says, "The wills above be done." But more than this, it is Gonzalo who suggests that everyone join the king and the prince at prayers, "For our case is as theirs," for only Gonzalo realizes that we are all in this boat of life together. Next, we learn from Prospero that Gonzalo's charity saved the banished duke's and Miranda's lives, and his compassion provided Prospero with the books that have given him his power. Gonzalo's optimism is the only ray of brightness in the shipwrecked party. While all the others lament their loss, only Gonzalo reminds them of their good fortune. When Sebastian sneers that Gonzalo "will carry this island home in his pocket, and give it his son for an apple," he speaks more truly than he knows, for the spirit of Prospero's island is within Gonzalo. It may be going too far to suggest that Antonio's and Sebastian's mocking of Gonzalo recalls the mocking of Jesus by the Romans, yet there is the same presence of innate holiness and others' blindness to it. As Gonzalo had saved Prospero, so does he save Alonso from Antonio and Sebastian (and even Antonio and Sebastian from Alonso a dozen lines later), just as he orders the party to save all three when they go mad after the banquet vanishes. If Ferdinand and Miranda embody the beauty of romantic love, Gonzalo personifies the sanctity of brotherly love. Many varieties of love operate in this play; Gonzalo's is perhaps the one which Shakespeare felt had the greatest chance of saving man from himself.

Samuel Johnson remarked that compared with Shakespeare's tragedies the factor most impressive about his comedies was the effortlessness with which they appear to have been created. Had Johnson been discussing characters rather than genres we can well imagine he would have observed that two types of characters came with remarkable ease from Shakespeare's pen: his clowns and his heroines. It is as though the wit of the clowns and the sweetness of the heroines flowed through Shakespeare's hand like a steady stream of honey from his blood. The final plays each have a heroine without whom there could be no play. Some are more fully drawn, but none is lovelier than Miranda.

Nature has raised Miranda and Prospero has educated her, but she has educated him too. In reading the final scene it seems hard to believe that Prospero could have spared the agents of his exile unless perhaps living in isolation for twelve years with the angelic Miranda has taught him the various attitudes of love and kindness. She seems less her father's daughter than he shall prove his daughter's father. Twice in the play she is called "goddess"; no other woman in Shakespeare is addressed by this word twice (although Diana of *All's Well*, Imogen, and Perdita are each called "goddess" once). Though a goddess she is also a young girl, a young girl of a special kind. The first quality in I.ii that impresses us after her beauty is her empathetic concern for those aboard the ship. Before explaining the story of her origin, Prospero lays aside his mantle, for he needs no magic with her; she carries magic within her. Her reactions to Prospero's narrative demonstrate a growing awareness of her newly acquired womanhood. Of her life before the exile she remembers only the women who attended her, for their figures were what hers must only recently have become. Three times Prospero demands her attention, and these cries of "Thou attend'st not!", whatever they may tell us of Prospero, also indicate that Miranda has reached the stage where she must observe the world for herself rather than have it related to her by her father. She has been the cherub that has preserved Prospero, but this must inevitably end soon, for Ferdinand is about to come into her life.

The pristine love-spell between Ferdinand and Miranda

invites comparison with those two other magnificent adolescent love affairs: Romeo and Juliet, and Florizel and Perdita. Mrs. Kemble—to many tastes hopelessly out-of-date, but possibly worth hearing on this point—observed of Miranda, "Her surrender of herself to the man she loves is so little feminine after the approved feminine fashion that it is simply angelic."[5] Mrs. Kemble went on to contrast this surrender with Juliet's, whose artificial upbringing forced her, once she realized she was overheard, to apologize for her honesty. Miranda has no need for apologies. She tells Ferdinand at first sight he is a "thing divine," and that he is the first man she ever sighed for. At the perfect moment, with total lack of coyness, she asks Ferdinand if he loves her, and fifteen lines later she actually proposes to him. She has no shame, nor should she have. She is perfectly willing to carry Ferdinand's logs or to follow him about if he refuses to marry her. If we are tempted to indulge or suspect her trusting innocence, let us also remember the price we must pay for our cynicism.

Neither is Ferdinand in the slightest degree unworthy of her. His nature is as noble, his love as pure. Enchanted by Ariel's music, Ferdinand immediately recognizes the wonders of the isle and the beauty of Miranda. Coleridge was the first to point out the full power of the phrase with which Prospero describes their meeting: "At first sight / They have changed eyes." In those last four words Shakespeare has expressed more even than the ecstasy of young love; he has made this meeting a transcendental experience.[6] The combined effect of Miranda's radiance and Prospero's magic transforms the prince: "Thy nerves are in their infancy again," says Prospero, which, to me, recalls the words of Jesus: "Except ye be converted and become as little children, ye shall not enter the kingdom of heaven." We are in the third act before Ferdinand even asks Miranda her name, for such superficialities are no longer important; Prospero's island is beyond Juliet's

Verona. Ferdinand does not prize the kingship which has cost him his father. The ambition which distorts Antonio, Sebastian, and Stephano is absent from the prince. All he desires is Miranda. Ariel and Caliban often resented the work Prospero required of them, but to Ferdinand his tasks are "joyful labours" for he realizes the truth of Macbeth's ill-spoken words, "The labour we delight in physics pain"; Falstaff had said, " 'Tis no sin for a man to labour in his vocation," and Ferdinand's vocation has become the winning of Miranda. His success has become evident by the end of the masque when he speaks for both in assuring Prospero, "We wish your peace."

The greatest achievement of Prospero is that, with Ariel's indispensable help, he brings these two young lovers together. If Prospero is Lear's second chance, Ferdinand and Miranda are Romeo and Juliet's second chance. In the earlier tragedy the enmity of the two houses destroys the two lovers; in *The Tempest* the two lovers help save the divided houses of Milan and Naples. How the parents learn the children's lesson is perhaps best demonstrated in the symbolism of the scene where Ferdinand and Miranda are revealed playing at chess.[7] Here the hostility which began twelve years earlier has diminished to a sporting contest between two young people who love each other deeply. The purity of their love conveys them ahead of even Prospero, and he knows it. "So glad of this as they I cannot be," he says. He could not be more pleased; yet, his joy must fall short of theirs for no pleasure approaches the intensity of falling deeply in love, for the first time, with someone who returns that love.

If any relationship in the play equals in beauty that of Ferdinand and Miranda, it is the relationship of Ariel and Prospero. Critics generally examine each separately and rarely bring to light the delicate love and mutual dependence of each for the other. For at least a moment they must be looked at as a pair, a team. The very appearance of Ariel in Act I instantly enlarges our opinion of Prospero; we cannot lightly dismiss the magic of one who has so exquisite a spirit in his service. Ariel serves Prospero, but he protects him, too. Ariel, no less than Miranda, has made Prospero's exile bearable. It is to Ariel that Prospero turns in his moment of deepest anxiety at the conclusion of the masque. "Do you love me master? no?" asks Ariel; "Dearly, my delicate Ariel," replies Prospero. The only tears of sadness at the conclusion of the play come when we realize that these two must now part forever.

What is Ariel? A fairy? An angel? A spirit neither human nor animal, Ariel is beyond sexual classification or definitive shape. He (and we choose this pronoun for convenience only) is Shakespeare's most ethereal abstraction, surreal in the pure sense of the word Apollinaire intended when he coined it.[8] His is the spirit of fire and air, the creative power of beautiful music, the healing magic of sympathy and forgiveness. That Ariel wants his freedom of Prospero is not at all surprising, since we find that the greater the freedom of action he has the more wonderful are his deeds. Under the foul witch Sycorax, whose tasks he found repulsive, he could do nothing. Under Prospero he is able to perform more useful service. He raises the tempest. He fetches dew from the Bermudas at midnight, and he brings Ferdinand to Miranda. He makes Alonso's banquet vanish, and he helps Prospero to produce the masque. Yet, when he acts on his own he performs his noblest miracles. He keeps the mariners safe. He, literally the "good angel" that preserves the king, wakes Gonzalo to save Alonso. He informs Prospero of Caliban's and Stephano's plot. Finally, when we witness the relative mercilessness of Prospero's treatment of Caliban and the relish he takes in gaining control over his enemies, we realize that Prospero's decision to forgive his enemies is itself largely Ariel's work.

In *The Passionate Pilgrim* Shakespeare had written, "If music and sweet poetry agree,/ As they must needs, the sister and the brother." In Ariel music and poetry unite. He personifies the power of music that had always fascinated Shakespeare. From *The Two Gentlemen of Verona*, which is remembered more for a single song than for anything else, to *The Winter's Tale*, whose most arresting moment is prompted by music, Shakespeare remains enchanted by the "concord of sweet sounds." The songs of Ariel represent the culmination of Shakespeare's music; they are the highest level we can be brought to by sound. But there is a higher level still, and it can only be reached in silence. Just before the masque begins, Prospero tells his children, "No tongue . . . all eyes . . . be silent." He cautions not only the young couple, however, but us as well that something beyond words is happening. He is telling us the manner in which Shakespeare had absorbed life to the point where he could mirror it more completely than any other mortal ever has. Shakespeare would never have put Montaigne's words into Gonzalo's mouth unless they expressed exactly what he felt men would do in an ideal community: "No occupation, all men idle, all:/ And women too." Fittingly, it is in Ariel's final song, as he anticipates his freedom, that we get what may be a glimpse of how Shakespeare wished to spend his last years in Stratford:

> Merrily, merrily, shall I live now,
> Under the blossom that hangs on the bough.

This is what freedom means to Ariel, not merely the freedom to do something, but the freedom to do nothing.[9] Rimbaud passed into silence because poetry had lost its magic for him; perhaps Shakespeare passed into silence because his poetry had taken us as far as words can.

However mystifying Ariel is, though, the most intriguing

question raised about the nature of any of the characters is that which examines Prospero: how much, if at all, does Prospero represent Shakespeare himself? Indeed, Prospero, probably the only figure in Shakespeare with a life story more fascinating than that which won Desdemona, would be perplexing enough even if we never made any equation between him and the poet. But since the identification was originally suggested by Coleridge[10] and later stated explicitly by Campbell[11] (significantly, both poets themselves), no serious critic has been able to ignore its implications. Dover Wilson has even proposed, quite credibly, that the actor who portrayed Prospero in 1611 very probably was Shakespeare himself.[12] Here lies one of Shakespeare's greatest challenges to our own "negative capability," for while we actually cannot know how real the Prospero-Shakespeare identity is, the temptation to venture some guess is enormous.

Whatever Prospero might be, he is certainly unique in many ways. Dramatically there has been no one quite like him in the earlier plays, particularly in the other romances. No character before him (except in a far different way and lesser degree, Iago) has ever so controlled the circumstances of the plot and the destinies of the other characters. Nor has there ever been a character with a nature quite like Prospero's, that magnificent mixture of majesty, studiousness, crustiness, and affection. With Miranda's first two lines we know that Prospero is a magician. While Prospero's is a powerful magic that can raise a tempest and dominate Sycorax's god, Setebos, it is also a virtuous magic that can stay Ferdinand's weapon and lull Miranda to a gentle sleep. In *The Merry Wives of Windsor*, Shallow asks Sir Hugh, "What, the sword and the word! Do you study them both, Master Parson?" and it would seem that in Prospero lies the fullest answer to Shallow's question, for his magic derives from just such a universal study. He makes his respect for learning obvious. Caliban's inability to learn frustrates Prospero as much as anything else in the play, and he considers himself his daughter's "schoolmaster" as well as her father. He often speaks to her as a gruff school teacher: "Dost thou attend?" "Thou attend'st not!" he scolds, and when she asks an intelligent question he seems about to put a gold star on her forehead, "Well demanded wench:/My tale provokes that question." When she dares question her schoolmaster's methods he snaps, "What, I say,/My foot my tutor!" Prospero is at least above partiality; he is equally crusty to everyone. He addresses Ferdinand in the first scene with little mercy, Caliban with none, and even the seraphic Ariel is a "dull thing" whom Prospero threatens to peg into the knotty entrails of an oak tree for twelve years. If we knew Prospero as his daughter does, however, we would take his remarks less seriously; her final words in I.ii are directed as much to the reader as to Ferdinand:

> Be of comfort,
> My father's of a better nature, sir,
> Than he appears by speech: This is unwonted
> Which now came from him.

And we need not wait until later in the play to realize she is right. We can already see beneath his brusque exterior a profound gratitude to Gonzalo and a deep love for Miranda. Furthermore, no one could seriously doubt that he loves Ariel even as much as he does his own child, that his harsh words to Ariel are part of an affectionate game they might call " 'That's my noble master!'—'That's my tricksy spirit!'." The clearest indications of Prospero's goodness, though, are his aside comments on the joy he feels in seeing Miranda fall in love.

Prospero's attitude toward the growing love of Ferdinand and Miranda gives us our truest initial insight into him. With "gentleness," in its now lost sense of "bigness of heart," love is the dominant emotional image in the play. Prospero's mature

understanding of the importance of love is the first indication
we have that he, more than any previous character in Shakespeare, has a full awareness of his world and his place in it.
Prospero's soul "prompts" this love, and when it is securely
launched his "rejoicing at nothing can be more." Looking at
the two lovers Prospero utters his blessing, "Heavens rain
grace/On that which breeds between 'em!" All the tasks
Prospero demands of Ferdinand we know are only trials of
the prince's love. How far we have progressed in a father's
understanding of love from Lord Capulet, Polonius, Brabantio, and Cymbeline to Prospero.

Yet, in the middle of this joy, in the middle of the masque
which is Prospero's engagement present, comes the moment
of greatest doubt. Infuriated by Caliban's plot on his life, the
intrusion of the foul elements of the outside world, Prospero
makes his most profound and memorable speech:

> Our revels now are ended . . . These our actors,
> As I foretold you, were all spirits, and
> Are melted into air, into thin air,
> And, like the baseless fabric of this vision,
> The cloud-capped towers, the gorgeous palaces,
> The solemn temples, the great globe itself,
> Yea, all which it inherit, shall dissolve,
> And, like this insubstantial pageant faded,
> Leave not a rack behind: we are such stuff
> As dreams are made on; and our little life
> Is rounded with a sleep . . .

The speech's meaning vexes even Prospero.

> We are such stuff
> As dreams are made on; and our little life
> Is rounded with a sleep.

Is Prospero, like Bottom awakening from his dream, incapable of articulating his experience, or is he amplifying, with

a mystical twist, the invitation in Puck's epilogue? Could we, involved as we are with "our little life," not comprehend the plane of reality[13] of the sleep which rounds it? Was Keats asking Prospero's same question:

> Was it a vision, or a waking dream?
> Fled is that music:—Do I wake or sleep?

Sleep and death had always been intimately tied together in Shakespeare, the former often referred to as "death's counterfeit." Even here, in his final play, Shakespeare knows he cannot venture a description of that undiscovered country from whose bourn no traveller returns, but he does what he can do for us: in the final scene he will show us how to prepare for it.

By the time the final scene opens Prospero has brought his daughter to the point where she can lead her own fruitful life, and he has brought all his enemies within his power. He must now decide on a course of justice. He reaches his decision in consultation with Ariel:

> *Ariel.*   . . . Your charm so strongly works 'em,
> That if you now beheld them, your affections
> Would become tender.
>   *Pros.*   Dost thou think so, spirit?
>   *Ariel.*   Mine would, sir, were I human.
>   *Pros.*   And mine shall . . .
> Hast thou—which art but air—a touch, a feeling
> Of their afflictions, and shall not myself,
> One of their kind, that relish all as sharply,
> Passion as they, be kindlier moved than thou art?
> Though with their high wrongs I am struck to th' quick,
> Yet, with my nobler reason, 'gainst my fury
> Do I take part: the rarer action is
> In virtue than in vengeance: they being penitent,
> The sole drift of my purpose doth extend
> Not a frown further. Go, release them Ariel.
> My charms I'll break, their senses I'll restore,
> And they shall be themselves.

Prospero and Ariel, in a purely poetic sense, are not two separate entities here, but two consulting limbs of man's highest spirit. Ariel is called "spirit" right in the midst of the decision to remind us that he is a surreal abstraction of the best that humans such as Prospero and we are capable of. He brings Prospero to empathize; he brings him to a Christ-like realization of the "Love your enemies" spoken on the mount. This is the climax of the play, the final climax in Shakespeare. From this point in the play on there remains only the conversion of the enemies. Prospero is almost ready to abjure his magic, and with the speedy rebirths of his enemies—all but Antonio[14]—he has at last finished with his work. At the end of the play Prospero is ready to bury his staff, with which he has accomplished all he could. He is ready to bid good-bye to Ariel, from whom he has learned all that was possible, and to bid good-bye, too, to his daughter, for whom he has done all that a father may. He will travel back to Milan reunited with Gonzalo and surrounded by men he has made into their new, best selves. Every third thought will be of his grave, and these can be gratified thoughts, for Prospero has set his life in order. With a full comprehension of his place in time and space Prospero has attained harmony with the grand order of his universe. He will enjoy however much of life remains, and he is fully prepared, when necessary, to die. There will be no final fears of having left something undone. The sleep which rounds Prospero's life will be tranquil.

Miranda's final words in *The Tempest* are:

> O, wonder!
> How many goodly creatures are there here!
> How beauteous mankind is! O brave new world,
> That has such people in't!

How ill-judged the crew before her would have been by these words minutes earlier. Miranda apprehends their new-creation quicker, no doubt, than we do. Prospero's " 'Tis new to thee," does not contradict Miranda's statement, but only tempers it to the point where she may realize that her words are true not as certainty, but as possibility. That mankind would not always show itself beauteous Shakespeare knew well, but that there was inherent in the human race the capability of making the world a Prospero's island he also knew. In his final complete play the darkness of the tragedies has finally dissolved into a mysterious kind of daylight in which we can see a vision of a better world.

Coupling Shakespeare with Dante, Northrop Frye has written, "In the greatest moments of Dante and Shakespeare, in, say, *The Tempest* or the climax of the *Purgatorio*, we have ... the feeling that here we are close to seeing what our whole literary experience has been about, the feeling that we have moved into the still center of the order of words."[15] Dover Wilson couples Shakespeare with Beethoven, saying that in their final utterances each was like a passive instrument yielding to "breezes blowing from some seventh heaven where there is neither speech nor language."[16] I could couple Shakespeare with no one, nor any of his plays, despite my deep love for so many of them, with *The Tempest*. This final play of Shakespeare takes us to the frontier of aesthetic experience via a kind of magic never rough, howsoever necessary to abjure.

1. *Œuvres Completes de Shakespeare*, 1865, Vol. II, Introduction, p. 87; quoted in *The Tempest*, New Variorum Edition, H. H. Furness, ed., (Philadelphia: Lippincott, 1892; rpt. New York: Dover, 1964), p. 357.

2. *The Meaning of "The Tempest,"* (Literary and Philosophical Society of Newcastle Upon Tyne, 1936), p. 12.

3. *The Meaning of Shakespeare*, 2 vols., (Chicago: University of Chicago Press, 1951; rpt. 1960), II, p. 277. See too the detailed explanation of psychological connections between the two plays in Ella Freeman Sharpe. "From *King Lear* to *The Tempest*," *International Journal of Psychoanalysis*, XXVII (1946) 19-30.

4. Sir Arthur Quiller-Couch, *Shakespeare's Workmanship* (1918: rpt. Cambridge, England: Cambridge University Press, 1931), p. 292.

5. *Notes Upon Some of Shakespeare's Plays*, 1882, p. 155f.; quoted in Furness, p. 375.

6. "God, it has been said, is the mode in which the subject-object distinction is transcended." G. Wilson Knight, *The Crown of Life* (1948; rev. rpt. London: Methuen, 1965), p. 28.

7. I owe full realization of this scene's symbolic importance to Dover Wilson, *Meaning of "The Tempest,"* pp. 18-19.

8. In *The Theater of the Absurd* (New York: Doubleday, 1961; rev. ed. 1969), p. 314, Martin Esslin quotes Apollinaire as saying, "[Surrealism] is not a renovation of the theatre, [but] at least a personal effort, [in which] I thought one should return to nature itself, but without imitating her in the manner of the photographers. When man wanted to imitate the action of walking, he created the wheel, which does not resemble a leg."

9. Goddard, pp. 285-286, has shown the full importance of Ariel's song.

10. Samuel Taylor Coleridge, *Shakespearean Criticism*, ed. Thomas Middleton Raysor (1930; rpt. New York: Dutton, 1960), I, p. 119.

11. *Dramatic Works of Shakespeare*, 1938, quoted in Furness, p. 356.

12. *Meaning of "The Tempest,"* p. 5.

13. I gratefully borrow the term "plane of reality" from E. M. W. Tillyard, *Shakespeare's Last Plays* (London: Chatto and Windus, 1938; rpt. 1964).

14. Admittedly, to our ironic age this has become an increasingly significant exception. See, for example, the second section of W. H. Auden's "The Sea and the Mirror," in *For The Time Being* (1944, rpt. in *The Collected Poetry of W. H. Auden*, New York: Random House, 1945, pp. 351-404).

15. *Anatomy of Criticism* (1957; rpt. New York: Atheneum, 1967), p. 117.

16. *Meaning of "The Tempest,"* p. 1.

THE CONTRIBUTORS

DIANA T. CHILDRESS
Brooklyn College, CUNY

THERESA COLETTI
University of Rochester

RICHARD C. CROWLEY

MIKE FRANK
Williams College

ELTON D. HIGGS
University of Michigan—Dearborn

L. C. KNIGHTS
King Edward VII Professor of English Literature, Cambridge

KENNETH MUIR
King Alfred Professor of English Literature, Liverpool

ALEX NEWELL
Concordia University

LEONARD POWLICK
University of Pittsburgh

GERALD SCHORIN
University of Pittsburgh

ANDREW SOLOMON
University of Pittsburgh

MICHAEL TINKER
Texas A & I University

RICHARD C. TOBIAS
University of Pittsburgh

ANDREW WELSH
Rutgers University

PAUL G. ZOLBROD
Allegheny College